MATHEMATICAL AND
ANALOGICAL REASONING
OF YOUNG LEARNERS

STUDIES IN MATHEMATICAL THINKING AND LEARNING
Alan H. Schoenfeld, Series Editor

Artzt/Armour-Thomas • *Becoming a Reflective Mathematics Teacher: A Guide for Observation and Self-Assessment*

Baroody/Dowker • *The Development of Arithmetic Concepts and Skills: Constructing Adaptive Expertise*

Boaler • *Experiencing School Mathematics: Traditional and Reform Approaches to Teaching and Their Impact on Student Learning*

Carpenter/Fennema/Romberg (Eds.) • *Rational Numbers: An Integration of Research*

Cobb/Bauersfeld (Eds.) • *The Emergence of Mathematical Meaning: Interaction in Classroom Cultures*

Cohen • *Teachers' Professional Development and the Elementary Mathematics Classroom: Bringing Understandings to Light*

Clements/Sarama/DiBiase (Eds.) • *Engaging Young Children in Mathematics: Standards for Early Childhood Mathematics Education*

English (Ed.) • *Mathematical and Analogical Reasoning of Young Learners*

English (Ed.) • *Mathematical Reasoning: Analogies, Metaphors, and Images*

Fennema/Nelson (Eds.) • *Mathematics Teachers in Transition*

Fennema/Romberg (Eds.) • *Mathematics Classrooms That Promote Understanding*

Lajoie (Ed.) • *Reflections on Statistics: Learning, Teaching, and Assessment in Grades K–12*

Lehrer/Chazan (Eds.) • *Designing Learning Environments for Developing Understanding of Geometry and Space*

Ma • *Knowing and Teaching Elementary Mathematics: Teachers' Understanding of Fundamental Mathematics in China and the United States*

Martin • *Mathematics Success and Failure Among African-American Youth: The Roles of Sociohistorical Context, Community Forces, School Influence, and Individual Agency*

Reed • *Word Problems: Research and Curriculum Reform*

Romberg/Fennema/Carpenter (Eds.) • *Integrating Research on the Graphical Representation of Functions*

Schoenfeld (Ed.) • *Mathematical Thinking and Problem Solving*

Senk/Thompson (Eds.) • *Standards-Based School Mathematics Curricula: What Are They? What Do Students Learn?*

Sternberg/Ben-Zeev (Eds.) • *The Nature of Mathematical Thinking*

Wilcox/Lanier (Eds.) • *Using Assessment to Reshape Mathematics Teaching: A Casebook for Teachers and Teacher Educators, Curriculum and Staff Development Specialists*

Wood/Nelson/Warfield (Eds.) • *Beyond Classical Pedagogy: Teaching Elementary School Mathematics*

Yoshida/Fernandez • *Lesson Study: A Japanese Approach to Improving Mathematics Teaching and Learning*

MATHEMATICAL AND ANALOGICAL REASONING OF YOUNG LEARNERS

Edited by

Lyn D. English
Queensland University of Technology

LEA
LAWRENCE ERLBAUM ASSOCIATES, PUBLISHERS
2004 Mahwah, New Jersey London

Lawrence Erlbaum Associates, Inc., Publishers
10 Industrial Avenue
Mahwah, New Jersey 07430

Cover design by Kathryn Houghtaling Lacey

Library of Congress Cataloging-in-Publication Data

Mathematical and analogical reasoning of young learners / edited by Lyn D. English.
       p.   cm.
   Includes bibliographical references and index.
   ISBN 0-8058-4102-4 (acid-free paper) — ISBN 0-8058-4945-9 (pbk. : acid-free paper)
   1. Mathetmatics—Study and teaching (Elementary).   2. Reasoning in children.   I. English,
Lyn D.

QA135.6.M374   2004
510′.19—dc22   2003064155
                                                                                        CIP

Books published by Lawrence Erlbaum Associates are printed on acid-free paper,
and their bindings are chosen for strength and durability.

Printed in the United States of America
10 9 8 7 6 5 4 3 2 1

To Ben, Jasmine,
Lauren, and Paige

Contents

Preface

This book is intended for those interested in the mathematical development of young children, in particular, the development of their reasoning processes. The book will appeal to mathematics educators, researchers in mathematics education, educational psychologists, and teachers in early childhood classrooms.

As we illustrate in the following chapters, young children spontaneously pose and solve problems that involve a broad range of mathematical ideas and processes. They enthusiastically embrace problems involving pattern, shape, number, and measurement as they explore their physical and social environments. Of particular significance in young children's mathematical development are the reasoning processes they use in learning about their world, such as spatial and quantitative reasoning, deduction and induction, and analogical reasoning. However, existing research has yet to capture the range and extent of young children's reasoning processes and the ways in which they use these in their informal and formal learning. In particular, longitudinal studies exploring the development of children's reasoning in the early informative years of schooling are lacking. This book is an attempt to redress this situation.

In compiling the book, we drew on rich data sets from a longitudinal crosscultural study of young children's reasoning development as they progressed from preschool through the end of Grade 2. The participants included the children and their teachers from schools in Australia and the United States. We pay special attention to the children's development of

mathematical and analogical reasoning in their informative years as our earlier studies had highlighted the importance of analogical reasoning in young
children's mathematical development. Background information on analogical and mathematical reasoning is provided in chapter 1 and is elaborated on
in subsequent chapters.

One of the key issues explored in the volume is the relation between mathematical and analogical reasoning. Until recently, this link has received little
interest from the research community, especially studies involving in-depth
analyses of young children's mathematical and analogical development over
time. In conducting our investigations, it was imperative that we design developmentally appropriate and theoretically sound ways to expose young
children's reasoning capabilities. Our approaches to doing so are addressed
in chapter 2 where the construction and validation of our measures of mathematical and analogical reasoning are described.

The crosscultural nature of our investigations enabled us to examine
whether developmental trends in the young children's reasoning are the same
for both American and Australian children. Our findings on this aspect are
presented in chapter 3, where profiles of children's analogical and mathematical reasoning development are examined. Chapter 5 presents in-depth case
studies of individual children's development across the three years.

Also of interest was how changes in children's reasoning relate to the
implicit instruction they receive in their classrooms. Although children's
learning is influenced by the way in which teachers construct a context for
classroom discourse, the way individual children interpret that discourse is
equally important. Hence, another aspect of our research was on individual
learners, their learning environments, and the interaction between the two.
Chapter 4 examines the role of classroom discourse in supporting the development of young children's mathematical and analogical reasoning.

During each of the three years of the study, we interviewed the teachers of
the participating children to gain insights into their knowledge, beliefs, and
practices with respect to mathematical and analogical reasoning. In chapter
6, we present interview data addressing these aspects and discuss how the
teachers viewed the teaching of early mathematics and the development of
young children's reasoning. Chapter 7 presents in-depth case studies of the
three teachers.

Commentaries on our investigations are presented in chapters 8 and 9;
chapter 10 addresses some ways we can promote the mathematical and analogical reasoning development of young children.

ACKNOWLEDGMENTS

To each chapter author in this book I express my sincere thanks and appreciation. It has been both professionally rewarding and personally exciting to work with all of you on this project. We are indebted to Alan Schoenfeld for his insightful and encouraging comments to the original manuscript. We also express our sincere appreciation to the editorial team at Lawrence Erlbaum Associates, in particular, Lori Hawver and Naomi Silverman for their unwavering support and encouragement. The significant contribution of Jill and Brad Waters in compiling the author and subject indexes is gratefully acknowledged.

The research reported in the volume was supported by a Large Grant from the Australian Research Council.

—Lyn D. English

1

MATHEMATICAL AND ANALOGICAL REASONING IN EARLY CHILDHOOD

Lyn D. English
Queensland University of Technology

Those who observe young children at play will notice how readily they engage in mathematical activity. Young children spontaneously pose and solve problems that involve a broad range of mathematical ideas and processes. They enthusiastically embrace problems involving pattern, shape, number, and measurement as they explore their physical and social environments. Of particular significance in young children's mathematical development are the reasoning processes they use in learning about their world, such as spatial and quantitative reasoning, deduction and induction, and analogical reasoning. Other processes such as classifying, comparing, representing, experimenting, and creating, also play a significant role in children's mathematical development. As we illustrate in this book, children's reasoning processes are powerful facilitators of their early learning, even more so than specific items of mathematical knowledge (Perry & Dockett, 2002).

Existing research, however, has yet to capture the range and extent of young children's reasoning processes and the ways in which they use these in their informal and formal learning. One reason for this is that past research has mainly relied on children's performance on specific reasoning tasks that were created by researchers and administered under test-like conditions. Typically, such studies focused on "the three c's," namely, "conservation (and related Piagetian and neo-Piagetian investigations), counting, and calculations" (Ginsburg, Pappas, & Seo, 2001, p. 8). These studies do not reveal the types of mathematical activities that children themselves instigate, nor the various ways in which children reason and learn during their free play. Natu-

1

ralistic studies, on the other hand, can provide important insights into these issues. The studies of Ginsburg, Balfanz, and Greenes (2000), for example, have shown that children engage in mathematical activity for nearly half of their free playtime and, in doing so, display sophisticated thinking and reasoning processes.

The chapters of this book provide further evidence of young children's reasoning abilities. We draw on rich sets of data from a longitudinal and cross-cultural study of young children's reasoning development as they progressed from preschool through to the end of second grade. The participants included the children and their teachers from schools in Australia and the United States. We pay special attention to the children's development of mathematical and analogical reasoning in their informative years, given that our earlier studies had highlighted the importance of analogical reasoning in children's mathematical development (Alexander, White, & Daugherty, 1997). The purpose of this first chapter is to provide background information on analogical and mathematical reasoning, and to highlight the issues that are the focus of this book. Consideration is given first to the nature, role, and development of analogical reasoning.

ANALOGIES AND ANALOGICAL REASONING

Analogy provides an important example of what appears to be a highly general cognitive mechanism that takes specific inputs from essentially any domain that can be represented in explicit propositional form, and operates on them to produce inferences specific to the target domain. (Holyoak & Hummel, 2001, p. 162)

The powerful role of analogies in communicating, exploring, or transferring ideas has been well recognized since early times. Around the second century B.C., the Greek Stoic Chrysippus first used water waves to suggest the nature of sound, whereas in 1630, Galileo used the known orbit of the moon as the basis for his theory that the earth moves. Analogies are equally important in today's society. We use analogies in many walks of life, such as decision making in law, business, and politics; scientific reasoning in the laboratory; and problem solving in daily living (Dunbar, 2001; English, 1999; Holyoak & Thagard, 1995).

Defined in a general sense, analogy is the ability to reason with relational patterns. Being able to detect patterns, to identify recurrences of the patterns in the face of variations in their elements, to abstract from the patterns, and to communicate these abstractions is a basic human achievement (Gentner, Holyoak, & Kokinov, 2001). In essence, analogy lies at the core of human cognition and appears to be closely linked to the development of general representational ability (Gentner & Rattermann, 1991; Hofstadter, 2001). Even children as young as 1 and 2 years of age display an ability to reason analogically (Goswami, 2001), where they use their understanding of familiar situations to help them construct new knowledge. For example, Hatano and Inagaki's (1997) work on naïve biology has shown how young children use their knowledge about humans as the source for reasoning about less familiar animate objects. In one of our preschool classrooms, which we address in later chapters, we observed 5-year-old Elliott and James applying their knowledge of the human anatomy to interpret how trees function:

James: *The tree's so fat. It's got lots of blood in it.*

Elliott: *Because inside the wood there's some very liquid black stuff and I know that's blood.*

James: *No, water! The water goes in the tree and it could easily. . . . . The water goes under, in the roots, and it goes up in the tree and gets blood.*

Teacher: *Why do you think the trees need to have blood?*

James: *Cos if they didn't have blood they would die.*

Teacher: *What does the blood do, do you think?*

James: *Helps them stay alive.*

As a fundamental process of human cognition, analogical reasoning has received considerable attention in the past 10–15 years. A good deal of the research, however, has focused on the reasoning of the adult population. It is only in recent years that studies have addressed young children's ability to reason by analogy, reflecting a long-held view that such reasoning is a late developing skill (e.g., Inhelder & Piaget, 1958). Many of these studies have addressed classical four-term analogy problems of the type, mother is to daughter as father is to ? (e.g., the work of Inhelder & Piaget, 1958; Sternberg, 1977). Other studies have employed specifically designed problem analogies based on simple causal relations (e.g., rolling, pulling, stretching) involving real objects and models (e.g., Freeman, 1996; Goswami, 2001; Holyoak, Junn, & Billman, 1984). For example, Freeman's base problem entailed a loose rubber band stretched between two poles to make a "bridge" for rolling an orange across, whereas the transfer problems included giving a doll a "ride" by stretching ribbon between two towers of different heights.

In contrast to the above types of study, children's reasoning with analogies in everyday life and in specific disciplines, such as mathematics, has received considerably less attention. This is of particular concern, given that young children reason with pedagogical analogies from their earliest school experiences (English & Halford, 1995; Warfield & Yttri, 1999).

In the following sections, I present an overview of some of the diverse perspectives on analogical reasoning, on how it develops, and on the nature of young children's capabilities in this domain. These perspectives are further examined in other chapters of this book.

Reasoning with Classical Analogies

Classical or conventional analogies take the form, A:B::C:D (e.g., tree:limb:: body:arm), where the C and D terms must be related in the same way as the A and B terms are linked. These analogies are basically proportional or relational problems and have been popular in IQ tests for many years. Structural theories, such as that of Piaget (e.g., Piaget, 1952; Inhelder & Piaget, 1958), have probably been the most frequently applied to analyses of reasoning with classical analogies. Such theories focus on the nature or sophistication of the relations that are drawn between the terms in a given analogy problem. These linkages between the A and B terms and between the C and D terms are defined as "lower order" relations. For example, in the analogy, tree:limb:: body:arm, it might be inferred that limb is a part of a tree and that arm is an appendage of the human body. These two associations between tree and limb and between body and arm are instances of lower order relations.

In contrast, higher order relations are those generated between more distant or removed concepts. These relations require the reasoner to determine some form of relational similarity between the more distant concepts. Thus, the ability to link the A:B pairing to the C:D pairing involves a higher order relation. For example, before the analogy, tree:limb::body:arm, can be solved, the reasoner must be able to determine what similarities are shared by trees and human bodies before she can generate a relation that would link tree:limb with body:arm. The reasoner might say that trees and bodies are both living and free-standing structures with outgrowths that serve some physiological or biological function. Such a superordinate relationship is an example of a higher order relation. The ability to identify these higher order relations is considered the "hallmark" of reasoning in solving these analogy types (Goswami, 1992).

Reasoning with classical analogies has also been analyzed in terms of the component processes involved, with Sternberg's (e.g., 1977, 1981) componential theory of information processing being widely used. Here, the ability to reason analogically is viewed in terms of a number of component or elemental cognitive and metacognitive processes that are applied. This approach provides a much broader perspective on analogical reasoning capability than do structural theories. In brief, these components involve first, identifying each term of the analogy by *encoding* the attributes or characteristics of each term. Encoding is required for every term of the analogy problem. Next, is the process of *inferring*, where the relationship between the terms within each pairing is determined. Although inferring might appear to correspond to the structuralist conceptualization of a lower order relation, information-processing theorists see the possibility of multiple relations within the pairs being inferred during initial processing. The component process of *mapping* involves the linking of the A:B pairing to the C:D pairing by building a bridging inference on their relational similarity (cf., identifying a higher order relation). Finally, the process of *applying* involves generating or selecting a suitable term to complete the analogy, that is, to give it the required "conceptual balance" (i.e., establishing equivalence between the first and second pairing; Alexander et al., 1997, p. 121).

Reasoning with Problem Analogies

Studies addressing the ability to reason by analogy in problem-solving tasks have increased in popularity in the past couple of decades (e.g., Clement, 1993; Holyoak & Koh, 1985; Novick, 1995; Reed, 1987; Robins & Mayer, 1993; Stavy & Tirosh, 1993). In these studies, the reasoner must recognize the similarity in relational structure between a known problem (termed the *base* or *source*) and a new problem (the *target*); that is, a "structural alignment" or "mapping" between the two problems must be found (Bassok, 2001; Holyoak, Gentner, & Kokinov, 2001; refer Fig. 1.1). Story problems that comprise causal relations in general domains, such as the frequently cited "Genie" problem (Holyoak et al., 1984), have been popular. Here, the base problem involves a magic genie that rolled his carpet into a tube to provide a pathway for some valuable jewels. The target problem entails transporting some small rubber balls from one location to another. For children to solve the problem, they must recognize the intended relational correspondence between the carpet and the paper. In other words, with this type of protagonist story problem, the need to apply analogical reasoning is implicit, whereas in classical analogies it is explicit in the task structure. As discussed later, this implied need to reason analogically is not readily apparent to children and is one of the performance factors that must be taken into account in analyzing the development of analogical reasoning.

Word problems involving specific educational content, such as mathematical concepts, have been less popular in studies of children's analogical reasoning than general story problems (English, 1997, 1998). This is in spite of the fact that solving such problems can contribute significantly to children's conceptual development during mathematical problem solving and can also provide us with insights into children's understanding of core content (English, 1997; Holyoak & Thagard, 1995; Silver, 1990). In one such study, for example, (English, 1997) 75 sixth graders (11-year-olds) were presented with sets of source (or base) problems involving comparison multiplication and division, combinatorial reasoning, and partitive division (sharing) with variable remainder use.

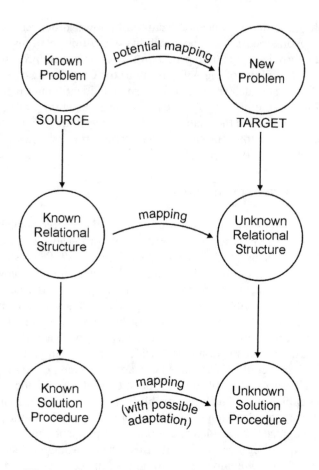

FIG. 1.1.   Reasoning by analogy in problem-solving tasks.

The source problems were designed so that problems with the same mathematical structure had different cover stories and those with different structures had the same cover stories (this is similar to the cross-mapping condition used in other studies, such as Pierce & Gholson, 1994; Quilici & Mayer,
1996). For example, one of the comparison multiplication problems took the
form, *Sarah has 52 books on her shelf. Sue has 4 times as many as Sarah. How
many books has Sue?* A comparison division problem had the same cover
story, namely, *Mary has 72 books on her shelf. This is 3 times as many as Peter
has. How many books has Peter?* This problem design provided insight into
children's abilities to look beyond the surface features of the problems to detect the underlying structural features.

After sorting, classifying, and solving the source problems, the children
were introduced to some target problems. These problems had a similar

structure to the source problems but were more inclusive; that is, they contained all the information needed to solve the source problems, plus some additional information (Reed, Ackinclose, & Voss, 1990). This meant the child had to adapt or extend the source solution procedure in order to use it to solve the target problem, as is the case with the combinatorial examples, *Sally's ice-cream store sells 12 different ice cream flavors and 3 different sized cones. How many different choices of ice cream do you have?* (source problem), and *The Select-A-Card company plans to make boxes of greeting cards that are either green or yellow, and have Christmas, birthday, or Easter greetings, and have either silver or gold lettering. How many different types of cards will there be in each box?* (target problem).

Of interest was the children's ability to recognize commonalities in problem structure and to reason with these in an analogical manner to solve the related target problems. However, it was found that children's representations of the problems often lacked the appropriate relational structures needed for reasoning by analogy, with the children focusing instead on the common surface features of the problems. Even when the children did display relational understanding, they tended not to spontaneously reason analogically and, if they did, they often experienced difficulty in adapting the source solution procedure to meet the new requirements of the target problem.

It is interesting that several studies have shown how subjects in experimental situations tend to focus on superficial features when attempting to use analogy, whereas people in nonexperimental contexts often use more structural features in reasoning analogically (Dunbar, 2001). Dunbar refers to this phenomenon as the "analogical paradox" (p. 313); that is, whereas subjects require specific training or assistance in reasoning analogically in formal research settings, they need no help in using structural analogies in naturalistic contexts. One possible explanation for this paradox is that the surface features of experimental problem situations can present conceptual difficulties that are more structural in nature than previously thought (Lobato & Siebert, 2002). Lobato's work (e.g., Lobato, 2003; Lobato & Siebert, 2002) has shown how traditional studies of transfer, which provide subjects with paired tasks that are similar from the researchers' perspective, can conceal a good deal of students' learning processes. By adopting an "actor-oriented" perspective of transfer (Lobato & Siebert, 2002), researchers can gain insights into how individuals generate their own similarities between problems. Such insights can reveal how a new situation might be connected with the learners' images of previous situations.

From traditional studies of reasoning by analogy in solving problems, it appears that learners require a specific knowledge base pertaining to the use of analogy. First, learners must know the generalizable relational structure of the source or known problem, and, if a source problem has to be retrieved from memory, it must be done so in terms of its relational structure (Gentner

& Gentner, 1983; Gholson, Dattel, Morgan, & Eymard, 1989; Vosniadou, 1989). Semantic alignment, that is, the ability to see the link between the cover story and the mathematical structure of a word problem, requires special attention (Bassok, 2001). The phrasing of many word problems allows students to solve them correctly without understanding the mathematical structure of the problems (i.e., students frequently look for key words, such as *times*, to decide on a solution procedure).

Second, the learner must know to look for and must be able to identify the relational correspondence between the target problem and the source problem. The source problem must be utilized in terms of its generalizable structure (Gholson et al., 1989; see Fig. 1.1). Third, the learner must know what to do with the relational commonalities between the source and target problems. That is, she must know *how* to reason analogically and must appreciate the benefits of doing so (English, 1998). This is particularly important when the target problem is not completely isomorphic with the source, that is, when the solution model from the base problem has to be adapted in some way to account for the unique aspects of the target problem (Novick, 1992).

Reasoning with Pedagogical Analogies

The third type of analogy study involves reasoning with pedagogical analogs. Such reasoning has received considerably less attention even though instructional analogs have long been in use in mathematics and science education, where they are designed to provide a concrete representation of abstract ideas. That is, these analogs serve as a tangible source from which the student can construct a mental representation of the abstract idea or process being conveyed. Although studies addressing scientific analogs have been reported frequently in the educational literature (e.g., Clement, 1993; Duit, 1991; Gentner, 1989; Kurtz, Miao, & Gentner, 2001; Wong, 1993), substantial reviews of mathematical analogs have been comparatively scarce, despite the frequency of their use in the school curriculum. It is thus not surprising, that, when the structural complexity of mathematical analogs has been largely ignored, mixed reports on their instructional effectiveness have appeared (Thompson, 1994).

Even the most basic of mathematical analogs present some complexity for young children. For example, when counters and other discrete items are used to represent numbers to 10, children have to make a relational mapping from the set of items to the corresponding number name, as illustrated in Fig. 1.2. This is not such an easy task because these discrete items do not possess inherent structure; that is, they do not display numerical relationships. It is the way in which the items are arranged and manipulated that conveys these relationships.

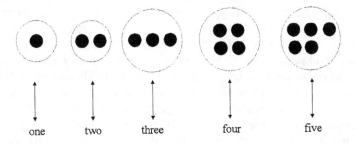

FIG. 1.2. Using counters to represent single-digit numbers. From English and Halford (1995). Reproduced with permission of Lawrence Erlbaum Associates.

Likewise, when children are introduced to the more structured base-10 blocks, they have to interpret the relationships that are inherent in the design of the materials. For example, to reason with the analog shown in Fig. 1.3, the child must focus on its relational properties and must map the base-ten structure of the two long blocks onto the digit "2" in the tens place of the numeral and likewise, map the structure of the seven single blocks onto the 7 ones in the ones place of the numeral. For children to make these mappings, they must understand fully the structure of the source analog and must be able to recognize the relational correspondence between the concrete source and the abstract target. Children must also be able to apply their understanding of these relational correspondences to activities in which the blocks model specific mathematical processes (e.g., those of addition). It is when children fail to develop this relational understanding that their learning becomes meaningless, which can account for many of the reported difficulties in chil-

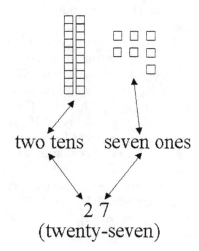

FIG. 1.3. Analogical representation of a two-digit number. From English and Halford (1995). Reproduced with permission of Lawrence Erlbaum Associates.

dren's mathematical learning (e.g., English & Halford, 1995; Hiebert & Wearne, 1992; Resnick, 1991).

Despite their obvious differences, classical analogies, analogous word problems, and pedagogical analogs share a basic similarity. That is, they all require the reasoner to recognize and understand relational or structural similarity and to make the appropriate relational mappings between analogous situations. Nevertheless, children have generally performed worse in studies of classical analogies than they have in studies involving analogous story problems. One explanation for this is that the classical analogies comprise more difficult relations than problem analogies and also lack the contextual framework of problem analogies (Goswami & Brown, 1989). As indicated in the next section, the nature of the classical analogies in traditional studies of young children's reasoning has been a major factor in reports of children's analogical incompetence (e.g., Lunzer, 1965).

CHILDREN'S DEVELOPMENT
OF ANALOGICAL REASONING

The development of young children's analogical reasoning ability has been a controversial issue for some time (e.g., Goswami, 1992; Piaget, 1952; Sternberg & Rifkin, 1979, Vosniadou, 1989). It is only in recent years that young children have been credited with the ability to reason analogically, despite the recognized importance of such reasoning in learning, problem solving, and discovery (Goswami, 1992; Holyoak & Thagard, 1995). This lack of attention has been due in part to the dominance of Piagetian theory (Piaget, 1952; Inhelder & Piaget, 1958), which has argued that children's failure to solve classical analogy tasks is due to their inability to reason about higher order relations. Hence, reasoning by analogy was considered a late developing skill, emerging around 11–12 years of age. Prior to this age, children were considered to rely on associative or lower order relations in solving analogy tasks. For example, in one of Piaget's studies (Piaget, Montangero, & Billeter, 1977), 6-year-old children would solve the classical analogy task, car:petrol as bicycle:?, by selecting a response such as "handlebars," because they "both go on the road." The belief that classical analogies involved proportional concepts (Inhelder & Piaget, 1958) further supported the notion that analogical reasoning required formal-operational thinking.

Most of the earlier studies that supported this view of analogical development, however, failed to test whether the children had the required knowledge base in order to solve the tasks (e.g., Gallagher & Wright, 1979; Lunzer, 1965; Sternberg & Rifkin, 1979). For example, Lunzer (1965) included sophisticated numerical classical analogies in his set of tasks, which clearly were beyond the mathematical knowledge and experience of elementary-grade children. Likewise, in some of the well-known studies of children's reasoning with analogy problems (e.g., Gentner & Toupin, 1986), the view that young children's difficulties are due to their inability to reason with higher order relations is questionable. Indeed, numerous studies of analogical problem solving have found that novice problem solvers, whether they are children or older students, often have difficulty in detecting structural similarities between problems that have different contextual features. This is largely because novice solvers tend to focus on the salient surface features, such as specific items or objects, rather than the underlying structural properties or domain principles (Chi, Feltovich, & Glaser, 1981; Novick, 1992; Silver, 1981; Stavy & Tirosh, 1993). With development however, children are said to display a relational shift in their ability to detect structural relations; that is, they progress from processing object-based commonalities to processing higher order relational similarities (Gentner, 1988; Gholson, Smither, Buhrman, Duncan, & Pierce, 1997).

On the other hand, if children do not have knowledge of the relational systems on which particular analogies are based, it is difficult to claim that they fail analogy tasks because they lack the ability to reason with higher order relations (Goswami, 2001). A lack of conditional knowledge is another performance factor to be considered, as alluded to earlier (Alexander, Schallert, & Hare, 1991; English, 1998). Even if young children (and indeed, adults) know the relations on which an analogy is based, they may fail to solve the particular analogy (i.e., in a manner expected by the experimenter) because they may not realize they have to seek relational similarities and may not know what to do with them (Brown, 1989; English, 1997; Goswami, 1992). One of the major factors, then, that needs to be considered in determining children's analogical reasoning ability is the nature and extent of their knowledge base, including their conceptual, relational, and conditional knowledge (Alexander et al., 1998; Brown, 1989; English, 1998; Goswami, 1992; Vosniadou, 1995). Otherwise, it is not analogical reasoning ability that is being tested, but rather, the richness of the required knowledge base.

When researchers have created situations in which the knowledge base of the young child was a specific consideration, the performance of those as young as 3 years old has demonstrated the processes associated with analogical reasoning (e.g., Alexander et al., 1989; Brown, 1989; Goswami, 1992; Goswami & Brown, 1989; Holyoak & Koh, 1987). Likewise, other researchers who have employed meaningful contexts and materials, such as games or riddles, have produced seemingly strong evidence of young children's capacity to reason about higher order relations; this has been the case for both classical and problem analogies (Alexander et al., 1997; Chen, Yanowitz, & Daehler, 1995; Goswami & Brown, 1989).

Young children have also been shown to respond positively to studies that incorporate a training component (Alexander et al., 1989; Chen & Daehler,

1989; White & Alexander, 1986; White & Caropreso, 1989). These studies have shown that even those children who were initially classified as non-analogical reasoners were able to solve a variety of classical analogy problems following several interventions that focused on the basic reasoning components of these problems (i.e., encoding, inferring, mapping, and applying). The processing of these elemental components was evidenced not only in the children's overall performance on geometric, figural, and concrete (i.e., physical objects) analogies that varied from those used in training, but also in the children's explanations of their thinking. In several of those studies (e.g., Alexander et al., 1989), much was uncovered from what even children as young as 3 and 4 shared about their reasoning. Basically, when asked to talk about how they arrived at their solutions, those classified as analogical reasoners displayed evidence of the basic reasoning components. Further, those classified as analogical reasoners either prior to or following training displayed a resistance to countersuggestion, an occurrence that conflicts with the theoretical premises of Piaget (1952). Alexander and colleagues have suggested that this resistance may be attributable to the game-playing format of the analogy task, which made the children more comfortable with displaying resistance to the arguments or suggestions presented by adults. Further discussion on this point appears in chapter 2.

At this point, it is worth noting that many studies have claimed that young children cannot reason analogically, but this is often because they do not provide the experimenter with the desired responses (personal communication, Alan Schoenfeld). This means that other responses, which could very well involve aspects of analogical reasoning, are ignored. In future studies, we need to look beyond the desired responses and explore the many varied approaches young children take to solving analogical reasoning problems.

In sum, the extensive work that has been completed on analogical reasoning indicates that analogies provide a powerful tool for children's learning about their world. This appears to be the case in many domains, including physics (e.g., Pauen, 1996), language (e.g., Gentner & Rattermann, 1991), mathematics (English, 1999), and naïve biology (Hatano & Inagaki, 1997). Analogies contribute to both the construction and reconstruction of children's knowledge, including mathematical knowledge, and play an important role in conceptual change.

THE NATURE OF MATHEMATICAL REASONING

It is only in recent years that the term, *mathematical reasoning*, has appeared frequently in the research and curriculum literatures (e.g., National Council of Teachers of Mathematics [NCTM], 2000; Stiff & Curcio, 1999). Prior to that, mathematical problem solving involving both routine and novel problems was the domain of focus, with problem-solving processes and strategies being of primary research interest (e.g., Schoenfeld, 1992; Silver, 1985). These days, mathematical reasoning has received the attention it warrants, as can be seen in the 1999 Yearbook of the National Council of Teachers of Mathematics devoted to the topic.

There exist numerous interpretations, however, of mathematical reasoning and of how it is manifested in students' mathematical development. The traditional view of mathematical reasoning as superior computational and analytical skills (Sternberg, 1999) has been revised to accommodate processes that are important in today's knowledge-based era. These include gathering evidence, analyzing data, making conjectures, constructing arguments, drawing and validating logical conclusions, and proving assertions (Malloy, 1999; NCTM, 2000; Peressini & Webb, 1999). Such processes also facilitate specific modes of thinking such as conditional, proportional, spatial, critical, and creative thinking, along with deductive and inductive reasoning (e.g., Baroody, 1998; English & Halford, 1995; Krulik & Rudnick, 1999). For example, deduction involves reasoning logically from generalized statements (often referred to as *premises*) to draw conclusions about particular cases (Greenes, 1996). Likewise, critical thinking involves drawing appropriate conclusions from a given set of data and being able to detect any inconsistencies or contradictions in the data.

Current views on mathematical reasoning also highlight the formation of generalizations, with the abstraction of ideas and relationships being paramount (e.g., NCTM, 2000; Peressini & Webb, 1999; Russell, 1999; Stiff & Curcio, 1999). Russell's (1999) definition illustrates this perspective; namely, mathematical reasoning is "essentially about the development, justification, and use of mathematical generalizations," which "leads to an interconnected web of mathematical knowledge within a mathematical domain" (p. 1). When students progress from considering the specific instance to the general case (i.e., reasoning about a whole class of mathematical objects), they are considered to display effective mathematical reasoning. The identification, extension, and generalization of patterns, for example, are powerful components of inductive reasoning. Indeed, mathematics itself, is frequently viewed as "the science of patterns" (Schoenfeld, 1992, p. 337), with "doing mathematics" seen as a search for patterns (National Research Council, 1989, p. 31).

It is now generally recognized that reasoning is fundamental to understanding and applying mathematics, and that mathematical reasoning should be fostered by engaging students in investigating, representing, conjecturing, explaining, and justifying mathematics (Baroody, 1998; Clements, Sarama, & DiBiase, 2003; NCTM, 2000; Russell, 1999; Stiff, 1999).

Young Children's Mathematical Reasoning

Young children reason mathematically for a variety of purposes in a variety of situations. The nature of this mathematical reasoning has been described variously in the literature. It is frequently viewed as the ability to perceive the basic attributes of objects or symbols, associate or relate objects or symbols with the abstract concepts they signify, and recognize and utilize the patterns and connections among various objects, symbols, and concepts (Baroody, 1998; English & Halford, 1995; Fuson, 1992; Resnick, 1991; Sophian, 1999; Wynn, 1992). Also incorporated in definitions of young children's mathematical reasoning is their understanding of various types of patterns and functional relationships (NCTM, 2000). This includes their ability to sort and classify items, to describe and predict change, and to recognize, construct, and extend patterns.

Argumentation is another component of young children's mathematical reasoning, one that has received limited attention to date (Perry & Dockett, 2002). Children use argumentation processes to learn about their world, query facts and opinions, make decisions, and convince others. Engaging in argumentation develops children's abilities to describe, explain, and justify their mathematical thinking, as well as critically analyze the thinking of others. The following excerpt from our study provides one instance of children engaging in argumentation. The group of preschool children were making "pizzas" out of sand and water when William and Belinda came to a disagreement over adding more water to the "mixture." William initially justified his decision to add more water but subsequently acceded that enough water had been added and recalled the number of cupfuls to support his decision.

William: *We've got plenty of water here.*

Belinda: *No, you can't put water on that* (pizza).

William (adding water):   *Well, that might be nice now, since I put some water in it. This one's (pizza) got lots of water. I might put some more. . . .*

Belinda: *Don't!*

William: *I'm just using a bit.*

Tina: *It keeps turning into a bath.*

William: *I know, cos' we got 1, 2, 3, 4, ah, 5 cups of water. We don't need 6.*

Tina: *Look, I made a pizza.*

William: *Actually, we have got 6. Now I need to put some sand in here. One cup of sand . . . one cup of sand. This will be very good; one cup of sand.*

When we observe young children at play, we see many such cases of mathematical reasoning. Traditionally, however, young children's mathematical reasoning abilities have been studied from a skills-based or product perspective, with a focus on the fundamental procedures of addition, subtraction, multiplication, and division (e.g., Bush, 1978; Carpenter, Moser, & Romberg, 1982). In the past decade or so, there has been a move away from a strong content perspective to one of process, with a focus on the thinking behind children's responses (e.g., Clements et al., 2003; Davis & Maher, 1997; Feeney & Stiles, 1996; Maher & Martino, 1996; Perry & Dockett, 2002). For example, it is no longer a simple issue of whether a kindergarten child can distinguish a circle from a triangle, but whether we can expose the thinking that contributed to the ability to make this distinction, such as whether the kindergarten child can recognize the shapes in less idealized forms or whether the child has the means to label or communicate any differences she may actually perceive.

With an increased focus on the thinking behind children's mathematical responses, research of the past decade has helped dispel common notions of young children as limited in their mathematical abilities. It is now well recognized that young children have a significant implicit understanding of numerous concepts and principles, and can reason with these ideas in mathematically sophisticated ways (Balfanz, 1999; Gelman, 1998; Greeno, 1989; NCTM, 2000). As the chapters of this book and other research demonstrate, young children apply a range of mathematical ideas in their daily lives and develop a substantive informal knowledge of mathematics even before they commence formal schooling (Alexander et al., 1997; Ginsburg, Choi, Lopez, Netley, & Chi, 1997; Ginsburg et al., 1999; Greeno, 1989; NCTM, 2000; Pepper & Hunting, 1998).

Nevertheless, there is still insufficient research on the range of reasoning processes that young children display in their informal learning activities (Ginsburg et al., 1999). We concur with Ginsburg et al. that psychological research on young children's mathematical reasoning is limited and is "disproportionately balanced toward consideration of elementary notions of quantity and whole number" (p. 89). These researchers conducted a series of investigations on young children's mathematical competence as they engaged in the informal mathematical activities of their preschool classroom. One of their findings revealed the relative frequencies of occurrence of the children's informal mathematical activities (i.e., mathematical activity evident in the children's play). Interestingly, of the total period of observation (469 minutes), 36% of the children's activities were devoted to reasoning with patterns and shapes (pattern and shape detection, prediction, creation), 22% to dynamics (exploration of the processes of change or transformation), 18% to relations (magnitude evaluation or comparison), 13% to classification (sorting, grouping, categorizing), and only 1% to enumeration (quantification or numerical judgment). Enumeration, the topic that is most frequently researched, occurred relatively rarely in the children's play. In contrast, the children favored pattern analysis and geometric thinking in their free play.

These findings highlight the need for substantial research on young children's informal mathematical reasoning processes in a diverse range of learning contexts. Importantly, such research needs to be disseminated widely to classroom teachers. A promising step in this direction is the recent book, *Engaging young children in mathematics: Findings from the 2000 National Conference on Standards for Preschool and Kindergarten Mathematics Education* (Clements et al., 2003). The book presents latest research findings concerning early mathematical thinking and learning, and targets classroom teachers as well as other mathematics educators. Further discussion on this work appears in chapter 10.

ANALOGICAL REASONING AND MATHEMATICAL REASONING

One of the key issues we explore in this book is the relationship between mathematical and analogical reasoning. Until recently, this link has received little interest from the research community, especially studies involving in-depth analyses of young children's mathematical and analogical development over time. This is in spite of the fact that major national documents, such as *Principles and Standards for School Mathematics* (NCTM, 2000), emphasize that young children enter school with "a natural tendency to connect everything they know" and that a major goal of instruction is to help children check new ideas against what they already know (p. 146).

As indicated in this chapter, the ability to see connections and relationships among mathematical ideas and to apply this understanding to the solution of new problems is a basic component of mathematical reasoning (Alexander et al., 1997; English, 1997; English & Halford, 1995; Fuson, 1992; Hiebert & Carpenter, 1992). Even at its most basic level, mathematical reasoning requires that young children recognize how a given term (or object or symbol) represents some abstract concept that is not directly conveyed. Yet, the building of relations or correspondences between some physical or symbolic entity and the abstract concept it conveys involves important analogical reasoning processes (English & Halford, 1995; Goswami, 1992; Vosniadou, 1995).

In developing our study, we sought to explore further these apparent links between analogical and mathematical reasoning, as well as deepen our existing understanding of how these forms of reasoning develop in young children from their preschool year through to the end of their second grade. The cross-cultural nature of our investigation enabled us to examine whether developmental trends are the same for American and Australian children. Our findings on these aspects are presented in chapter 3, where profiles of children's analogical and mathematical reasoning development are examined. Chapter 5 presents more in-depth case studies of individual children's development across the three years. In conducting our investigations, it was imperative that we design developmentally appropriate and theoretically sound ways to expose these reasoning capabilities. Our approaches to doing so are addressed in the next chapter, where the construction and validation of our measures of mathematical and analogical reasoning are described.

Also of interest in our study was how changes in children's reasoning relate to the implicit instruction children receive in their classrooms. In recent years, there has been increased attention on the role of classroom discourse in supporting children's mathematical growth (Corwin, 1995; Perry & Dockett, 1998). Although children's learning is influenced by the way in which teachers construct a context for classroom discourse, the way individual children interpret that discourse is equally important (Cobb, Boufi, McClain, & Whitenack, 1997). Hence, another aspect of our research was on individual learners, their learning environments, and the interaction between the two. Specifically, our goal here was to examine the role of classroom discourse in supporting the development of young children's mathematical and analogical reasoning. Chapter 4 addresses the issues and outcomes of this component of our study.

During each of the three years of the study, we interviewed the teachers of the participating children to gain insights into their knowledge, beliefs, and practices with respect to mathematical and analogical reasoning. In chapter 6, we present interview data addressing these aspects and discuss how the teachers viewed the teaching of early mathematics and the development of young children's reasoning. The chapter also includes a theoretical overview of teachers' knowledge, beliefs, and practices, along with a cross-case analysis of teachers displaying different orientations. In chapter 7, in-depth case studies of three teachers are presented.

Commentaries on our work are presented in chapters 8 and 9 by Usha Goswami and Giyoo Hatano, respectively, eminent researchers on children's reasoning and development. In the final chapter, I address some ways in which we might promote the mathematical and analogical reasoning development of young children.

REFERENCES

Alexander, P. A., Murphy, P. K., & Kulikowich, J. M. (1998). What responses to domain-specific analogy problems reveal about emerging competence: A new perspective on an old acquaintance. *Journal of Educational Psychology, 90,* 397–406.

Alexander, P. A., Schallert, D. L., & Hare, V. C. (1991). Coming to terms: How researchers in learning and literacy talk about knowledge. *Review of Educational Research, 61*, 315–343.

Alexander, P. A., White, C. S., & Daugherty, M. (1997). Children's use of analogical reasoning in early mathematics learning. In L. English (Ed.), *Mathematical reasoning: Analogies, metaphors, and images* (pp. 117–147). Mahwah, NJ: Lawrence Erlbaum Associates.

Alexander, P. A., White, C. S., Haensly, P. A., & Crimmins-Jeanes, M. (1978). Training in analogical reasoning. *American Educational Research Journal, 24*, 387–404.

Alexander, P. A., Willson, V. L., White, C. S., Fuqua, J. D., Clark, G. D., Wilson, A. F., & Kulikowich, J. M. (1989). Development of analogical reasoning in 4- and 5-year-old children. *Cognitive Development, 4*, 65–88.

Balfanz, R. (1999). Why do we teach young children so little mathematics? Some historical considerations. In J. Copley (Ed.), *Mathematics in the early years* (pp. 3–10). Reston, VA: National Council of Teachers of Mathematics.

Baroody, A. J. (with Coslick, R. T.). (1998). *Fostering children's mathematical power: An investigative approach to K–8 Mathematics Instruction.* Mahwah, NJ: Lawrence Erlbaum.

Bassok, M. (2001). Semantic alignments in mathematical word problems. In D. Gentner, K. J. Holyoak, & N. Kokinov (Eds.), *The analogical mind: Perspectives from cognitive science* (pp. 401–434). Cambridge, MA: MIT Press.

Brown, A. L. (1989). Analogical learning and transfer: What develops? In S. Vosniadou & A. Ortony (Eds.), *Similarity and Analogical Reasoning* (pp. 369–412). Cambridge, England: Cambridge University Press.

Bush, L. R. (1978). Preschool children's knowledge of addition and subtraction. *Journal for Research in Mathematics Education, 9*, 44–54.

Carpenter, T. P., Moser, J. M., & Romberg, T. A. (Eds.). (1982). *Addition and subtraction: A cognitive perspective.* Hillsdale, NJ: Lawrence Erlbaum Associates.

Chen, Z., & Daehler, M. W. (1989). Positive and negative transfer in analogical problem solving by 6-year-old children. *Cognitive Development, 4*, 327–344.

Chen, Z., Yanowitz, K. L., & Daehler, M. W. (1995). Constraints on accessing abstract source information: Instantiation of principles facilitates children's analogical transfer. *Educational Psychology, 87*(3), 445–454.

Chi, M. T. H., Feltovich, P. J., & Glaser, R. (1981). Categorization and representation of physics problems by experts and novices. *Cognitive Science, 5*, 121–152.

Clement, J. (1993). Using bridging analogies and anchoring intuitions to deal with students' preconceptions in physics. *Journal of Research in Science Teaching, 30*(10), 1241–1257.

Clements, D. H., Sarama, J., & DiBiase, A. M. (Eds.). (2003). *Engaging young children in mathematics: Findings of the 2000 National Conference on Standards for Preschool and Kindergarten Mathematics Education.* Mahwah, NJ: Lawrence Erlbaum Associates.

Cobb, P., Boufi, A., McClain, K., & Whitenack, J. (1997). Reflective discourse and collective reflection. *Journal for Research in Mathematics Education, 28*(3), 258–277.

Corwin, R. B. (1995). *Talking mathematics: Supporting children's voices.* Westport, CT: Heinemann.

Davis, R. B., & Maher, C. A. (1997). How students think: The role of representations. In L. D. English (Ed.), *Mathematical reasoning: Analogies, metaphors, and images* (pp. 93–116). Mahwah, NJ: Lawrence Erlbaum Associates.

Duit, R. (1991). On the role of analogies and metaphors in learning science. *Science Education, 75*(6), 649–672.

Dunbar, K. (2001). The analogical paradox: Why analogy is so easy in naturalistic settings, yet so difficult in the psychological laboratory. In D. Gentner, K. J. Holyoak, & N. Kokinov (Eds.), *The analogical mind: Perspectives from cognitive science* (pp. 313–334). Cambridge, MA: MIT Press.

English, L. D. (1997). Children's reasoning processes in classifying and solving computational word problems. In L. D. English (Ed.), *Mathematical reasoning: Analogies, metaphors, and images* (pp. 191–220). Mahwah, NJ: Lawrence Erlbaum Associates.

English, L. D. (1998). Reasoning by analogy in solving comparison problems. *Mathematical Cognition, 4*(2), 125–146.

English, L. D. (1999). Reasoning by analogy: A fundamental process in children's mathematical learning. In L. V. Stiff & F. R. Curcio (Eds.), *Developing mathematical reasoning, K–12* (pp. 22–36). Reston, VA: National Council of Teachers of Mathematics.

English, L. D., & Halford, G. S. (1995). *Mathematics education: Models and processes*. Mahwah, NJ: Lawrence Erlbaum Associates.

Feeney, S. M., & Stiles, J. (1996). Spatial analysis: An examination of preschoolers' perception and construction of geometric patterns. *Developmental Psychology, 32*, 933–941.

Freeman, K. E. (1996). *Analogical reasoning in 2-year-olds: A comparison of formal and problem-solving paradigms*. Unpublished doctoral dissertation, University of Minnesota.

Fuson, K. (1992). Research on whole number addition and subtraction. In D. A. Grouws (Ed.), *Handbook of research on mathematics teaching and learning* (pp. 243–275). New York: Macmillan.

Gallagher, J. M., & Wright, R. J. (1979). Piaget and the study of analogy: Structural analysis of items. In J. Magary (Ed.), *Piaget and the helping profession* (Vol. 8, pp. 114–119). Los Angeles: University of Southern California.

Gelman, S. (1998, February). *Concept development in preschool children*. Paper presented at the Forum on Early Childhood Science, Mathematics, and Technology, Washington, DC.

Gentner, D. (1988). Metaphor as structure mapping: The relational shift. *Child Development 59*(1), 47–59.

Gentner, D. (1989). The mechanisms of analogical learning. In S. Vosniadou & A. Ortony (Eds.), *Similarity and analogical reasoning* (pp. 199–241). Cambridge, England: Cambridge University Press.

Gentner, D., & Gentner, D. R. (1983). Flowing waters or teaming crowd: Mental models of electricity. In D. Gentner & A. L. Stevens (Eds.), *Mental models* (pp. 99–129). Hillsdale, NJ: Lawrence Erlbaum Associates.

Gentner, D., Holyoak, K. J., & Kokinov, B. N. (Eds.). (2001). *The analogical mind: Perspective from cognitive science*. Cambridge, MA: MIT Press.

Gentner, D., & Rattermann, M. J. (1991). Language and the career of similarity. In S. A. Gelman & J. P. Byrnes (Eds.), *Perspectives on thought and language: Interrelations in development* (pp. 225–277). London: Cambridge University Press.

Gentner, D., & Toupin, C. (1986). Systematicity and surface similarity in the development of analogy. *Cognitive Science, 10*, 277–300.

Gholson, B., Dattel, A. R., Morgan, D., & Eymard, L. A. (1989). Problem solving, recall, and mapping relations in isomorphic transfer and non-isomorphic transfer among preschoolers and elementary school children. *Child Development, 60*(5), 1172–1187.

Ginsburg, H. P., Balfanz, R., & Greenes, C. (2000). Challenging mathematics for young children. In A. L. Costa (Ed.), *Teaching for intelligence II: A collection of articles* (pp. 245–258). Arlington Heights, IL: Skylight Professional Development.

Ginsburg, H. P., Choi, Y. E., Lopez, L. S., Netley, R., & Chi, C. Y. (1997). Happy birthday to you: Early mathematical thinking of Asian, South American, and U. S. children. In T. Nunes & P. Bryant (Eds.), *Learning and teaching mathematics: An international perspective* (pp. 163–207). East Sussex, England: Taylor & Francis.

Ginsburg, H. P., Inoue, N., & Seo, K. H. (1999). Young children doing mathematics: Observations of everyday activities. In J. Copley (Ed.), *Mathematics in the early years* (pp. 88–99). Reston, VA: National Council of Teachers of Mathematics.

Ginsburg, H. P., Pappas, S., & Seo, K. H. (2001). Everyday mathematical knowledge: Asking young children what is developmentally appropriate. In S. L. Golbeck (Ed.), *Psychological perspectives on early childhood education: Reframing dilemmas in research and practice* (pp. 181–219). Mahwah, NJ: Lawrence Erlbaum Associates.

Goswami, U. (1992). *Analogical reasoning in children*. Hove, UK: Lawrence Erlbaum Associates.

20   ENGLISH

Goswami, U. (2001). Analogical reasoning in children. In D. Gentner, K. J. Holyoak, & B. N. Kokinov (Eds.), *The analogical mind: Perspective from cognitive science* (pp. 437–470). Cambridge, MA: MIT Press.

Goswami, U., & Brown, A. L. (1989). Melting chocolate and melting snowmen: Analogical reasoning and causal relations. *Cognition, 35*, 69–95.

Greenes, C. (1996). Investigations: Vehicles for learning and doing mathematics. *Journal of Education, 178*(2), 35–50.

Greeno, J. G. (1989). A perspective on thinking. *American Psychologist, 44*, 134–141.

Hatano, G., & Inagaki, K. (1997). Qualitative changes in intuitive biology. *European Journal of Psychology of Education, 12*(2), 111–130.

Hiebert, J., & Carpenter, T. P. (1992). Learning and teaching with understanding. In D. A. Grouws (Ed.), *Handbook of research on mathematics teaching and learning: A project of the National Council of Teachers of Mathematics* (pp. 65–97). New York: Macmillan.

Hofstadter, D. R. (2001). Epilogue: Analogy as the core of cognition. In D. Gentner, K. J. Holyoak, & B. N. Kokinov (Eds.), *The analogical mind: Perspective from cognitive science* (pp. 499–538). Cambridge, MA: MIT Press.

Holyoak, K. J., Gentner, D., & Kokinov, B. N. (2001). Introduction: The place of analogy in cognition. In D. Gentner, K. J. Holyoak, & B. N. Kokinov (Eds.), *The analogical mind: Perspective from cognitive science* (pp. 1–20). Cambridge, MA: MIT Press.

Holyoak, K. J., & Hummel, J. E. (2001). Toward an understanding of analogy within a biological symbol system. In D. Gentner, K. J. Holyoak, & B. N. Kokinov (Eds.), *The analogical mind: Perspective from cognitive science* (pp. 161–196). Cambridge, MA: MIT Press.

Holyoak, K. J., Junn, E. N., & Billman, D. O. (1984). Development of analogical problem-solving skill. *Child Development, 55*, 2042–2055.

Holyoak, K. J., & Thagard, P. (1995). *Mental leaps: Analogy in creative thought.* Cambridge, MA: MIT Press.

Inhelder, B., & Piaget, J. (1958). *The growth of logical thinking from childhood to adolescence.* New York: Basic Books.

Krulik, S., & Rudnick, J. A. (1999). Innovative tasks to improve critical and creative thinking skills. In L. V. Stiff & F. R. Curcio (Eds.), *Developing mathematical reasoning, K–12* (pp. 138–145). Reston, VA: National Council of Teachers of Mathematics.

Kurtz, K. J., Miao, C. H., & Gentner, D. (2001). Learning by analogical bootstrapping. *The Journal for the Learning Sciences, 10*(4), 417–446.

Lobato, J. (2003). How design experiments can inform a rethinking of transfer and vice versa. *Educational Research, 32*(1), 17–20.

Lobato, J., & Siebert, D. (2002). Quantitative reasoning in a reconceived view of transfer. *The Journal of Mathematical Behavior, 21*(1), 87–116.

Lunzer, E. A. (1965). Problems of formal reasoning in test situations. In P. H. Mussen (Ed.), European research in child development. *Monographs of the Society for Research in Child Development, 30*(2, Serial No. 100), pp. 19–46.

Maher, C., & Martino, A. (1996). The development of the idea of mathematical proof: A five-year case study. *Journal for Research in Mathematics Education, 27*, 194–214.

Malloy, C. (1999). Developing mathematical reasoning in the middle grades: Recognizing diversity. In L. V. Stiff & F. R. Curcio (Eds.), *Developing mathematical reasoning, K–12* (pp. 13–21). Reston, VA: National Council of Teachers of Mathematics.

National Council of Teachers of Mathematics. (2000). *Principles and standards for school mathematics.* Reston, VA: National Council of Teachers of Mathematics.

National Research Council. (1989). *Everybody counts: A report to the nation on the future of mathematics education.* Washington, DC: National Academy Press.

Novick, L. R. (1992). The role of expertise in solving arithmetic and algebra word problems by analogy. In J. I. D. Campbell (Ed.), *The nature and origins of mathematical skills* (pp. 155–188). Amsterdam: Elsevier.

Novick, L. R. (1995). Some determinants of successful analogical transfer in the solution of algebra word problems. *Thinking and Reasoning, 1*(1), 5–30.

Pauen, S. (1996). Children's reasoning about the interaction of forces. *Child Development, 67*, 2728–2742.

Pepper, K. L., & Hunting, R. P. (1998). Preschoolers' counting and sharing. *Journal for Research in Mathematics Education, 29*(2), 164–183.

Peressini, D., & Webb, N. (1999). Analyzing mathematical reasoning in students' responses across multiple performance assessment tasks. In L. V. Stiff & F. R. Curcio (Eds.), *Developing mathematical reasoning, K–12* (pp. 156–174). Reston, VA: National Council of Teachers of Mathematics.

Perry, B., & Dockett, S. (1998). Play, argumentation and social constructivism. *Early Childhood Development and Care, 140*, 5–15.

Perry, B., & Dockett, S. (2002). Young children's access to powerful mathematical ideas. In L. D. English (Ed.), *Handbook of international research in mathematics education* (pp. 81–112). Mahwah, NJ: Lawrence Erlbaum Associates.

Piaget, J. (1952). *The origins of intelligence in children.* New York: Norton.

Piaget, J. (1962). *The language and thought of the child* (M. Gabain, Trans.). Cleveland, OH: Meridian. (Original work published 1923)

Piaget, J., Montangero, J., & Billeter, J. (1977). La formation des correlats. In J. Piaget (Ed.), *Recherches sur l'abstraction reflechissante I* (pp. 115–129). Paris: Presses Universitaires de France.

Pierce, K. A., & Gholson, B. (1994). Surface similarity and relational similarity in the development of analogical problem solving: Isomorphic and nonisomorphic transfer. *Developmental Psychology, 30*(5), 724–737.

Quilici, J. L., & Mayer, R. E. (1996). Role of examples in how students learn to categorize statistics word problems. *Journal of Educational Psychology, 88*, 144–161.

Reed, S. (1987). A structure-mapping model for word problems. *Journal of Experimental Psychology: Learning, Memory, and Cognition, 13*, 124–139.

Reed, S. K., Ackinclose, C. C., & Voss, A. A. (1990). Selecting analogous problems: Similarity versus inclusiveness. *Memory & Cognition, 18*(1), 83–98.

Resnick, L. B. (1991). *From protoquantities to operators: Building mathematical competence on a foundation of everyday knowledge.* Pittsburgh, PA: Learning Research and Development Center, University of Pittsburgh.

Robins, S., & Mayer, R. E. (1993). Schema training in analogical reasoning. *Journal of Educational Psychology, 85*(3), 529–538.

Russell, S. J. (1999). Mathematical reasoning in the elementary grades. In L. V. Stiff & F. R. Curcio (Eds.), *Developing mathematical reasoning, K–12* (pp. 22–36). Reston, VA: National Council of Teachers of Mathematics.

Schoenfeld, A. H. (1992). Learning to think mathematically: Problem solving, metacognition, and sense making in mathematics. In D. A. Grouws (Ed.), *Handbook of Research on Mathematics Teaching and Learning* (pp. 334–370). New York: Macmillan.

Silver, E. A. (1981). Recall of mathematical problem formulation: Solving related problems. *Journal for Research in Mathematics Education, 12*(1), 54–64.

Silver, E. A. (1985). *Teaching and learning mathematical problem solving: Multiple research perspectives.* Hillsdale, NJ: Lawrence Erlbaum Associates.

Silver, E. A. (1990). Contributions of research to practice: Applying findings, methods, and perspectives. In T. J. Cooney & C. R. Hirsch (Eds.), *Teaching and learning mathematics in the 1990s* (pp. 1–11). Reston, VA: National Council of Teachers of Mathematics.

Sophian, K. (1999). Children's ways of knowing: Lessons from cognitive development research. In J. Copley (Ed.), *Mathematics in the early years* (pp. 11–20). Reston, VA: National Council of Teachers of Mathematics.

Stavy, R., & Tirosh, D. (1993). When analogy is perceived as such. *Journal of Research in Science Teaching, 30*(10), 1229–1239.

Sternberg, R. J. (1977). *Intelligence, information processing, and analogical reasoning: The componential analysis of human abilities.* Hillsdale, NJ: Lawrence Erlbaum Associates.

Sternberg, R. J. (1981). Intelligence and nonentrenchment. *Journal of Educational Psychology, 73*, 1–16.

Sternberg, R. J. (1999). The nature of mathematical reasoning. In L. V. Stiff & F. R. Curcio (Eds.), *Developing mathematical reasoning, K–12* (pp. 37–44). Reston, VA: National Council of Teachers of Mathematics.

Sternberg, R. J., & Rifkin, B. (1979). The development of analogical reasoning processes. *Journal of Experimental Child Psychology, 27*, 195–232.

Thompson, P. W. (1994). Concrete materials and teaching for understanding. *Arithmetic Teacher, 41*(9), 556–558.

Vosniadou, S. (1989). Analogical reasoning as a mechanism in knowledge acquisition: A developmental perspective. In S. Vosniadou & A. Ortony (Eds.), *Similarity and analogical reasoning* (pp. 413–437). New York: Cambridge University Press.

Vosniadou, S. (1995). Analogical reasoning in cognitive development. *Metaphor and symbolic activity, 10*(4), 297–308.

Warfield, J., & Yttri, M. J. (1999). Cognitively guided instruction in one kindergarten classroom. In J. V. Copely (Ed.), *Mathematics in the early years* (pp. 103–111). Reston, VA: National Council of Teachers of Mathematics.

White, C. S., & Alexander, P. A. (1986). Effects of training on four-year-olds' ability to solve geometric analogy problems. *Cognition and Instruction, 3*(3), 261–268.

White, C. S., & Caropreso, E. J. (1989). Training in analogical reasoning processes: Effects on low socioeconomic status preschool children. *Journal of Educational Research, 83*(2), 112–118.

Wong, E. D. (1993). Understanding the generative capacity of analogies as a tool for explanation. *Journal of Research in Science Teaching, 30*, 1259–1272.

Wynn, K. (1992). Addition and subtraction by human infants. *Nature, 358*, 749–751.

2

SEEING THE POSSIBILITIES: CONSTRUCTING AND VALIDATING MEASURES OF MATHEMATICAL AND ANALOGICAL REASONING FOR YOUNG CHILDREN

Patricia A. Alexander
Michelle M. Buehl
University of Maryland

Throughout this volume, two powerful forces in human learning and development will be discussed, analogical reasoning and mathematical reasoning. Through the process of analogical reasoning, humans build conceptual bridges between objects and ideas that would otherwise sit in experience or thought as distinct, divorced entities. As Polya (1957) stated, "Analogy pervades all our thinking, our everyday speech and our trivial conclusions as well as artistic ways of expression and the highest scientific achievement" (p. 37). Thus, the child who describes his room to friends as a *garbage dump*, or the famous scientist who envisioned the molecular structure of benzene as a snake grasping its tail are both manifesting analogical reasoning. It is through this analogical process that we forge associations, build theories, transfer understandings, and endow abstract notions with concrete, colorful, and memorable qualities (Vosniadou, 1989).

The nature of mathematical reasoning is no less fundamental to human growth. Mathematics has been described as the science of patterns. Through mathematical reasoning, humans seek to understand and represent the infinite array of patterns that exist everywhere in nature. As with analogical thought, mathematical reasoning is the means by which humans of all ages or expertise attempt to bring order and rhythm to what would otherwise be a chaotic world. This is true whether the reasoner is a toddler who realizes that she can count the dolls on her shelf the same way she counts the fingers on her hand, or a theoretical physicist trying to count the stars in the universe. Moreover, in research and in practice, the phrase *mathematical reasoning* became a marker from many more specific skills or abilities that apply to numeric, spatial, and temporal quantities.

In recent work, our focus has been on the emergence of both analogical and mathematical reasoning (e.g., Alexander, Murphy, & Kulikowich, 1998; White, Alexander, & Daugherty, 1998). We have also been invested in understanding the way that formal educational experiences spark or spurn further growth and elaboration of these fundamental processes during early childhood (e.g., Alexander, 2000). This program of research required that we discover developmentally appropriate and theoretically sound ways to expose the capabilities of young children to reason analogically and mathematically. Researchers concerned with the nature and development of young minds have long faced the formidable task of locating or devising valid and reliable measures that assess children's thoughts and feelings (e.g., Daehler & Chen, 1993; Gelman, 1979; Goswami, 1995; Wynn, 1992). Here we share efforts at constructing and validating measures used to examine the reasoning of young children engaged in analogical (i.e., relational) and mathematical (i.e., numeric/quantification) tasks.

Our first decision in identifying or constructing measures of analogical or mathematical reasoning pertained to the measurement course we would pursue. That is to say, measurement of cognitive processes has generally followed one of two courses (Cronbach, 1990). The first course, such as that pursued in the formulation of classroom-based assessments, involves the assessment of *typical* performance. Measures devised within this framework seek to understand what children are apt to do under normal or typical conditions. When teachers develop tasks or tests to gauge their students' academic strengths and needs as part of the curriculum, they are likely interested in typical performance.

The second course, and the one we chose for this study, entails the exploration of what children can do when placed in situations that stimulate or motivate them to perform at their best. This represents a focus on *maximum* or *optimal* performance (Ackerman & Heggestad, 1997; Alexander, Willson, White, & Fuqua, 1987). The question is no longer what children *typically* do, but rather what these developing minds can *potentially* do (Alexander, White, & Daugherty, 1997; Vygotsky, 1934/1986). Cronbach's (1990) initial distinction between maximum and typical performance rested on the assumption that maximum performance would result when there are significant consequences involved—as in the case of high-stakes testing (Cohen, 2000). In other words, the argument is made that the importance ascribed to such test propels students to function better than they would under more typical educational conditions.

In our work, we take an alternative approach to maximum performance, however (e.g., Alexander, Willson et al., 1987). We hold that tasks that include familiar, manipulative elements cast within low-risk but highly motivating contexts (e.g., game playing) will promote high levels of thinking and responding among young children. Our findings to date have supported this contention and prompted us to take a similar approach to task development as part of this longitudinal investigation (Alexander et al., 1997; White & Alexander, 1986).

Moreover, our rationale for pursuing this maximum course of action addresses other significant psychological and practical issues. For example, the work of Piaget and others (e.g., Inhelder & Piaget, 1958; Sternberg & Rifkin, 1979) offered evidence that higher order cognitive processes, such as that required to reason analogically or to engage in complex mathematical problem solving, were not generally within the grasp of young minds. Thus, it was concluded that children younger than 11 or 12, who had not reached the stage of formal operations, would not manifest complex relational or numeric thought (Piaget, 1952).

Yet, many developmental researchers and theorists hold to alternative views about reasoning development. There are those who regard reasoning as a nascent ability that develops over time as children's language and world knowledge expands (Chen & Daehler, 1989). For example, in terms of analogical reasoning, there is growing evidence (cf. Goswami, 1992) that even the very young can manifest the type of relational thought previously judged beyond their cognitive capabilities. Likewise, researchers and educators have become sensitive to the mathematical understanding and reasoning that children reveal even before they are exposed to formal instruction (English, 1997; Resnick & Omanson, 1987; Saxe, 1991).

Results from our own programs of research give credence to the arguments that children far younger than 11 or 12 manifest analogical and mathematical reasoning (e.g., Alexander, Willson et al., 1989; White et al., 1998). For us, the issue is how these two forms of reasoning (i.e., analogical and mathematical) co-develop. However, we realized that we would be exploring emergent abilities that are highly constrained by young children's rather limited linguistic abilities and conceptual knowledge. Therefore, it made more sense for us to consider familiar, manipulative measures where children's emergent abilities would be more likely to reveal themselves.

Still, efforts to uncover the possibilities within young minds remain hampered by the availability of measures and methods that are statistically reliable and valid, as well as practically useful and motivating (Alexander et al., 1997). Moreover, it was essential that our measures of analogical and mathematical reasoning would be adaptive to changes in children's abilities over time. Specifically, we wanted to track development in children's reasoning from kindergarten through Grade 2. To achieve this end, our instruments had to be able to keep pace with the expanded knowledge and processing skills of our young learners. Finally, our intentions were to look at analogical and mathematical reasoning of children in the United States and Australia. For that reason, we had to be sensitive to cultural and linguistic properties of the measures that could interfere with optimal performance (Goswami, 1992).

In the ensuing discussion, we outline the dimensions of our initial analogical and mathematical reasoning measures and their subsequent iterations. However, there were several salient attributes of these measures that we judged as essential if we were to gauge maximum performance. First, young children generally function well when tasks involve more familiar, concrete, and manipulative objects (White & Coleman, 2000). Therefore, we decided to use simple objects found in preschool and early childhood settings (e.g., attribute blocks and toy dinosaurs) when building the items for the base measures. Further, the degree of abstraction and manipulation would be elements that we took into account when we created more advanced versions of the reasoning tasks.

Second, young children perform better when they work in familiar surroundings with individuals with whom they are comfortable (Bronfenbrenner, 1986). In light of this observation, we decided that all measures should be administered in as close proximity to the children's classroom as possible, and that children should be free to participate or not on any given day. Further, all those involved in the administration of the analogical and mathematical reasoning measures were introduced to the children before testing began and became frequent visitors to the children's classrooms over the course of the three-year study.

Third, we felt it was essential that the tasks we chose or constructed would be stimulating and enjoyable to the children (Crisafi & Brown, 1986; Gelman & Gallistel, 1978). Maximum performance is not just predicated on whether young children can manifest some particular ability or trait, but whether they are willing to do so (Alexander, 1997). That is, motivation is a key factor when assessing young children who are not always as compliant as adults in testing situations. Their attention span is also understandably limited (Byrnes, 1996). Therefore, we structured both the analogical and mathematical measures as "games." In these games, children understood they would be presented with "tricky" problems.

Our previous experience had shown us that this game-playing context was effective at maintaining young children's interest (Alexander, Willson et al., 1987). It also proved beneficial in that the children seemed less susceptible to adult suggestion when they assumed that the adult may try to "trick them." Finally, in establishing the "rules" for the game, we made sure that the children understood that part of their task was to explain their choices or actions. This allowed us to consider not only children's choices, but also to weigh the reasons underlying those choices.

With these salient attributes as our starting points, we set out to identify or design suitable measures that would produce reliable and valid data about young children's analogical and mathematical reasoning capabilities. For each of these reasoning measures, we will address issues of construct validity, describe specifics about the task content and format, overview steps in devising subsequent iterations, and present reliability data.

STUDY BACKGROUND

Participants for this phase of the study were children enrolled in two public schools in the United States and two public schools in Australia. These children were tested at the beginning and end of kindergarten, first grade, and second grade (referred to as Year 1, Year 2 and Year 3 in Australia). Initially, testing began with 61 children, 31 from the United States and 30 from Australia. There were 28 males and 33 females distributed over four classrooms. One classroom in the United States had 5 males and 9 females, and the other had 8 males and 9 females. For the two Australian schools, one classroom had 9 males and 6 females, whereas the other had 6 males and 9 females.

Due to a loss of participants across the span of the study and some variation in testing procedures in Australia, reliability assessments presented here will be based primarily on the responses from the children in American schools. Specifically, the full sample of Australian children was tested at the outset of Year 1. After this initial testing, only 9 case study children were periodically assessed. For the final testing in Year 3, 20 of the Australian children who were initially tested Year 1 were located and assessed. However, the small sample of Australian children for the other time points precluded separate analyses of the data. Consequently, we will present reliability analyses for both American and Australian children for the Year 1 pretests and the Year 3 posttests. The reliability of measures for the other assessments given throughout the course of the study will be based solely on the American data.

ANALOGICAL REASONING MEASURES

Construct Validity

Although there are varied conceptions of analogical reasoning in the research literature, most revolve around a core definition. In essence, analogical reasoning entails the comparison of conceptual and perceptual experiences based on recognized relationships or shared attributes (Case, 1985; Holyoak & Thagard, 1995). As with the earlier examples of the child comparing his room to a garbage dump or the scientist using the image of a snake biting its tail to conceptualize the structure of a benzene molecule, there are relationships or parallels drawn between seemingly dissimilar objects or ideas. Consequently, any measure identified or created must build on relational reasoning in some form.

Further, most theories of analogical reasoning make mention of levels of relational thinking (e.g., Gentner & Toupin, 1986; Inhelder & Piaget, 1958; Sternberg, 1977). For instance, Inhelder and Piaget (1958) framed their theory of analogical reasoning around the notion of lower order (first-order) and higher order (second-order) relations. Lower order relations are associations that remain within the same conceptual category, whereas higher order relations require the individual to cross conceptual realms. For instance, a child is presented with the problem, nest:bird::house:?. In order to solve this analogy, the child must first grasp the relation between nest and bird, a relation that is conceptual in that birds live in nests (lower order relations). The child must also form an association between nest and house, which is more demanding because these terms represent distinct concepts (higher order relations). Ultimately, the child may recognize that a nest and a house are both residences, although for different creatures.

Sternberg's (1977) componential theory of analogical reasoning, which appeared in the 1980s, extends the theoretical work of Piaget. In this theory, Sternberg focuses on underlying processes from which particular relations or responses arise. Therefore, Sternberg labels the process involved in deducing the relationship between nest and bird as *inferring*. The cross-domain associations, as represented by the relationship between nest and house, require a varied form of mental processing that Sternberg refers to as the process of *mapping*.

Similarly, in her extensive program of research on analogical reasoning, Gentner and colleagues (e.g., Gentner & Toupin, 1986) examined the degree of conceptual or perceptual similarity that exists between the terms of analogy problems. According to Gentner and Toupin (1986), high-similarity comparisons result when individuals form associations between objects, people, or events that appear relatively similar on the surface. Low-similarity comparisons, on the other hand, require individuals to forge relations between objects, people, or events that bear little perceptual similarity. For instance, a young child who says that a lemon is like the sun may be inferring their surfaces shared a common feature; that is, a lemon is round and yellow like the pictures of the sun she has seen. This would constitute high perceptual similarity and make the process of analogical reasoning easier. If that same child proclaims that trees are like people because both have arms and need food and water, she would be building relations that are less structurally evident. This would be considered low-similarity reasoning and would represent a more complex form of analogical reasoning.

Our previous work on analogical reasoning was founded on Sternberg's componential theory of analogical reasoning (e.g., Alexander, Pate, Kulikowich, Farrell, & Wright, 1989; Alexander, White, Haensley, & Crimmins-

Jeanes, 1987; White & Alexander, 1986). Because this proved to be an effective theoretical framework for assessing and training analogical reasoning in younger and older children, we retained it as the theoretical model for measure selection and development. However, in evaluating or devising the specific terms of the analogy problems, we also considered the degree of perceptual and conceptual similarity each term represented and used this criterion as a means of creating more demanding items within and across measures (e.g., high similarity—hand:glove::foot:[sock]; low similarity—airplane:parachute::6:[9]).

Finally, there are various ways that analogical reasoning problems can be cast. For example, Gick and Holyoak (1980) framed much of their research around story problems in which analogical relationships are implied. In one of their classic problems, the tumor/fortress dilemma, college students are presented with a situation in which a doctor must treat a patient with a malignant stomach tumor. The problem is that this tumor cannot be irradiated at the requisite intensity because a ray of this magnitude would also destroy the surrounding health tissue. Some students are first given another story about a wise general who must storm an impenetrable fortress. The problem is that all the roads to the fortress have been rigged so that the weight of any approaching army would set off land mines. To avoid this trap, the general breaks his army down into smaller forces. Each force approaches the castle at the same time but by different roads. In that way, the army arrives at the castle in sufficient force to destroy it, but none of the forces are of sufficient weight to trigger the mines planted in the roads. Students who are reasoning analogically will use the content of the fortress story to help them solve the dilemma posed in the tumor problem.

Although story-based analogy problems have been used with younger children (Crisafi & Brown, 1986), we chose to use the classical analogy form in this research. Our rationale for this choice was predicated on several factors. First, far fewer story problems can be used in an assessment measure, and we were concerned about basing reliability and validity of measures on only one or two items. Second, our population would be ethnically and culturally diverse. Therefore, it would be more difficult to find story problems that would be equally understood by all participants. Third, story problems are inherently linguistic problems. Our intention was to cast analogy problems in multiple forms (i.e., pictorial, graphic, and linguistic). We felt that this multimodal approach would contribute to maximum performance among young children. Consequently, we relied on classical analogy problems.

Classical analogies follow the form A:B::C:?, like the nest:bird::house:? problem described earlier. In our research, we have found classical analogy problems to be effective at assessing the inferences (lower order relations) and mappings (higher order relations) children make when solving such problems. Additionally, the terms of these problems can be pictorial, graphic, or linguistic in form.

Base (Year 1) Measure

For the base measures of analogical reasoning, we chose the Test of Analogical Reasoning in Children or TARC (Alexander, Willson et al., 1987). The TARC is a 16-item task in which each problem is constructed from plastic attribute blocks that vary on the dimensions of color (red, blue, and yellow), shape (rectangle, square, circle, and triangle), and size (large and small). Each A:B::C:? problem is displayed on a 30" × 10" wooden gameboard consisting of four 4" × 4" boxes. The first two item boxes are separated from the second two by means of a wooden divider. The 16 problems are arranged in order of increasing difficulty with the first two serving as orienting items. This order is achieved by systematically transforming the relations between A:B on the dimensions of color, shape, and size. Therefore, item 1 (displayed in Fig. 2.1) is the simplest form of problem because there is a direct perceptual similarity between terms. By comparison, the association between the A and B terms of item 16, also displayed in Fig. 2.1, requires a transformation of color, shape, and size.

Four response options are placed to the right of the gameboard. Each distractor was chosen to represent a deviation from the correct response by one or more attributes. For example, for item 5, option 4 was the wrong shape, option 1 deviated by color and shape, and option 4 varied by size, color, and shape. The directions for the TARC were as follows:

> Today, you will be playing a game and in this game we have a gameboard (pointing to the board) and different pieces that go on the board (holding up attribute block). When we play the game, I am going to take different pieces and put them on the board like this (holding up blocks used in item 1). Each time we play the game, I am going to put a piece here (inserting block in first box), here (placing piece in second box), and here (inserting block in third box), but I am not going to put a piece here (indicating the fourth box). What you have to do is choose the piece from over here (pointing to the four choices vertically arranged to the right) that you think should go in this box (pointing to the fourth box). Now, the way you decide is to look at this piece (first block) and this piece (second block) and see how they go together. Then, you look at this piece (third block), and you find the piece from over here (pointing to the options) that goes with this one (third block) the way these two (first and second blocks) go together.

The children were also told that part of the game was explaining why they chose a particular block. To test resistance to suggestion, the researcher would substitute an alternative block for the child's selection (whether correct or incorrect) and ask whether it was a better choice. As a way to fit this within the game context, the children were warned that the researcher may try to "trick them." One researcher sat on the floor and conducted the testing,

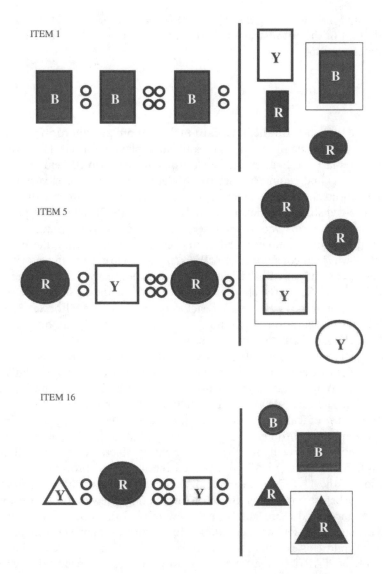

FIG. 2.1. Sample items from TARC.

as the second investigator recorded the children's choices and verbal explanations. Testing took approximately 30 minutes to complete.

Scoring for the TARC was based on the total number of items that the children answered correctly, excluding the initial two practice problems (maximum score = 14). Specifically, incorrect items received a score of 0 and correct items were scored as 1. The Cronbach alphas for the TARC for the 31

American kindergartners was $\alpha = .80$ at pretest and $\alpha = .91$ at posttest (29 children). For the 30 Australian children, the Cronbach alpha for the TARC at pretest was .64.

Task Iteration: Year 2

As a way to transform the TARC to make it more age appropriate for the children, we decided to retain the overall game-playing format. However, we chose to replace the 16 attribute block problems with two 10-item sets of pictorial (Set A) and geometric (Set B) problems (see Fig. 2.2). A variation of these pictorial and geometric sets was used in previous research involving elementary-aged students (Alexander, Wilson, et al., 1987). The use of pictorial and geometric terms was also in keeping with the curricular materials to which the children were exposed in first grade. Further, while the problem structure was held constant (i.e., A:B::C:?), and while each term was set in its proper box on the gameboard, the number of response options was increased. Specifically, for Set A, the children could select from among 10 picture cards, which were presented to them after each problem was posed. For Set B, there were 20 response options, including several that deviated only by one attribute (i.e., color) from the correct answer.

The pictorial and geometric items varied by difficulty. For the pictorial items, difficulty was manipulated by varying the degree of perceptual similarity between the A and B terms. (See items 1 and 10 in Fig. 2.2 as examples of simple and hard items, respectively.) Difficulty for the geometric items was based on the number of features transformed. (See items 3 and 9 in Fig. 2.2 as examples of simple and hard items.) Further, we felt that the marked increase in response options, especially for the geometric items, increased the overall difficulty of the measure. Finally, we piloted the items and procedures for this iteration of the TARC on a sample of American and Australian children of similar age before proceeding. Based on this piloting, a few of the line drawings were enhanced and more suitable colors were used for some of the objects.

Whereas the TARC was scored only for correct or incorrect response, we included children's explanations as part of the scoring procedure for this iteration of the TARC (hereafter referred to as TARC2). Specifically for the TARC2, incorrect selections received a score of 0. If the children chose the correct option but offered no explanation or one that was incoherent or illogical, they received a score of 1 for that item. A score of 2 was given when children not only selected the correct response option, but also provided a reasonable explanation for their choice. By reasonable, we mean that the explanation reflected some attention to the attributes of the terms or to the processes of analogical reasoning (e.g., "I knew that the bird lived in the nest, so I picked this one [house] because a man lives in a house.").

Set A: Pictorial Problems

Item 1

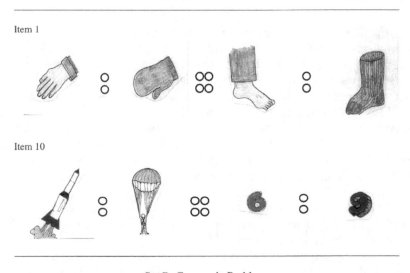

Item 10

Set B: Geometric Problems

Item 3

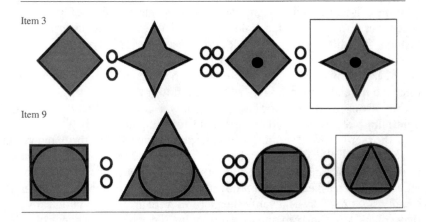

Item 9

FIG. 2.2.   Sample items from Set A and Set B of TARC2.

Interrater agreement for the scoring was .94 (maximum score = 40). The Cronbach alphas for Set A, Set B, and the total measure at pretest were .63, .67, and .70, respectively (26 American first graders). For the posttest, completed at the end of first grade, the alphas for the 26 children were .59 (Set A), .79 (Set B), and .81 (Total). The somewhat low reliability for the pictorial analogy problems at posttest was attributable to the reduced variability in students' performance on those items.

Task Iteration: Year 3

For the final year of the three-year study, we retained the geometric set of analogy problems from Year 2. This became Set A for Year 3. For Set B, we created 10 verbal analogies of the form A:B::C:? Difficulty for these verbal analogies was based on the familiarity of the concepts and on the level of similarity between terms. For example, one of the easier verbal analogies in Set B was bird:fly::fish:(swim), whereas a more difficult item was perfume:woman:: aftershave:(man). It should be noted that even though most of the children in the study were reading to a certain degree, the researcher would read the words aloud to the children or permit them to read the words themselves. In addition, if children did not know the meaning of a particular word, it would be defined briefly for them.

For this final year, we also included two items in the reasoning measure, which required the children to generate their own analogy items (Set C). For these items, the children were provided with 19 picture cards and asked to create and then explain their own problem. The gameboard was used in this portion of the task, as well as for the items in Sets A and B. These generated analogies were scored on a 0–3 scale.

If the child failed to create an appropriate problem, a score of 0 was given. A score of 1 was given if the child used the pictures in some linear or logical fashion, but did not exhibit analogical reasoning. This typically occurred when children used the four pictures to tell a story (e.g., "There was this *boy* and he had a toy *car* . . ."). This also occurred when children created two distinct and unrelated pairings (e.g., "This is a flower [buds] and this is the bush it came from [blooming flowers], and this is a hot thing [hand touching a lightbulb] but this is a cold thing" [hand touching an icecube]).

If the pictures were seemingly analogically arranged, but the explanation was missing or illogical, the response was scored as 2 (e.g., The child first selects pictures of a bird and a nest and then pictures of a person and a house. However, when asked to explain how the pictures "go together," he cannot.) Finally, a score of 3 was given if the pictures were arranged analogically and the explanation displayed analogical thinking (i.e., showed evidence of inferring and mapping; e.g., "The flowers [blooming flowers] go on the stems [buds with stems]. The leaf [leaf] goes on the tree [tree].").

The pretest data for Year 3 was based on the responses of 23 American second graders. The Cronbach alphas for Set A, Set B, Set C, and for the total analogy measure (including the "create-your-own" problems) were .53, .65, .25, and .75. Results for Year 3 were based on data from 22 American second graders. The Cronbach alphas were .76 for Set A, .64 for Set B, .59 for Set C, and .80 for the total analogy measure. Twenty Australian children also completed the Year 3 TARC at posttest. The Cronbach alphas for Set A, Set B, Set C, and for the total analogy measure were .63, .42, .36, and .58.

MATHEMATICAL REASONING

Construct Validity

As with analogical reasoning, there are diverse perspectives on the nature of mathematical reasoning. In much of the educational literature, mathematical reasoning is de facto defined as the thinking or understanding required to perform the mathematical tasks that are part of school curricula (Dreyfus & Eisenberg, 1996; English, 1997; National Council of Teachers of Mathematics [NCTM], 1999). Still, according to Dreyfus and Eisenberg (1996), there are several facets of thought that are common to most implicit and explicit characterizations of mathematical reasoning, such as analogy, representation, visualization, and reversibility of thought.

We found support for Dreyfus and Eisenberg's (1996) position. For instance, we examined various volumes and documents that specifically address mathematical learning (e.g., Mayer, 1998; Resnick & Ford, 1981; Sternberg & Ben-Zeev, 1996). In doing so, we found that mathematical reasoning was generally implicitly rather than explicitly defined. However, whether implicitly or explicitly explained, mathematical reasoning was conveyed as the mental activities associated with the performance of mathematic tasks, especially the solution of mathematic problems of a "schooled" nature (Stewart, 1987).

In keeping with Dreyfus and Eisenberg's (1996) analysis, we gave consideration to the mental processes underlying performance of such problem-solving tasks. For instance, when specifically delineated in NCTM's Principles and Standards for School Mathematics, mathematical reasoning is described as "habits of thinking clearly and checking new ideas against what they already know," "chains of deduction," and "making sense of mathematics" (1999, Standard 7, p. 1). The NCTM document also states that pattern recognition and classification skills are central to mathematical reasoning, and that children's development of logical reasoning is dependent on [students'] ability to explain their reasoning for the responses they make.

Indeed, despite the definitional variations in the literature, there appear to be basic processes that underlie mathematical reasoning, as Dreyfus and Eisenberg (1996) posited. Those basics include quantification, patterning, abstraction and generalization, and representation and translation. In effect, children must acquire a sense of quantity, amount, or number (quantification), if they are to think mathematically. They must also have the ability to perceive regularities in nature or to conceive of such patterns in the abstract (patterning). These children must also understand that the marks or symbols they see represent more than their explicit physical nature (abstraction).

Similarly, individuals, including young children, must come to accept that the imperfect objects or representations in their physical environment stand for "perfect" mathematical forms (idealization). For example, if we were to draw a circle on this page with a compass, we would discover that it was far from a perfect circle, as a result of flaws in the paper, the drawing implements, and our artistic ability. Yet, that would not prevent us from conceiving it as a perfect circle for the purpose of mathematical performance. Over time, individuals must also acquire the ability to consolidate information into a more parsimonious, more encompassing, statement (generalization). In fact, without generalization, there would be no means for mathematicians to cope with the infinite amount of information in the physical world or in the realm of the abstract.

Finally, mathematical thinking can be characterized by representation and translation. Representation is the process by which individuals form an external depiction or an internal, mental model of information they encounter. Translation, on the other hand, refers to the ability to convey that internal or external model in some alternative format, as when ideas are symbolically represented in words, pictures, or numbers. Butterworth (1999) calls this process *transcoding*.

For the purpose of this longitudinal study, we targeted several of these basic processes of mathematical reasoning that seemed particularly relevant to the emergence of mathematical understanding in young children. Specifically, our interests were on quantification, patterning, representation, and translation, with the latter demonstrated in children's construction of problems and their verbal explanations. In addition, we looked carefully at the curricula for the early grades to ensure that the tasks used as catalysts for these thinking processes were developmentally appropriate for these children.

Base (Year 1) Measure

Unlike the situation for analogical reasoning, we were unable to locate an existing measure to serve as our test of mathematical reasoning. We initially considered the Georgia Kindergarten Assessment Program [GKAP], which had been used in an earlier study of the relationship of analogical and mathematical reasoning for 26 preschoolers and kindergartners (Alexander et al., 1997). The GKAP consists of 24 items and focused on the logical-mathematical skills of sorting, comparison, numerical recognition and counting, and extending patterns. However, Alexander and colleagues reported that this measure was a rather limited gauge of the children's mathematical reasoning. We concurred with this assessment of the GKAP and determined to expand the scope of this measure for this study.

The curricular and empirical work of Lyn English, editor of this volume, was central to the development of this new measure. For example, to form the base measure, hereafter referred to as the Mathematics Reasoning Test for Young Students [MRTYS], the research team relied heavily on problems and manipulative tasks illustrated in *Sunshine Maths Year 1*, a curricular guide written for Australian children by English and Baturo (1984). A similar curricular program was in place in the American schools, as well. The resulting test, which was piloted on a comparable group of children, consisted of four components.

The first component (18 items, maximum score = 49), Attributions and Patterning, assessed the children's ability to identify salient features in given manipulatives (e.g., attribute blocks or toy dinosaurs). The children then arranged the manipulatives into groups of their choosing. We scored the children's groupings on a 0–2 scale based on the number (i.e., 1 or more than 1) and level of sophistication (i.e., strong or weak reliance on perceptual features) of the attributes they used to form those groups. For example, if the children stated that they put the dinosaurs together by color, they received a score of 2. We awarded 1 point for the use of only 1 attribute and 1 point for the selection of color, a surface-level feature, as that grouping variable. However, if the children said the dinosaurs in their groups were the same kind (e.g., T-Rex or triceratops) and ate different things, their explanation was scored as 4. This 4 represented the use of multiple attributes (2 points), including features like eating habits that are less reliant on physical attributes (2 points). As part of this problem set, children also identified, completed, and created linear patterns using the given manipulatives (e.g., ABC or ABBA patterns). For example, using dinosaurs that varied by type and by color, we created a pattern of an orange triceratops followed by two purple T-Rexes and then another orange triceratops (i.e., ABBA). We asked the children to show us which dinosaurs would come next.

Two item sets in this base measure targeted quantification. The first of these (9 items, maximum score = 10) assessed the children's understanding of relations that dealt primarily with length (Quantification-Relations). All materials for these relational comparisons were concrete, manipulative objects such as sticks of varying sizes. For one item in this set, the children were asked to reorder sticks into ascending lengths. We scored their responses as 0, 1, or 2 depending on whether that reordering was completely inaccurate (0), partially correct (1), or entirely correct (2).

The second set examined quantification pertaining to numbers (Quantification-Numbers). Within this set (23 items, maximum score = 23), the children counted to 10 and beyond. Specifically, the children were told, "Teddy would like to hear you count. He would like you to start at the number 1 and count to 10 . . . Can you count higher than 10?" The children also gave the name for a particular numerical symbol (e.g., 3 or 8) and counted an appropriate number of manipulatives (e.g., "Can you tell me how many teddy bears are here?"). In addition, the children used number cards to provide the appropriate symbol for a particular named quantity name (e.g., "Can you find the number 2 for me?"). The movement back and forth from counter symbols to labels was also illustrative of the children's representation and translation abilities. We independently scored all tests with an interrater agreement of .95. The Cronbach alphas at pretest for the 31 American kindergartners were .71 for the overall test and .61, .63, and .69 for the Attributions and Patterning, Quantification-Relations, and Quantification-Numbers, respectively. For the 24 Australian students (6 students were eliminated from this analysis due to missing data), the pretest Cronbach alphas were .88 for the overall test and .67, .82, and .91 for Attributions and Patterning, Quantification-Relations, and Quantification-Numbers, respectively. At posttest, the Cronbach alphas (29 American children) were .45 for the overall test and .44, .52, and .46 for the Attributions and Patterning, Quantification-Relations, and Quantification-Numbers, respectively. As we found for several analogical reasoning posttests, the low alphas were largely attributable to reduced variability. Posttest reliabilities for the Australian students could not be conducted due to the substantially reduced sample size.

Task Iteration: Year 2

In extending and modifying the base measure for the second year of the study, we maintained the same three components of the MRTYS. With the assistance of Lyn English, we expanded the Attributions and Patterning set for Year 2 (referred to as the MRTYS2) by including more pattern completions and pattern creations. The MRTYS2 also required finer discriminations among blocks varying on multiple attributes (15 items, maximum score = 36). As with the MRTYS, the children's explanations were considered in scoring items in this set.

For the Quantification-Relation set (10 items, maximum score = 13), we replaced the concrete manipulatives with line drawings of three houses differing on various dimensions (see Fig. 2.3). We asked the children questions pertaining to relational aspects of the pictures (e.g., "Which house is the tallest?"). We also asked the children to illustrate the position of certain objects. For instance, we asked them to "[d]raw a bird flying OVER the house that has three windows." We scored these items as 0 (inappropriate) or 1 (appropriate). For three questions in this segment, we asked the children to make comparisons based on multiple spatial dimensions such as width and height (e.g., "Does the highest house have the tallest TV antenna?"). The children had to provide justifications for their yes or no responses to these spatial problems, resulting in a 0–2 scale.

For the Quantification-Number set (34 items, maximum score = 34), the children were asked to recognize, produce, compare, and sequence numbers between 1 and 40, with the aid of manipulatives. For example, the children were shown a display of 12 number cards and asked to "pick any number that is GREATER THAN 25" or to "pick any number BETWEEN 10 and 15."

FIG. 2.3. Drawing used for MRTYS2 Quantification-Relations items.

Also, the children listened to simple story problems and were asked to represent and solve the problem using counters (e.g., "Penny is a hungry dog. On Sunday, she ate four dog biscuits for breakfast, two for lunch, and three for afternoon snack. How many dog biscuits did she eat on Sunday?").

We independently scored the Year 2 measure with a resulting level of agreement of .93. At pretest, the Cronbach alphas were .84 for the overall MRTYS2 test (26 American first graders) and .29, .65, and .91 for the Attributions and Patterning, Quantification-Relations, and Quantification-Numbers, respectively. At posttest, the alphas were .79 (26 American children) for the overall test and .53, .61, and .84 for the aforementioned problem sets.

Task Iteration: Year 3

Changes involving increased complexity and decreased use of concrete manipulatives characterized the Year 3 measure (MRTYS3). In addition, several of the prior problem sets were expanded and restructured into separate components. For instance, there was a set of 10 items focusing on attribute identification or completion on the MRTYS3 (Attributions). As illustrated in the sample problems in Fig. 2.4, performance targeted drawings rather than concrete objects and entailed multiple attributes that the children identified or produced. In addition, a set of seven problems assessed the children's sequencing and patterning abilities (Sequencing and Patterning). For this set, children dealt with pictures and figures like those seen in Fig. 2.4 that they ordered and explained. When requested to explain their order, this explanation was considered in scoring. Thus, an incomplete or illogical order was scored as 0, whereas a seemingly viable sequencing accompanied by no clear or reasonable explanation received a score of 1. A score of 2 was given when both

Attribution Problems

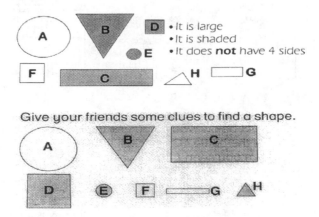

Sequencing Problem

Write the numbers 1, 2, 3, 4, 5 to show the ORDER in which each of these has happened:

FIG. 2.4.   Sample items from MRTYS3 Attributions and Sequencing and Patterning.

the ordering and the explanation were judged as appropriate (maximum score = 14).

The 6 items dealing with Quantification-Relations focused on the children's understanding of length, mass, and spatial comparisons. Each of these items, scored on a 0–2 scale, required students to justify their answers (maximum score =12). For example, we asked the children whether the book displayed would weigh "LESS THAN 2 pounds (1 kilogram for the Australian children), ABOUT 2 pounds, or MORE THAN 2 pounds?" They were then asked to explain why that was so. The Quantification-Number set consisted of 9 items in which the children not only had to display an understanding of numbers between 1 and 100, but also a conception of place value. For example, the children were given an array of place value blocks arranged by hundreds, tens, and ones and asked to show the number 217. Once the children created their arrangement, they were asked to explain how they knew they had produced the number 217.

For the final year of testing, we also extended the section on word problems to include 14 items (Story Problems). We did this to match the transformations that were occurring in the schools' curricula where increasingly more instructional attention was devoted to understanding mathematical problems embedded in text. As part of this assessment, the children solved several word problems like the following: "Lara saved 32 dollars to go to the Spring Fair. However, she would like to save 40 dollars to spend at the fair. How many more dollars does she need to save?" In addition, the children were given a traditional problem, such as 10 − 3, and asked to create their story to go with that problem (maximum score = 25).

As in the prior two years, we scored the MRTYS3 tests independently with an interrater agreement of .94. For the Year 3 pretest data, the Cronbach alpha was .88 for the overall test (23 American second graders). The alphas for the various sets were .64 (Attributions), .61 (Sequencing and Patterning), .66 (Quantification-Relations), .77 (Quantification-Number), and .77 (Story Problems). The alphas for the posttest data (22 American second graders) were .69 (Attributions), .45 (Sequencing and Patterning), .54 (Quantification-Relations), .69 (Quantification-Number), and .74 (Story Problems). The alpha for the overall test was .90. Twenty Australian children also completed the MRTYS3 at the conclusion of the study. The alphas for the 20 Australian students were .44 (Attributions), .30 (Sequencing and Patterning), .04 (Quantification-Relations), .68 (Quantification-Number), and .61 (Story Problems). The alpha for the overall test was .81 for the Australians.

CONCLUSIONS AND IMPLICATIONS

In this investigation, we tested the reliability and validity of data from measures chosen or created to assess the analogical and mathematical reasoning of young children. To this end, we believe that we have been generally successful. We built our measures on what we saw as best practices in the assessment of maximum performance in the young, and on theory and research in analogical and mathematical thinking. Further, we were able to extend and expand our base measures, so that they could keep pace with the developmental changes taking place in the minds of our young participants.

Of course, the findings of our study must be considered in light of the limitations. Foremost, this longitudinal investigation was conceptualized as cross-cultural. Yet, while the measures were in fact used in both the American and Australian classrooms with success, we were unable to incorporate the

Australian children in all of these analyses. We hope that there will be subsequent occasions to use the TARC and MRTYS measures with children from various cultural and ethnic groups and thereby gauge the reliability and validity of their resulting data more broadly.

Further, in conducting a longitudinal investigation, we found it necessary to formulate iterations of our base measures for Years 2 and 3. Perhaps, in the future, we can devise a single measure that can more readily adapt to the changes in learning and development that occur for young children as they progress in their education. Related to this latter point, we did not consider the impact of classroom instruction on children's performance. However, the observations that were an ongoing part of this longitudinal study of young children's analogical and mathematical reasoning development point to the potential influence of instruction on student development. Specifically, there was a continued and explicit focus on young children's mathematical learning both in the American and Australian schools. No such continued or explicit attention to analogical reasoning was demonstrated in any of the classrooms we observed. Therefore, even though we may wish to speculate on the impact of schooling on reasoning development, the direct or indirect effects of such curricular and pedagogical emphases on the children's reasoning abilities remain indeterminable.

Despite these limitations, the present study has contributed to current understanding about young children's learning and development on several fronts. First, we found clear evidence that young children engage in both analogical reasoning and mathematical reasoning—concerns to the contrary not withstanding. Second, we were able to use or devise measures that not only proved informative, but which the children also found entertaining. Assessment, it appears, need not be painful to be effective. Third, we saw evidence of analogical and mathematical reasoning in these young children even from the outset of the study. If we personally had any doubts about the remarkable capacity of these young minds to reason, the results of this investigation would have put those doubts to rest.

That is not to say that individual differences in reasoning were nonexistent. Quite to the contrary, there was tremendous variability in the reasoning of these children both within and across domains. There were preschoolers who initially manifested the process of analogical thinking and never wavered in that ability. Similarly, there were children who, even after three years of formal learning, had not achieved analogical reasoning to any consistent degree. This same degree of variability was evident for these young children's mathematical reasoning. There were those preschoolers who surprised us with their mathematical prowess, just as there were children whose mathematical reasoning remained rudimentary.

However, by examining how children engage in analogical and mathematical reasoning, we may be better able to promote optimal growth for all students—whether their abilities be strong or weak. For example, we may be able to devise learning environments and instructional activities that nurture these emergent abilities and consequently foster children's continued reasoning development. At the very least, such exploration of children's thinking may enlighten us as to the workings of the young mind and allow us to make more informed choices in our research and in our educational practice.

REFERENCES

Ackerman, P. L., & Heggestad, E. D. (1997). Intelligence, personality, and interests: Evidence for overlapping traits. *Psychological Bulletin, 121,* 219–245.

Alexander, P. A. (1997). Mapping the multidimensional nature of domain learning: The interplay of cognitive, motivational, and strategic forces. In M. L. Maehr & P. R. Pintrich (Eds.), *Advances in motivation and achievement* (Vol. 10, pp. 213–250). Greenwich, CT: JAI Press.

Alexander, P. A. (2000). Toward a model of academic development: Schooling and the acquisition of knowledge: The sequel. *Educational Researcher, 29*(2), 28–33, 44.

Alexander, P. A., Murphy, P. K., Kulikowich, J. M. (1998). What responses to domain-specific analogy problems reveal about emerging competence: A new perspective on an old acquaintance. *Journal of Educational Psychology, 90,* 397–406.

Alexander, P. A., Pate, P. E., Kulikowich, J. M., Farrell, D. M., & Wright, N. L. (1989). Domain-specific and strategic knowledge: Effects of training on students of differing ages or competence levels. *Learning and Individual Differences, 1,* 283–325.

Alexander, P. A., White, C. S., & Daugherty, M. (1997). Children's use of analogical reasoning in early mathematics learning. In L. English (Ed.), *Mathematical reasoning: Analogies, metaphors, and images* (pp. 117–147). Mahwah, NJ: Lawrence Erlbaum Associates.

Alexander, P. A., White, C. S., Haensly, P. A., & Crimmins-Jeanes, M. (1987). Training in analogical reasoning. *American Educational Research Journal, 24,* 387–404.

Alexander, P. A., Willson, V. L., White, C. S., & Fuqua, J. D. (1987). Analogical reasoning in young children. *Journal of Educational Psychology, 79,* 401–408.

Alexander, P. A., Willson, V. L., White, C. S., Fuqua, J. D., Clark, G. D., Wilson, F., & Kulikowich, J. M. (1989). Development of analogical reasoning in four- and five-year-old children. *Cognitive Development, 4,* 65–88.

Alexander, P. A., Wilson, A. F., White, C. S., Willson, V. L., Tallent, M. K., & Shutes, R. E. (1987). Effects of teacher training on children's analogical reasoning performance. *Teaching and Teacher Education, 3*(4), 275–285.

Bronfenbrenner, U. (1986). Ecology of the family as a context for human development: Research perspectives. *Developmental Psychology, 22,* 723–742.

Byrnes, J. P. (1996). *Cognitive development and learning in instructional context.* Boston: Allyn and Bacon.

Butterworth, B. (1999). *What counts: How every brain is hardwired for math.* New York: Free Press.

Case, R. (1985). *Intellectual development: Birth to adulthood.* New York: Academic Press.

Chen, Z., & Daehler, M. W. (1989). Positive and negative transfer in analogical problem solving by 6-year-old children. *Cognitive Development, 4,* 327–344.

Cohen, A. S. (2000). High-stakes testing in grades K–12: Comments on Paris et al. *Issues in Education, 6*(1/2), 133–138.

Crisafi, M. A., & Brown, A. L. (1986). Analogical transfer in very young children: Combining two separately learned solutions to reach a goal. *Child Development, 57,* 953–968.

Cronbach, L. J. (1990). *Essentials of psychological testing* (5th ed.). New York: Harper & Row.

Daehler, M. W., & Chen, Z. (1993). Protagonist, theme, and goal object: Effects of surface features on analogical transfer. *Cognitive Development, 8,* 211–229.

Devlin, K. (1994). *Mathematics: The science of pattern.* New York: Freeman.

Dreyfus, T., & Eisenberg, T. (1996). On different facets of mathematical thinking. In R. J. Sternberg & T. Ben-Zeev (Ed.), *The nature of mathematical thinking* (pp. 253–284). Mahwah, NJ: Lawrence Erlbaum Associates.

English, L. D. (1997). *Mathematical reasoning: Analogies, metaphors, and images.* Mahwah, NJ: Lawrence Erlbaum Associates.

English, L. D., & Baturo, A. (1984). *Sunshine Maths Year 1.* Melbourne, Australia: Longman.

Gelman, R. (1979). Preschool thought. *American Psychologist, 34,* 900–905.

Gelman, R., & Gallistel, C. R. (1978). *The child's understanding of number.* Cambridge, MA: Harvard University Press.

Gentner, D., & Toupin, C. (1986). Systematicity and surface similarity in the development of analogy. *Cognitive Science, 10,* 277–300.

Gick, M. L., & Holyoak, K. J. (1980). Analogical problem solving. *Cognitive Psychology, 12,* 306–355.

Goswami, U. (1992). *Analogical reasoning in children.* Hove, UK: Lawrence Erlbaum Associates.

Goswami, U. (1995). Transitive relational mappings in three- and four-year olds: The analogy of Goldilocks and the three bears. *Child Development, 66,* 877–892.

Holyoak, K. F., & Thagard, P. (1995). *Mental leaps: Analogy in creative thought.* Cambridge, MA: MIT Press.

Inhelder, B., & Piaget, J. (1958). *The growth of logical thinking from childhood to adolescence.* New York: Basic Books.

Mayer, R. E. (1998). *The promise of educational psychology: Learning in the content areas.* Columbus, OH: Merrill.

National Council of Teachers of Mathematics. (1999). *Curriculum standards for teaching mathematics.* Reston, VA: Author.

Piaget, J. (1952). *The origins of intelligence.* New York: Norton.

Polya, G. (1957). *How to solve it.* Princeton, NJ: University Press.

Resnick, L. B., & Ford, W. (1981). *The psychology of mathematics for instruction.* Hillsdale, NJ: Lawrence Erlbaum Associates.

Resnick, L. B., & Omanson, S. F. (1987). Learning to understand arithmetic. In R. Glaser (Ed.), *Advances in instructional psychology* (Vol. 3, pp. 41–95). Hillsdale, NJ: Lawrence Erlbaum Associates.

Saxe, G. B. (1991). *Culture and cognitive development: Studies in mathematical understanding.* Hillsdale, NJ: Lawrence Erlbaum Associates.

Sternberg, R. J. (1977). *Intelligence, information processing, and analogical reasoning: The componential analysis of human abilities.* Hillsdale, NJ: Lawrence Erlbaum Associates.

Sternberg, R. J., & Ben-Zeev, T. (1996). *The nature of mathematical thinking.* Mahwah, NJ: Lawrence Erlbaum Associates.

Sternberg, R. J., & Rifkin, B. (1979). The development of analogical reasoning processes. *Journal of Experimental Child Psychology, 27,* 195–232.

Stewart, I. (1987). *The problem of mathematics.* New York: Oxford University Press.

Vosniadou, S. (1989). Analogical reasoning as a mechanism in knowledge acquisition: A developmental perspective. In S. Vosniadou & A. Ortony (Eds.), *Similarity and analogical reasoning* (pp. 413–437). New York: Cambridge University Press.

Vygotsky, L. (1986). *Thought and language* (A. Kozulin, Trans.). Cambridge, MA: MIT Press. (Original work published in 1934).

White, C. S., & Alexander, P. A. (1986). Effects of training on four-year-olds' ability to solve geometric analogy problems. *Cognition and Instruction, 3,* 261–268.

White, C. S., Alexander, P. A., & Daugherty, M. (1998). The relationship between young children's analogical reasoning and mathematical learning. *Mathematical Cognition, 4*(2), 103–123.

White, C. S., & Coleman, M. (2000). *Early childhood education: Building a philosophy for teaching*. Columbus, OH: Merrill.

Wynn, K. (1992). Addition and subtraction by human infants. *Nature, 358*, 749–751.

3

LONGITUDINAL AND CROSS-CULTURAL TRENDS IN YOUNG CHILDREN'S ANALOGICAL AND MATHEMATICAL REASONING ABILITIES

Michelle M. Buehl
University of Memphis

Patricia A. Alexander
University of Maryland

As discussed in the other chapters of this book, analogical and mathematical reasoning are cognitive processes that are essential in our daily lives. Every day we reason analogically and mathematically to acquire new knowledge, understand abstract concepts, and make sense of the world around us (English, 1999; Holyoak & Thagard, 1995). Further, those processes are used regularly in both informal and formal learning environments, underscoring the pervasiveness of these forms of reasoning (e.g., Resnick & Omanson, 1987; Saxe, 1991; Vosniadou, 1989). But how do these processes emerge? What fosters their development and how do they change over time? These are some of the questions that led us initially to explore the analogical and mathematical reasoning abilities of young children.

Complex reasoning abilities were initially believed to be faulty or non-existent until later childhood (e.g., Inhelder & Piaget, 1958). The recognition that young children are able to reason at higher levels than once thought possible has opened the field to new areas of research (Chen & Daehler, 1989; Goswami, 1992). The last 20 years, in particular, has witnessed a burgeoning of research examining the cognitive and reasoning processes of young children. This research indicates that children do indeed display more advanced forms of reasoning early in life. However, researchers are still working to understand (a) what are the most advanced forms of reasoning in which young children engage in and under what conditions, (b) what such reasoning looks like, and (c) how it changes over time.

Within the cognition and reasoning literatures, some researchers have specifically addressed the onset and development of analogical reasoning (e.g., Goswami, 1992, 1995; Holyoak & Thagard, 1995; Sternberg, 1977). This work demonstrates that young children evidence analogical reasoning under certain conditions. For example, the task must be appealing to children, appropriate to their knowledge base, and presented in a familiar and welcoming context (Chen, 1996; Goswami & Brown, 1989; Holyoak & Koh, 1987). In an effort to design tasks to meet these criteria, some researchers have employed story analogies in which children were told a story and then asked to solve a problem that was analogous to the problem discussed in the initial story (e.g., Holyoak, Jull, & Billman, 1984). Such tasks either drew from or provided the children with necessary background knowledge. Further, the story format was familiar to the young children.

In contrast, Alexander and colleagues developed the Test of Analogical Reasoning in Children (TARC; Alexander, Willson, White, & Fuqua, 1987; Alexander et al., 1989), a measure that also met the criteria for an appropriate task, but presented problems in the classic A:B::C:? format. Specifically, the TARC, presented as a fun but tricky game, used objects that were familiar to the children (e.g., triangles and squares, birds and fish). One advantage of using the TARC as opposed to story-based problems is the ability to present multiple analogy problems in a reasonable amount of time, consequently providing children with more opportunities to demonstrate their abilities.

Multiple investigations with the story problems and the TARC have indicated that young children can reasoning analogically (e.g., Alexander, Wilson, et al., 1987; Alexander, White, & Daugherty, 1997; Holyoak & Thagard, 1995; White & Alexander, 1986). The research on children's analogical reasoning also suggests that children's reasoning abilities improve over time. For example, White, Alexander, and Daugherty (1998) administered the TARC to assess preschool children's analogical reasoning on two occasions, eight months apart. Comparisons of children's reasoning scores revealed that they performed significantly better on the analogy task at the end of the eight-month period. Additionally, research by Alexander and colleagues has also indicated that children's analogical reasoning can be improved with specific instruction from either researchers or the children's classroom teachers (Alexander, White, Haensly, & Crimmins-Jeanes, 1987; Alexander, Wilson, et al., 1987; White & Alexander, 1986).

Examined as a whole, this research suggests that young children do reason analogically and that their reasoning becomes more advanced over time due to cognitive maturation and experience. However, the literature has not examined how analogical reasoning develops in young children over an extended period of time. For instance, what changes in children's analogical reasoning occur over the course of their early elementary years? Further, how are these changes related to the implicit instruction children receive in their classrooms? These are some of the questions we wanted to address in this investigation.

As with analogical reasoning, interest in young children's mathematical reasoning has grown in recent years (e.g., National Council of Teachers of Mathematics [NCTM], 1998; Stiff & Curcio, 1999). Researchers and mathematics practitioners have become attentive to children's abilities to recognize patterns and to form generalizations and abstractions (e.g., English & Halford, 1995; Hiebert & Carpenter, 1992; Wynn, 1992). Further, under the umbrella term of *mathematical reasoning*, others have explored children's abilities to draw conclusions from evidence, employ inductive and deductive reasoning, and reason spatially (e.g., Baroody, 1999; Malloy, 1999; Peressini & Webb, 1999; Russell, 1999; Stiff & Curcio, 1999). Even when these researchers and practitioners espouse varied perspectives as to what constitutes mathematical reasoning, they concur that such reasoning is the basis for the later mathematical development (Devlin, 1994; Dreyfus & Eisenberg, 1996). The importance of mathematical reasoning is further demonstrated by the emphasis that the National Council of Teachers of Mathematics (NCTM, 2000) places on developing children's reasoning abilities. Within their *Principles and Standards for School Mathematics*, NCTM (2000) strongly encourages teachers to attend to the thinking behind children's responses.

Evidence from empirical studies suggests that even before children enter school, they possess and apply a range of numerical concepts and principles in their everyday lives and actions (e.g., English, 1997; Pepper & Hunting, 1998). Once the children enter school, the role for teachers is to offer experiences that develop, deepen, and expand students' rudimentary understandings of mathematics and numbers (NCTM, 2000). For example, within this growing empirical base, there has been an increase in the discussion of pedagogical methods that foster mathematical reasoning in students, such as presenting game-like tasks (e.g., Dominick & Clark, 1996). There have also been studies to improve preservice teachers' in-depth mathematical reasoning abilities so that they are better prepared to teach their students (e.g., Lubinski, Fox, & Thomason, 1998). Still other research has focused on the emergence of specific skills and concepts such as understanding place value or probability (Metz, 1998; Nagel & Swingen, 1998). In addition, there is increased attention to mathematical reasoning within specific populations including those who have been labeled as mathematically talented (Robinson, Abbot, Berninger, & Busse, 1996).

Yet even with a growing base of empirical evidence for the early manifestation of reasoning abilities and the creation of instructional standards intended to support and extend the reasoning abilities of young children, few longitudinal studies have charted the development of mathematical reasoning in young children. Moreover, studies that have addressed young children's reasoning over time have tended to look at the impact of specific social and contextual factors such as maternal work force participation (Horwood & Fergusson, 1999) and interventions (e.g., Wade & Moore, 1998) on children's subsequent development. Thus, although there is ample evidence that children can and do engage in mathematical reasoning, there are few longitudinal studies addressing how those reasoning capabilities change over the course of time, especially in light of formal educational experiences.

Although understanding of mathematical reasoning development remains limited, there are certain hypotheses about its association with analogical reasoning that have been substantiated by the available evidence. For one, both analogical and mathematical reasoning are contingent on individuals' abilities to recognize and apply patterns whether these patterns consist of concrete objects or abstract ideas (Goswami, 1992; English & Sharry, 1996; Sternberg, 1977). Thus, it would appear that analogical and mathematical reasoning as related processes (English, chap. 1, this volume; White et al., 1998). Several programs of research have begun to explore this potential relationship. For example, in the White et al. study (1998), children's mathematical reasoning was also assessed. The researchers found that young children's mathematical reasoning, particularly their patterning abilities, significantly predicted their analogical reasoning abilities eight months later. However, this study did not examine how the relationship between analogical and mathematical reasoning changes over an extended period of time. Additionally, the analyses employed in the investigation only examined the impact of mathematical reasoning on analogical reasoning. It is quite plausible that children's early analogical reasoning abilities may support the development of later mathematical reasoning abilities. Specifically, we believe there is a reciprocal relationship between children's abilities to recognize and apply patterns in an analogical manner and their abilities to perceive numerical patterns and form the appropriate abstractions and generalizations (English, chap. 1, this volume; White et al., 1998).

Thus, the purpose of this study was to deepen our understanding of how young children's analogical and mathematical reasoning develop as well as how those processes relate to one another over a span of three years. Further, the cross-cultural nature of this investigation allowed us to examine whether such developmental trends are the same for American and Australian children. Specifically, the following questions guided this investigation:

- How do young children's analogical and mathematical reasoning develop over time?
- What is the nature of the relationship between young children's analogical and mathematical reasoning?
- What are the differences in the analogical and mathematical reasoning of young American and Australian children?

- What are the specific developmental profiles of analogical and mathematical reasoning that emerge over time?

STUDY BACKGROUND

The Children

Children from four different schools, two in the United States and two in Australia, participated in this investigation. Sixty-one children—31 in the United States and 30 in Australia—completed the first assessment, administered early in the first year of formal schooling (i.e., kindergarten in the United States and Year 1 in Australia). At this initial testing, our American sample included 13 males and 18 females, and our Australian samples consisted of 15 males and 15 females. The majority of the children sampled from the United States were Caucasian and all of the Australian children were Caucasian. The children were primarily from middle- and upper-middle-class families, reflective of the schools' general student populations.

Due to differences in testing procedures as well as the expected attrition in a longitudinal study, we did not have complete data for all children across the three years. Specifically, only 22 American and 6 Australian children had analogy and mathematics data for the duration of the study. With regard to the American children, 10 were male and 12 were female. Three of the Australian children were male and three were female. Therefore, we chose to conduct analyses on those children with complete data sets with few exceptions.

The Measures

The TARC and the Mathematical Reasoning Test for Young Students (MRTYS) were used in this investigation to assess children's analogical and mathematical reasoning abilities. The details of the TARC and the MRTYS as well as associated reliability and validity data are discussed at length in Alexander and Buehl (chap. 2, this volume). It is important to note that there were variations of the TARC and the MRTYS developed for each year of the study. These variations were made to increase test difficulty. However, these yearly changes resulted in different numbers of items and different maximum scores per measure. Consequently, to aid in the analysis and interpretation of results, we used proportion scores for both the analogical and mathematical reasoning measures. These proportion scores were calculated by dividing each child's raw score by the maximum number of points. Further, the TARC and MRTYS consist of various subsets of items. Given the low reliabilities on some subsets, as well as the lack of information available for the Australian sample on certain assessments, we tended to focus on the total analogy and mathematics reasoning scores in the analyses presented in this discussion of longitudinal development.

The Procedures

This longitudinal study was conducted over the course of three academic years (i.e., kindergarten, first, and second grades), herein referred to as Year 1, Year 2, and Year 3. At the beginning and end of each school year (i.e., pretest and posttest), the children were assessed with appropriate versions of the TARC and the MRTYS. The order in which the two tests were administered varied. The children also completed the two tests separately, often on different days. These assessments were administered in the school environment, close to the children's classrooms, and the test administrators were familiar to the children.

However, there were some differences in the testing procedures followed in the United States and Australia. Specifically, all available American children were assessed at the beginning and end of each year for a total of six different time points. In Australia, after the initial testing (Year 1 pretest), only 12 case study children were followed over the three-year period. This number was further reduced to six children due to attrition and missing data. Additionally, as a result of variations in testing, the mathematical reasoning scores for the Australian children at the end of the second year of the study (Year 2 posttest) were not comparable to the American reasoning scores. This prohibited us from comparing the American and Australian data for Year 2. For the final testing (Year 3 posttest), the research team made efforts to locate as many of the originally sampled Australian children as possible. Due to those efforts, 20 Australian children were assessed at the Year 3 posttest.

STUDY FINDINGS

Changes in Reasoning Abilities

One of the purposes of this investigation was to examine changes in children's analogical and mathematical reasoning abilities over time. To achieve this goal, first we needed to ascertain whether the children with complete data were statistically different from the children lost to attrition or to variations in testing procedures. Thus, we created two comparison groups, complete and incomplete cases. Complete cases were those children who had complete data for all three years, whereas incomplete cases only had data for some of the assessments.

The means and standard of the TARC and MRTYS scores for the complete and incomplete cases are displayed in Table 3.1. For each assessment, t-tests were conducted separately for American and Australian samples to determine if the complete cases were statistically different from the incomplete cases. There was no evidence of statistical differences between the American children retained for the longitudinal analyses and those lost due to attrition ($ts < .91$, $ps > .05$). For the Australian children, those children with complete data performed statistically better than the incomplete children on the MRTYS Year 1 pretest ($t = 2.96$, $df = 22$, $p < .01$).

Although there were no other statistical differences for the Australian children, it should be remembered that proportionally few were assessed more than once. There are also noticeable descriptive differences that may not have been statistically significant given such small samples. Consequently, due to problems of generalizability, we feel that the longitudinal trends for the Australian children should be interpreted with great caution and best treated as primarily exploratory analyses.

Changes in Analogical Reasoning.   To assess longitudinal changes in the children's reasoning abilities, we visually examined plottings for the analogical reasoning proportion scores, as seen in Fig. 3.1. Note that for each year, there was some increase in children's analogical reasoning scores from pretest to posttest. This was true for both the American and Australian children.

To determine if such pretest to posttest increases were statistically significant, we conducted a series of dependent sample t-tests, pairing the pretest and posttest scores for each year. This form of analysis was chosen due to the nature of the tests administered. That is, only the pretest and posttest assessments of each year were comparable as the measures increased in difficulty each year. Consequently, the children's proportion scores were expected to be lower at the start of each year than they were at the end of the prior year. Our main concern, therefore, focused on the changes children demonstrated over the course of an academic year.

These analyses revealed that the American children did not statistically significantly improve in their analogical reasoning for the first two years of the study ($ts < 1.80$, $ps > .05$). However, there was a statistically significant increase in the children's analogical reasoning scores from the Year 3 pretest to the Year 3 posttest ($t = 3.74$, $df = 21$, $p = .001$). In contrast, the Australian children demonstrated statistically significant improvements in their analogical reasoning for Year 1 ($t = 2.67$, $df = 5$, $p < .05$) and Year 3 ($t = 2.58$, $df = 5$, $p < .05$).

Changes in Children's Mathematical Reasoning.   A similar analysis was conducted for the children's mathematical reasoning scores. We first examined a plot of the American and Australian mathematical reasoning data

TABLE 3.1

TARC and MRTYS Proportion Scores for American and Australian Complete and Incomplete Cases

	American				Australian			
	Complete Cases		Incomplete Cases		Complete Cases		Incomplete Cases	
Year / Assessment	n	M(SD)	n	M(SD)	n	M(SD)	n	M(SD)
Year 1								
TARC Pretest	22	.76 (.21)	9	.69 (.24)	6	.74 (.17)	24	.63 (.19)
MRTYS Pretest	22	.78 (.12)	9	.81 (.09)	6	.75 (.10)[a]	18	.53 (.17)[b]
TARC Posttest	22	.80 (.28)	7	.90 (.08)	6	.85 (.12)	5	.77 (.18)
MRTYS Posttest	22	.80 (.07)	7	.79 (.08)	6	.83 (.11)	2	.62 (.12)
Year 2								
TARC Pretest	22	.79 (.13)	4	.81 (.12)	6	.72 (.15)	3	.63 (.13)
MRTYS Pretest	22	.74 (.12)	4	.68 (.17)	6	.78 (.10)	0	
TARC Posttest	22	.85 (.15)	4	.91 (.06)	6	.72 (.12)	3	.65 (.12)
MRTYS Posttest	22	.77 (.11)	4	.74 (.09)	0		0	
Year 3								
TARC Pretest	22	.83 (.11)	1	.76 (- -)	6	.74 (.18)	3	.81 (.04)
MRTYS Pretest	22	.72 (.16)	1	.69 (- -)	6	.81 (.07)	3	.68 (.11)
TARC Posttest	22	.90 (.10)	0		6	.87 (.07)	14	.82 (.09)
MRTYS Posttest	22	.85 (.14)	0		6	.81 (.07)	14	.74 (.12)

Note. Superscripts indicate significant ($p < .05$) differences between groups.

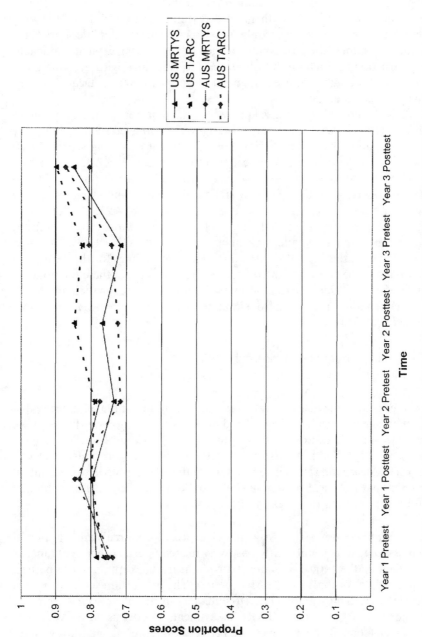

FIG. 3.1. TARC and MRTYS proportion scores for American and Australian longitudinal cases.

55

(Fig. 3.1). This visual examination revealed that similar to their analogical reasoning, the children's mathematical reasoning increased at least slightly each year. In some ways, we would have expected more dramatic shifts in the children's mathematical reasoning as they were receiving explicit mathematics instruction throughout the school year, whereas analogical reasoning was not explicitly taught nor even frequently mentioned (White, Deal, & Deniz, chap. 6, this volume).

To determine if the changes apparent in the plot were statistically significant, a series of dependent sample t-tests were conducted separately for the American and Australian children's mathematical reasoning scores. These analyses revealed that the American children did not demonstrate a significant change in mathematical reasoning during Year 1 ($t = .66$, $df = 21$, $p > .05$). However, they did evidence statistically significant increases during Year 2 ($t = 2.17$, $df = 21$, $p < .05$) and Year 3 ($t = 6.35$, $df = 21$, $p < .001$). With regard to the Australian children, there were no statistically significant changes in their mathematical reasoning scores posttest ($ts < 1.83$, $df = 5$, $ps > .05$). However, this lack of statistically significant findings for the Australian children may be related to the reduced sample size. From these longitudinal analyses, it was evident that these young children increased in their analogical and mathematical reasoning from kindergarten (Year 1) to the end of second grade (Year 3).

Relationships Between Analogical and Mathematical Reasoning

Another goal of the analysis was to explore the nature of the relationship between young children's analogical and mathematical reasoning. To do so, we examined the correlations between children's TARC and MRTYS proportion scores (Table 3.2). We also conducted several regression analyses. Due to the small Australian sample, our analysis of the relationship between analogical and mathematical reasoning was based only on the American children with complete data ($n = 22$).

Correlational Analysis.   As would be expected, children's analogical reasoning scores were significantly positively related to each other over time, as were their mathematical reasoning scores. The main exception to this pattern were the data for the Year 2 TARC pretest. The proportion scores from this measure were significantly related to outcomes for the Year 3 TARC pretest, but not to any of the other TARC assessments. As discussed in Alexander and Buehl (chap. 2, this volume), the TARC Year 2 pretest had the lowest reliability (i.e., .70), which reduces the strength of any potential relationship. The few additional relationships that were not statistically significant (i.e., the correlations between the Year 1 TARC pretest and posttest and the 3

TABLE 3.2
TARC and MRTYS Correlations for the American Children

Reasoning Measure Assessment	2	3	4	5	6	7	8	9	10	11	12
TARC											
1. Year 1 Pretest	.79**	.24	.66**	.40	.54**	.58**	.54**	.58**	.61**	.47*	.48*
2. Year 1 Posttest		.26	.54**	.37	.55**	.41	.43*	.56**	.65**	.50*	.78**
3. Year 2 Pretest			.42	.61**	.32	.50*	.62**	.22	.23	.55*	.41
4. Year 2 Posttest				.78**	.80**	.65**	.63**	.79**	.71**	.66**	.82**
5. Year 3 Pretest					.65**	.71**	.64**	.60**	.62**	.62**	.84**
6. Year 3 Posttest						.75**	.49*	.77**	.74**	.59**	.84**
MRTYS											
7. Year 1 Pretest							.74**	.61**	.75**	.51**	.65**
8. Year 1 Posttest								.58**	.61**	.66**	.61**
9. Year 2 Pretest									.81**	.66**	.81**
10. Year 2 Posttest										.67**	.75**
11. Year 3 Pretest											.76**
12. Year 3 Posttest											

Note. * indicates statistical significance at the .05 level; ** indicates statistical significance at the .01 level.

TARC pretest) were relatively large ($r = .40$ and $r = .37$, respectively), suggesting that the lack of significance may also be related to the small sample size. All of the MRTYS assessments were significantly related to each other (Table 3.2).

When we examined the correlations between the analogical and mathematical reasoning measures, there were numerous statistically significant relationships. In fact, all but two correlations were greater than .41. The two exceptions were the relationships between the Year 3 TARC pretest and the Year 3 MRTYS pretest ($r = .21$) and posttest ($r = .23$). As already discussed, the Year 3 TARC pretest appears to be somewhat aberrant. These significant correlations suggest that analogical and mathematical reasoning are significantly related.

Regression Analyses.   In addition to examining the simple correlations between children's analogical and mathematical reasoning scores, we wanted to explore the potential reciprocal relationship between analogical and mathematical reasoning. That is, does children's analogical reasoning contribute to their future mathematical reasoning and, conversely, does mathematical reasoning support future analogical reasoning? Specifically, we first investigated how well children's Year 1 TARC pretest scores predicted their Year 3 MRTYS posttest scores. Using simple regression, children's Year 1 TARC pretest scores were found to be a significant predictor of their Year 3 MRTYS scores ($\beta = .48$, $p = .022$). Further, children's prior analogical reasoning abilities accounted for 24% of the variance in their later mathematical reasoning.

In an effort to understand how analogical reasoning was related to children's mathematical reasoning, we also used the Year 1 TARC pretest to predict each of the Year 3 MRTYS subtests (i.e., Attributions, Sequencing and Patterning, Quantification–Relations, Quantification–Number, and Story Problems). Five simple regressions were conducted, each with children's Year 1 TARC scores as the predictor and one of the Year 3 MRTYS subtest scores as the dependent variable. These analyses indicated that children's TARC scores significantly predicted the children's scores on the Sequencing and Patterning ($\beta = .45$, $p = .036$) and Story Problems ($\beta = .43$, $p = .044$) subtests. Specifically, children's analogical reasoning explained 20% of the variance in their patterning abilities and 19% of the variance in their success with the story problems. Children's TARC scores did not significantly predict their scores on the Attributions ($\beta = .42$, $p > .05$), Quantification–Relations ($\beta = .36$, $p > .05$), or Quantification–Number ($\beta = .39$, $p > .05$) subtests.

We also wanted to determine if children's prior mathematical reasoning predicted their analogical reasoning. To do so, we first conducted a simple regression using the children's Year 1 MRTYS pretest scores as a predictor of their Year 3 TARC posttest scores. This analysis revealed that the Year 1 MRTYS pretest scores significantly predicted the Year 3 TARC posttest scores ($\beta = .75$, $p < .001$), explaining 57% of the variance in children's analogical reasoning.

Finally, to explore the nuances of the relationship between analogical and mathematical reasoning, we entered the Year 1 MRTYS subtest scores (i.e., Attributions and Patterning, Quantification–Relations, and Quantification–Number) as predictors of children's Year 3 TARC posttest scores. Using stepwise regression techniques, the Year 1 Attributions and Patterning ($\beta = .37$, $p = .013$) and Quantification–Relations ($\beta = .61$, $p < .001$) subtests significantly predicted children's Year 3 TARC performance, together explaining 71% of the variance in children's analogical reasoning.

These analyses suggest that children's analogical reasoning abilities contributed to their future mathematical reasoning abilities and children's mathematical reasoning influenced their future analogical reasoning. Such findings provide additional support for the reciprocal relationship between analogical and mathematical reasoning. Further, mathematical patterning appeared to be a strong link between these two forms of reasoning. In this way, the current investigation replicates previous findings (e.g., White et al., 1998).

Cross-Cultural Differences

As discussed, the differences in testing procedures in America and Australia resulted in a substantially smaller Australian sample for comparison purposes. Consequently, cross-cultural statistical comparisons could not be conducted for all assessments. However, a sufficient number of children in both countries completed the TARC and MRTYS at the beginning (Year 1 pretest) and end of the study (Year 3 posttest) to allow for statistical comparison. Specifically, for Year 1, 31 American and 30 Australian children completed both the TARC and MRTYS pretests. Due to missing data, however, MRTYS scores were only available for 24 Australian children. Further, for Year 3, 22 American and 20 Australian children completed both the TARC and MRTYS posttest. Cross-cultural comparisons were conducted on those samples.

The means and standard deviations for the participants who completed the Year 1 pretest and Year 3 posttest measures are presented in Table 3.3. Four independent sample t-tests were conducted with country as the independent variable and TARC and MRTYS scores at Year 1 pretest and Year 3 posttest as the respective dependent variables. These analyses indicated certain cross-cultural differences. That is, although there were no statistical differences in children's analogical reasoning at the Year 1 pretest ($t = 1.76$, $df = 59$, $p = .083$), as assessed by the TARC, children in the United States performed statistically better than the Australian children on the Year 3 TARC posttest ($t = 2.13$, $df = 40$, $p < .05$). Additionally, the American children performed statistically better than the Australian children on the MRTYS at

TABLE 3.3
Means and Standard Deviations for American and Australian Children
Completing Year 1 Pretest and Year 3 Posttest Measures

| Year | American | | Australian | |
Assessment	n	M(SD)	n	M(SD)
Year 1 Pretest				
TARC	31	.74 (.22)	30	.65 (.19)
MRTYS	31	.79 (.11)[a]	24	.59 (.19)[b]
Year 3 Posttest				
TARC	22	.90 (.10)[a]	20	.84 (.08)[b]
MRTYS	22	.85 (.14)[a]	20	.76 (.11)[b]

Note. Superscripts indicate significant ($p < .05$) differences between groups.

both the Year 1 pretest ($t = 5.14$, $df = 53$, $p < .001$) and the Year 3 posttest ($t = 2.27$, $df = 40$, $p < .05$). These differences in scores indicate some cross-cultural variations in children's analogical and mathematical reasoning abilities. We speculate that this may be due to differences in classroom instruction as well as the children's experiences before entering school.

Although we did not statistically compare the American and Australian children on all assessments, due to the small Australian sample, we visually compared their patterns of development throughout the course of this study by examining the plot of the longitudinal proportion means (Fig. 3.1). This plotting of the children's mean performance on the analogical and mathematical reasoning measures indicates that the reasoning abilities appear somewhat similar for children in the United States and Australia. However, there are several differences. For one, the American children's reasoning scores tend to be slightly higher than those for the Australian children, but the Australians demonstrated more dramatic increases over the course of each year. Further, there are differences with regard to when the children displayed their greatest increase. The American children's performance increased most in Year 3, whereas the performance for Australian children showed the greatest increase in Year 1.

Profiles of Children's Analogical and Mathematical
Reasoning Development

The final research question for this investigation focused on the individual differences in children's reasoning abilities. In particular, we wanted to explore the performance patterns of children who followed varied developmental paths in the analogical and mathematical reasoning. For this analysis, we grouped the children based on similarities in their TARC and MRTYS proportion scores. We performed this grouping separately for the children's analogical and mathematical reasoning scores. Specifically, we created two graphs, one for analogical reasoning and one for mathematical reasoning, plotting the individual children's reasoning scores over the three years (Figs. 3.2 and 3.3). Based on a visual examination of these individual plots, we formed clusters of children who exhibited differential performance trajectories.

Analogical Reasoning Profiles.   For the analogical reasoning task, there were five children who consistently scored high (i.e., .85 or greater) on the TARC from the first testing in Year 1 to the final testing in Year 3 (Fig. 3.2). We refer to those children as Strong Analogical Reasoners. In contrast, there were five children whose performance was relatively low (i.e., below .75) for three or more assessments. We considered those children to be Weak Analogical Reasoners. The remaining 12 students evidenced more variability in their analogical reasoning performance from the onset to the conclusion of our study. Children in this group were considered to be Variable Analogical Reasoners.

The means and standard deviations for these three groups on the analogical and mathematical reasoning are shown in Table 3.4. Further, we plotted both the mean analogical and mathematical reasoning scores for the children in each of the three profile groups (Fig. 3.4). This plotting allowed us to see how children we considered to be strong, weak, or variable analogical reasoners performed on the measures of mathematical reasoning. What we found was that Strong Analogical Reasoners also displayed the highest levels of mathematical reasoning across the three years of the study. Similarly, the children in the Weak Reasoners groups also performed at the lowest level on the measures of mathematical reasoning from Year 1 to Year 3. For the more Variable Analogical Reasoners, we found a close alignment between the mean level of performance in analogical reasoning with that recorded for mathematical reasoning. In general, these correspondences in analogical and mathematical performance for the three profile groups provides further substantiation for the reciprocal relationship between these fundamental processes.

These profile plots also reveal periods during the longitudinal study when marked improvements in children's analogical and mathematical reasoning were evidenced. For instance, there was an appreciable improvement in the mathematical performance of the Strong Analogical Reasoners from Year 3 pretest to Year 3 posttest ($t = 2.76$, $df = 4$, $p = .051$). Although there were yearly improvements in the analogical performance of these Strong Analogical Reasoners, none of their pretest to posttest analogical gains were statistically significant, a reflection of their high, consistent performance.

For the Weak Analogical Reasoners, we observed an unusual decrease in the analogical reasoning performance during Year 1. A slight decrease was also exhibited in Year 2 for these children, followed by a nonsignificant increase in their analogical performance over the course of Year 3. Although

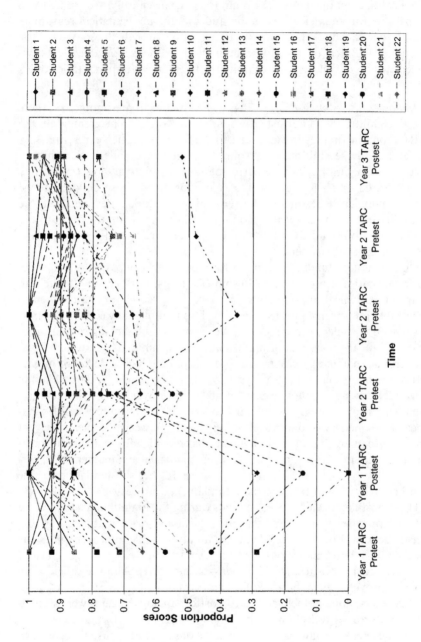

FIG. 3.2. TARC proportion scores for individual American cases.

Student 1
Student 2
Student 3
Student 4
Student 5
Student 6
Student 7
Student 8
Student 9
Student 10
Student 11
Student 12
Student 13
Student 14
Student 15
Student 16
Student 17
Student 18
Student 19
Student 20
Student 21
Student 22

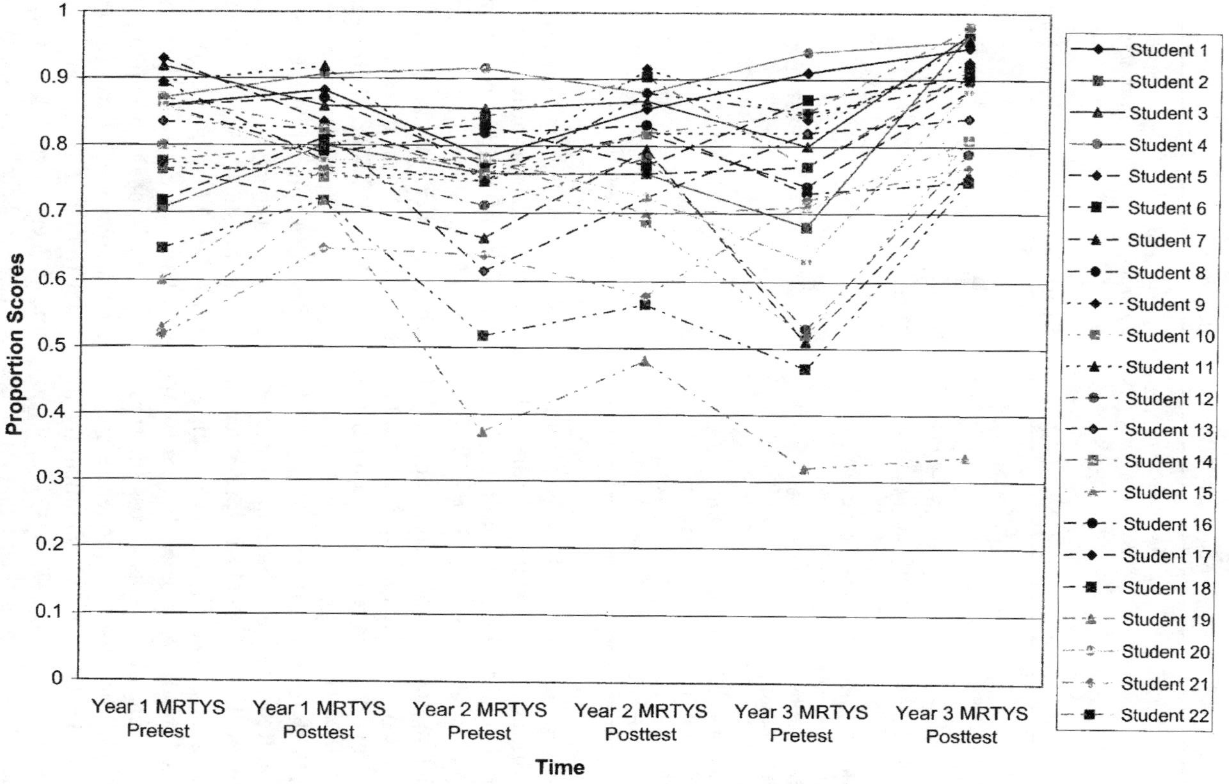

Proportion Scores
1
0.9
0.8
0.7
0.6
0.5
0.4
0.3
0.2
0.1
0
Year 1 MRTYS Pretest
Year 1 MRTYS Posttest
Year 2 MRTYS Pretest
Year 2 MRTYS Posttest
Year 3 MRTYS Pretest
Year 3 MRTYS Posttest
Time
Student 1
Student 2
Student 3
Student 4
Student 5
Student 6
Student 7
Student 8
Student 9
Student 10
Student 11
Student 12
Student 13
Student 14
Student 15
Student 16
Student 17
Student 18
Student 19
Student 20
Student 21
Student 22

FIG. 3.3. MRTYS proportion scores for individual American cases.

TABLE 3.4
Means and Standard Deviations for the
Analogical Reasoning Profile Groups

Year	Strong Analogical Reasoners (n = 5)	Weak Analogical Reasoners (n = 5)	Variable Analogical Reasoners (n = 12)
Assessment	M(SD)	M(SD)	M(SD)
Year 1			
TARC Pretest	.94 (.06)	.46 (.12)	.82 (.14)
MRTYS Pretest	.86 (.09)	.67 (.15)	.80 (.09)
TARC Posttest	.94 (.06)	.36 (.31)	.93 (.05)
MRTYS Posttest	.86 (.04)	.73 (.06)	.80 (.06)
Year 2			
TARC Pretest	.92 (.05)	.70 (.10)	.78 (.13)
MRTYS Pretest	.81 (.07)	.63 (.19)	.75 (.06)
TARC Posttest	.96 (.06)	.68 (.20)	.87 (.07)
MRTYS Posttest	.82 (.06)	.65 (.17)	.80 (.07)
Year 3			
TARC Pretest	.92 (.06)	.72 (.15)	.83 (.08)
MRTYS Pretest	.82 (.10)	.58 (.19)	.73 (.14)
TARC Posttest	.94 (.04)	.80 (.17)	.92 (.06)
MRTYS Posttest	.95 (.03)	.73 (.23)	.86 (.08)

there were no significant changes in the Weak Reasoners' analogical reasoning within each academic year, these children show marked improvement in their abilities from the beginning of Year 1 to the end of Year 3. In fact, by the end of Year 3, children in the Weak Analogical Reasoning group were approaching the level of performance exhibited by the other two groups. Further, the Weak Analogical Reasoners showed a marked gain in analogical reasoning during the school summer recess (e.g., Year 1 TARC posttest to Year 2 TARC pretest), which may be indicative of developmental maturation. With regard to their mathematical reasoning development, Weak Analogical Reasoners exhibited at least slight gains for all three years. For Year 3, the Weak Analogical Reasoners demonstrated a statistically significant increase in their mathematical reasoning abilities ($t = 2.93$, $df = 4$, $p = .043$).

The Variable Analogical Reasoners are somewhat more erratic in their analogical reasoning skills across the three years. That is, at the beginning of each year, they display a moderate level of analogical reasoning. However, by the end of each year, they significantly improved with regard to their analogical reasoning ($ts > 2.41$, $df = 11$, $ps < .034$) and in Years 1 and 3, they approached the level of the Strong Analogical Reasoners. Perhaps this pattern reflects the influence of the implicit use of analogies within their classrooms throughout each school year (White et al., chap. 6, this volume). Addi-

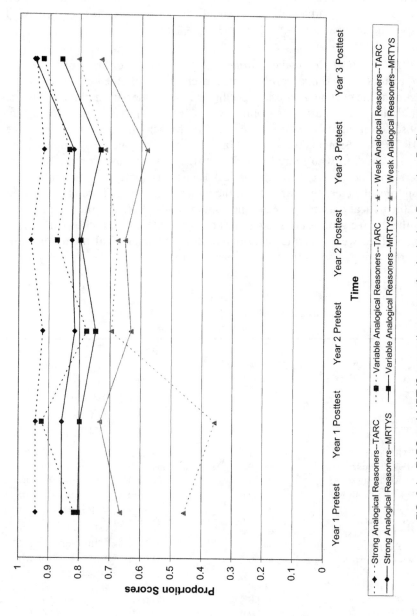

FIG. 3.4. TARC and MRTYS proportion scores for Analogical Reasoning Profile groups.

Legend:
- - ◆ - - Strong Analogical Reasoners--TARC
———◆——— Strong Analogical Reasoners--MRTYS
- - ■ - - Variable Analogical Reasoners--TARC
———■——— Variable Analogical Reasoners--MRTYS
· · ▲ · · Weak Analogcal Reasoners--TARC
———▲——— Weak Analogcal Reasoners--MRTYS

Proportion Scores (y-axis): 0, 0.1, 0.2, 0.3, 0.4, 0.5, 0.6, 0.7, 0.8, 0.9, 1

Time (x-axis): Year 1 Pretest, Year 1 Posttest, Year 2 Pretest, Year 2 Posttest, Year 3 Pretest, Year 3 Posttest

tionally, the Variable Analogical Reasoners are relatively stable in their mathematical reasoning for Year 1. However, they do exhibit a slight increase in Year 2 and a statistically significant increase in their mathematical reasoning in Year 3 ($t = 4.53$, $df = 11$, $p = .001$).

Mathematical Reasoning Profiles.   As a form of confirmatory analysis, we conducted a similar profile analysis children's mathematical reasoning scores as the grouping criteria. Specifically, after observing a plot of all of the children's mathematical reasoning scores (Fig. 3.3), we decided to classify those seven children who scored a .85 or higher on three or more of the MRTYS assessments as Strong Mathematical Reasoners. By comparison, the six children who scored below .75 three or more times on the MRTYS were considered Weak Mathematical Reasoners, with the remaining nine children labeled as the Variable Mathematical Reasoners. The analogical and mathematical reasoning means and standard deviations for the performance of these three groups are shown in Table 3.5. As with the analogical reasoning profiles, we also created a plotted of the mean analogical and mathematical reasoning scores for the three groups (Fig. 3.5).

TABLE 3.5
Means and Standard Deviations for the Mathematical
Reasoning Profile Groups

Year	Strong Mathematical Reasoners (n = 7)	Weak Mathematical Reasoners (n = 6)	Variable Mathematical Reasoners (n = 9)
Assessment	M(SD)	M(SD)	M(SD)
Year 1			
TARC Pretest	.89 (.11)	.60 (.24)	.78 (.20)
MRTYS Pretest	.88 (.02)	.64 (.12)	.80 (.07)
TARC Posttest	.94 (.05)	.62 (.39)	.81 (.27)
MRTYS Posttest	.86 (.05)	.72 (.04)	.79 (.03)
Year 2			
TARC Pretest	.88 (.06)	.68 (.07)	.79 (.15)
MRTYS Pretest	.80 (.06)	.62 (.15)	.76 (.07)
TARC Posttest	.93 (.06)	.70 (.20)	.88 (.07)
MRTYS Posttest	.85 (.03)	.63 (.11)	.80 (.07)
Year 3			
TARC Pretest	.91 (.05)	.73 (.14)	.82 (.07)
MRTYS Pretest	.84 (.07)	.54 (.15)	.74 (.11)
TARC Posttest	.94 (.03)	.78 (.14)	.94 (.04)
MRTYS Posttest	.94 (.04)	.71 (.18)	.88 (.07)

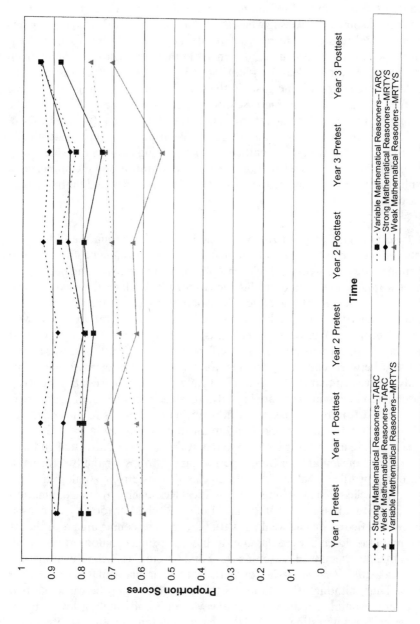

FIG. 3.5. TARC and MRTYS proportion scores for Mathematical Reasoning Profile groups.

67

This plotting shows that children in each profile group tended to score higher on the analogical reasoning measure than on the measure of mathematical reasoning. However, whereas all three groups evidenced some gains in analogical reasoning during each academic year, only the Variable Reasoners demonstrated a significant increase in their analogical reasoning from pretest to posttest for Year 3 ($t = 4.07$, $df = 5$, $p = .004$). Further, during Year 2, there were noticeable increases in the mathematical reasoning for all three profile groups. In fact, the increase from pretest to posttest for Year 2 for the Strong Mathematical Reasoners was statistically significant ($t = 2.59$, $df = 6$, $p = .041$). Finally, in Year 3, all three profile groups evidenced statistically significant increases in their mathematical reasoning abilities ($ts > 3.37$, $ps < .020$). Again, this could reflect both cognitive maturation and the influence of explicit instruction in the processes underlying analogical and mathematical reasoning.

Consistency of Profile Groups.   In addition to exploring the differences between the various analogical and mathematical reasoning profiles, we also examined the consistency of children's placement in the reasoning profiles. In other words, were the children classified as Strong Analogical Reasoners also those in the Strong Mathematical Reasoning group? Conversely, were the children placed in the Weak Analogical Reasoning group also those who were identified as Weak Analogical Reasoners? To address this issue, we first calculated a Spearman correlation coefficient to determine if there was a relationship between children's rankings on the two types of reasoning. This analysis revealed that there was a statistically significant correlation between the children's assignment to analogical and mathematical reasoning groups ($r = .53$, $p = .016$). In our view, this offers further evidence as to the reciprocal relationship between analogical and mathematical reasoning.

Second, we examined each case to determine whether individual children were placed in similar or different performance groups for the two forms of reasoning profiles. That is, are children classified as Strong Analogical Reasoners also classified as Strong Mathematical Reasoners? In our examination of the individual cases, we found that 11 of the 22 children (50%) were consistently classified as strong, weak, or variable across reasoning area. For the remaining 11 children, 5 were classified as having stronger analogical reasoning skills than mathematical reasoning skills and 6 were classified as demonstrating weak analogical skills in comparison to their mathematical reasoning skills. Thus, although there appears to be a relationship between the two types of reasoning, children are not always consistently high or low in both. However, it is interesting to note that when children's profile classifications were not consistent, they did not span more than one group. In other words, there were no instances of a child being a strong reasoner in one area and a weak reasoner in the other.

CONCLUSIONS AND IMPLICATIONS

The purpose of this investigation was to explore the development of young children's analogical and mathematical reasoning over a period of three years. Additionally, we had the opportunity to examine potential differences in reasoning development between children from the United States and Australia. Although this research has shed some light on our understanding of children's reasoning, it is not without its limitations. For example, our relatively small initial sample size was further reduced over the course of the investigation due to attrition. Additionally, somewhat different testing procedures were followed in the United States and Australia, substantially reducing the available data for the Australian students. Consequently, we were not able to perform some of the more advanced statistical analyses that we initially intended. Further, we were limited with regard to making cross-cultural comparisons between children in the United States and Australia. Moreover, those comparisons that we present herein must be interpreted with caution due to problems associated with generalizing from such a small sample.

In addition to the small sample sizes, our analogical and mathematical reasoning measures, although generally effective and innovative, were not perfect. For instance, the children were not assessed with the same measures throughout the course of the study. Instead, to adequately assess children's developing abilities, we had to increase the difficulty of the measures each year. Consequently, increases in children's reasoning between the school years could have been obscured. For future research, it may be useful to develop singular measures that can adequately assess children's analogical and mathematical reasoning over the course of several years. Although care would have to be taken to create a measure that could assess the intricacies of young children's reasoning at various ages in a reasonable amount of time, such an endeavor might be successfully undertaken via item response theory (IRT).

Also, because some of the reliabilities for the subtests on both the TARC and the MRTYS assessments were relatively low, we tended to focus on the children's total proportion scores in this study. Indeed, these scores provided us with useful information about children's reasoning from kindergarten (Year 1) through second grade (Year 3). However, reliable measures of the subcomponents of children's mathematical reasoning could offer even more insight into children's developing reasoning abilities and the relationships that exist among those abilities.

Despite these limitations, this study has afforded us valuable insights into the development of young children's reasoning abilities, and led to implications for both educational theory and instructional practice. First, we saw that over the course of the three-year investigation, the children increased in their analogical and mathematical reasoning abilities, even as we enhanced the difficulty of the assessment measures. This pattern suggests some role for cognitive maturation in the development of children's analogical and mathematical reasoning. However, there was also evidence of significant gains in the children's reasoning within a single school year. We feel that outcome indicates a role for classroom instruction on children's reasoning development. That is to say, it is reasonable to assume that documented changes in these children's mathematical reasoning would be partially attributable to the time and attention devoted to mathematics processes in the school curriculum. Although analogical reasoning does not receive the same level of instructional attention, teachers sometimes made analogical references during their interactions with the children (see Chiu & Tron; White et al., this volume). The use of case studies and in-class observations may allow us to understand such connections between children's reasoning and classroom interactions more fully (see Chiu & Tron; White et al., this volume).

Additionally, the outcomes of this investigation underscored the relationship between analogical and mathematical reasoning. Plotting children's mean performance on the two measures over time suggests that their analogical and mathematical reasoning abilities follow similar trajectories. The significant correlations between the measures also provides evidence of the link between these two types of reasoning as do the regression analyses. However, more work in this area is needed to fully understand the relationship between analogical and mathematical reasoning. For instance, we could not determine when the abilities to reason analogically or mathematically first emerged for our study participants. Concurrently, we could not ascertain whether one of these modes of reasoning evidences an earlier onset than the other, an outcome that would help to explain their complex relationship. Perhaps with larger samples and more precise measures, researchers can use more advanced techniques to model the linkages between analogical and mathematical reasoning.

Finally, there was evidence of differential patterns in children's analogical and mathematical reasoning development. With regard to cross-cultural differences, our findings suggest that although the overall developmental trajectories were similar, children from the United States demonstrated stronger analogical and mathematical reasoning skills than children in Australia. Perhaps these differences are due to instructional variations and emphases. Future research may explore these differences more deeply.

In addition to cross-cultural differences, individual differences in children's reasoning development were also identified. Specifically, in focusing on the American children, we discovered distinct profiles in both analogical and mathematical reasoning development. We identified strong, weak, and variable reasoners in both reasoning areas. It was also informative to learn that the developmental trajectories for analogical and mathematical reasoning within these performance groups were closely aligned. We determined that the performance designations assigned to half of the study children remained consistent across the two measures of reasoning (i.e., TARC and MRTYS). Finally, by the end of this investigation, the majority of the children appeared to be at least approaching similar ability levels. However, additional explorations of these individual differences may be fruitful. For example, do children's analogical and mathematical reasoning abilities eventually catch up to one another? What are the consequences for the children who continue to have disparate abilities in the two areas? Are there any long-term effects on the children who display reasoning difficulties early on? Can specific interventions prevent such difficulties?

As adults, we employ our analogical and mathematical reasoning abilities daily. From this study, it is evident that even young children engage in these foundational forms of reasoning abilities that improve over time. Yet, only with additional research can we come to understand the nuances in the performance of those fundamental processes and grasp the significance they hold for subsequent learning and development.

REFERENCES

Alexander, P. A., White, C. S., & Daugherty, M. (1997). Children's use of analogical reasoning in early mathematics learning. In L. English (Ed.), *Mathematical reasoning: Analogies, metaphors, and images* (pp. 117–147). Mahwah, NJ: Lawrence Erlbaum Associates.

Alexander, P. A., White, C. S., Haensly, P. A., & Crimmins-Jeanes, M. (1987). Training in analogical reasoning. *American Educational Research Journal, 24*, 387–404.

Alexander, P. A., Willson, V. L., White, C. S., & Fuqua, J. D. (1987). Analogical reasoning in young children. *Journal of Educational Psychology, 79*, 401–408.

Alexander, P. A., Willson, V. L., White, C. S., Fuqua, J. D., Clark, G. D., Wilson, F., & Kulikowich, J. M. (1989). Development of analogical reasoning in four- and five-year-old children. *Cognitive Development, 4*, 65–88.

Alexander, P. A., Wilson, A. F., White, C. S., Willson, V. L., Tallent, M. K., & Shutes, R. E. (1987). Effects of teacher training on children's analogical reasoning performance. *Teaching and Teacher Education, 3*(4), 275–285.

Baroody, A. J. (1999). Children's relational knowledge of addition and subtraction. *Cognition and Instruction, 17*, 137–175.

Chen, A. (1996). Children's analogical problem solving: The effects of superficial, structural, and procedural similarity. *Journal of Experimental Child Psychology, 62*, 410–431.

Chen, Z., & Daehler, M. W. (1989). Positive and negative transfer in analogical problem solving by 6-year-old children. *Cognitive Development, 4*, 327–344.

Devlin, K. (1994). *Mathematics: The science of pattern.* New York: Scientific American Library.

Dominick, A., & Clark, F. B. (1996). Using games to understand children's understanding. *Childhood Education, 72*, 286–288.

Dreyfus, T., & Eisenberg, T. (1996). On different facets of mathematical thinking. In R. J. Sternberg & T. Ben-Zeev (Eds.), *The nature of mathematical thinking* (pp. 253–284). Mahwah, NJ: Lawrence Erlbaum Associates.

English, L. D. (1997). *Mathematical reasoning: Analogies, metaphors, and images.* Mahwah, NJ: Lawrence Erlbaum Associates.

English, L. D. (1999). Reasoning by analogy: A fundamental process in children's mathematical learning. In L. V. Stiff & F. R. Curcio (Eds.), *Developing mathematical reasoning in grades K–12. 1999 Yearbook* (pp. 22–36). Reston, VA: National Council of Mathematics Teachers.

English, L. D., & Halford, G. S. (1995). *Mathematics education: Models and processes.* Mahwah, NJ: Lawrence Erlbaum Associates.

English, L. D., & Sharry, P. (1996). Analogical reasoning and development of algebraic abstraction. *Educational Studies in Mathematics, 30,* 137–159.

Goswami, U. (1992). *Analogical reasoning in children.* Hove, UK: Lawrence Erlbaum Associates.

Goswami, U. (1995). Transitive relational mappings in three- and four-year olds: The analogy of Goldilocks and the three bears. *Child Development, 66,* 877–892.

Goswami, U., & Brown, A. L. (1989). Melting chocolate and melting snowmen: Analogical reasoning and causal relations. *Cognition, 34,* 9–95.

Hiebert, J., & Carpenter, T. P. (1992). Learning and teaching with understanding. In D. A. Grouws (Ed.), *Handbook of research on mathematics teaching and learning: A project of the National Council of Teachers of Mathematics* (pp. 65–97). New York: Macmillan Publishing.

Holyoak, K. J., Jull, E. N., & Billman, D. O. (1984). Development of analogical problem-solving skill. *Child Development, 55,* 2042–2055.

Holyoak, K. J., & Koh, K. (1987). Surface and structural similarity in analogical transfer. *Memory and Cognition, 15,* 332–340.

Holyoak, K. J., & Thagard, P. (1995). *Mental leaps: Analogy in creative thought.* Cambridge, MA: MIT Press.

Horwood, L. J., & Fergusson, D. M. (1999). A longitudinal study of maternal labor force participation and child academic achievement. *Journal of Child Psychology & Psychiatry & Allied Disciplines, 40,* 1013–1024.

Inhelder, B., & Piaget, J. (1958). *The growth of logical thinking from childhood to adolescence.* New York: Basic Books.

Lubinski, C. A., Fox, T., & Thomason, R. (1998). Learning to make sense of division of fractions: One K–12 preservice teacher's perspective. *School Science and Mathematics, 98,* 247–253.

Malloy, C. E. (1999). Developing mathematical reasoning in the middle grades: Recognizing diversity. In L. V. Stiff & F. R. Curcio (Eds.), *Developing mathematical reasoning in grades K–12* (pp. 13–21). Reston, VA: National Council of Mathematics Teachers.

Metz, K. E. (1998). Emergent ideas of chance and probability in primary grade children. In S. P. Lajoie (Ed.), *Reflections on statistics: Learning, teaching, and assessing in grades K–12: Studies in mathematical thinking and learning* (pp. 149–174). Mahwah, NJ: Lawrence Erlbaum Associates.

Nagel, N. G., & Swingen, C. C. (1998). Students' explanations of place value in addition and subtraction. *Teaching Children Mathematics, 5,* 164–170.

National Council of Teachers of Mathematics. (1998). *Principles and standards for school mathematics: Discussion Draft.* Reston, VA: Author.

National Council of Teachers of Mathematics. (1999). *Curriculum standards for teaching mathematics.* Reston, VA: Author.

National Council of Teachers of Mathematics. (2000). *Principles and standards for school mathematics: Electronic Edition.* Reston, VA: Author.

Pepper, K. L., & Hunting, R. P. (1998). Preschoolers' counting and sharing. *Journal for Research in Mathematics Education, 29,* 164–183.

Peressini, D., & Webb, N. (1999). Analyzing mathematical reasoning in students' responses across multiple performance assessment tasks. In L. V. Stiff & F. R. Curcio (Eds.), *Developing mathematical reasoning in grades K–12* (pp. 156–174). Reston, VA: National Council of Teachers of Mathematics.

Resnick, L. B., & Omanson, S. F. (1987). Learning to understand arithmetic. In R. Glaser (Ed.), *Advances in instructional psychology* (Vol. 3, pp. 41–95). Hillsdale, NJ: Lawrence Erlbaum Associates.

Robinson, N. M., Abbott, R. D., Berninger, V. W., & Busse, J. (1996). Structure of abilities in math-precocious young children: Gender similarities and differences. *Journal of Educational Psychology, 88*, 341–352.

Russell, S. J. (1999). Mathematical reasoning in elementary grades. In L. V. Stiff & F. R. Curcio (Eds.), *Developing mathematical reasoning in grades K–12* (pp. 1–12). Reston, VA: National Council of Teachers of Mathematics.

Saxe, G. B. (1991). *Culture and cognitive development: Studies in mathematical understanding.* Hillsdale, NJ: Lawrence Erlbaum Associates.

Sternberg, R. J. (1977). *Intelligence, information processing, and analogical reasoning: The componential analysis of human abilities.* Hillsdale, NJ: Lawrence Erlbaum Associates.

Stiff, L. V., & Curcio, F. R. (1999). *Developing mathematical reasoning in grades K–12.* Reston, VA: National Council of Teachers of Mathematics.

Vosniadou, S. (1989). Analogical reasoning as a mechanism in knowledge acquisition: A developmental perspective. In S. Vosniadou & A. Ortony (Eds.), *Similarity and analogical reasoning* (pp. 413–437). New York: Cambridge University Press.

Wade, B., & Moore, M. (1998). An early start with books: Literacy and mathematical evidence for a longitudinal study. *Educational Review, 50*, 135–145.

White, C. S., & Alexander, P. A. (1986). Effects of training on four-year-olds' ability to solve geometric analogy problems. *Cognition and Instruction, 3*, 261–268.

White, C. S., Alexander, P. A., & Daugherty, M. (1998). The relationship between young children's analogical reasoning and mathematical learning. *Mathematical Cognition, 4*(2), 103–123.

Wynn, K. (1992). Addition and subtraction by human infants. *Nature, 358*, 749–751.

4

CLASSROOM DISCOURSE AND THE DEVELOPMENT OF MATHEMATICAL AND ANALOGICAL REASONING

Shuhui Chiu
National TaiChung Teachers College

Myriam O. Tron
University of Maryland

In recent years, mathematics education has placed considerable value on the role of classroom discourse in supporting children's conceptual development (Corwin, 1995; Dockett & Perry, 2000; Lampert, 1998; Lilburn & Rawson, 1994; Perry & Dockett, 1998; Putt et al., 2000). Discourse refers to any verbal exchange that may arise within the classroom. Researchers focusing on classroom discourse have emphasized the role that teachers play in facilitating such discourse (e.g., O'Connor, 1998; Rittenhouse, 1998). While the manner in which teachers build a context for classroom discourse may influence student learning, the individual participant's active interpretation of that discourse also plays a crucial role in the development of his or her understanding (Cobb, Boufi, McClain, & Whitenack, 1997). The focus of this component of our study is on the individual learners, their learning environments (classroom context), and the interaction between them. Our goal was to examine the role of classroom discourse in supporting the development of young children's mathematical and analogical reasoning.

CONSTRUCTION VERSUS ENCULTURATION

Piaget (1972) contended that children's reflections when operating on concrete objects serve as the platform for cognitive development. Mathematics educators have referred to this as *integration* (Steffe, von Glasersfeld, Richards, & Cobb, 1983) and *encapsulation* (Dubinsky, 1991). Those who re-

75

search integration and encapsulation emphasize action-oriented development. Generally, they assume that students' sensory-motor and conceptual activities act as catalysts for cognitive development and that teachers should provide activities and ask significant questions to facilitate children's thinking (Duckworth, 1996).

Vygotsky (1978) emphasized two primary influences on conceptual development, referred to as *social interaction* and *semiotic mediation* (van der Veer & Valsiner, 1991). Vygotsky posited that the internalization of psychological planes occurs through interpersonal interaction. Thus, based on Vygotsky's theory, children's conceptual development is profoundly influenced by cultural practices, such as the discourse community in which they participate. In addition, Vygotsky argued that cultural tools, such as language, are internalized and become psychological tools for thinking during the course of conceptual development (Rogoff, 1990, 1998).

Contemporary mathematics educators generally acknowledge the importance of the different learning perspectives emphasized by Piaget or Vygotsky, such as the contribution of individual reflection (i.e., the individuals' active construction of knowledge) versus enculturation (i.e., the internalization of culturally specific knowledge), respectively (e.g., McClain & Cobb, 1998). According to Cobb et al. (1997), both viewpoints are needed to explain the qualitative difference in individual children's thinking as they apply the same discourse processes. Thus, in this chapter, we examine the utterances of individual children and the guiding statements made by their teachers during verbal exchanges. Further, we explore how these factors are associated with the development of mathematical and analogical reasoning abilities in children over the course of three years.

MATHEMATICAL REASONING

The different forms and interpretations of mathematical reasoning have been addressed in chapter 1. In this chapter, we focus on children's mathematical reasoning in terms of their use of formal and informal knowledge (Ginsburg, Klein, & Starkey, 1998). There is little consensus among researchers regarding the boundary between these knowledge forms, however. For example, counting is referred to as informal knowledge by Ginsburg et al. (1998), whereas Resnick (1989) categorized it as formal. Nonetheless, this categorization scheme serves as a helpful framework to understand the development of young children's mathematical knowledge. Here, we integrate the concepts proposed by Ginsburg et al. (1998) and Resnick (1989) and refer to informal mathematical knowledge as knowledge acquired through a child's interactions with the physical and social world while using nonnumeric quantity knowledge or nonsystematic symbol systems to solve real-world problems (e.g., comparisons that do not involve exact quantities). In contrast, formal mathematical knowledge entails the manipulation of a system of symbols (e.g., writing numerals such as 1, 2, 3, using ABAB to refer a pattern, or using + and −). Formal mathematical knowledge, which allows children to make judgments precisely, is usually acquired in organized classroom contexts.

Young children develop a certain level of informal mathematical understanding even though they may not be able to articulate it clearly. Resnick (1989) summarized children's nonnumeric quantity knowledge into four categories: (a) quantity judgments of absolute size of labels (e.g., big, small, lots, and little), (b) linguistic labels on the comparisons of sizes (e.g., bigger, smaller, taller, and shorter), (c) changes as increases or decreases in quantity (e.g., if one of cookies is taken away, they would have less than before), and (d) part–whole schema (e.g., each piece of cake is smaller than the whole cake). For example, preschoolers may display difficulty in articulating set and subset relationships as seen in Piaget's experiments (e.g., "Which is more? The brown beads or the brown and white beads together?" Inhelder & Piaget, 1964).

Yet, research has shown that if the question is stated clearly to focus children's attention on the whole collection (e.g., use of the word *forest* rather than both *pine trees* and *oak trees*), young children do display an understanding of part–whole relationships (Resnick, 1989). Based on their informal mathematical knowledge, young children can make basic, although not precise, mathematical judgments. In contrast, counting is an example of a culturally transmitted formal knowledge that allows young children to make more exact mathematical judgments (Resnick, 1989). To understand counting, children must at least implicitly know that number names must match the objects one for one and that the order of the number names matters but not the order of objects being counted (Baroody & Wilkins, 1999; Gelman & Gallistel, 1978). It is worthwhile to note that although counting is categorized as formal mathematical knowledge in this chapter, children as young as 4 (before formal schooling) can readily count to a small number (Baroody & Wilkins, 1999; Ginsburg, Pappas, & Seo, 2001).

Children's informal mathematical knowledge is a necessary foundation for assimilating formal mathematical knowledge (Ginsburg et al., 2001; Nunes, 1993; Resnick, 1989; Tang & Ginsburg, 1999). The literature has documented how children's informal mathematical knowledge facilitates their understanding of systematic symbol systems. For example, young children may incorporate their informal comparison schema with counting to create a mental number line (Resnick, 1983) so as to quickly identify which number is more among a pair of numbers.

Children can also incorporate their informal mathematical concept of change with counting to compute the effects of addition and subtraction on sets of objects (Ginsburg, 1989). When entering the formal educational system,

children's informal mathematical knowledge can be enriched by codified arithmetic, which allows the user to deal with imaginary mathematical objects.
However, few studies have examined how evolving classroom contexts support
young children's transition from working primarily on informal mathematical
knowledge to applying formal mathematical knowledge effectively.

ANALOGICAL REASONING

While working with concrete materials, young children's ability to make analogical associations facilitates their learning of more formal mathematical
concepts (English & Halford, 1995). As is the case with mathematical reasoning, few studies have examined the role of classroom discourse specifically on
the development of analogical reasoning. However, researchers have examined the relationship between children's verbalizations and the development
of analogical reasoning ability. For example, White, Alexander, and Daugherty (1998) investigated the relationship between the private and social
speech of learners and their mathematical and analogical reasoning abilities.
The researchers found that children with a higher proficiency in mathematical and analogical reasoning verbalized conceptual relationships more frequently. In fact, it is a common paradigm to examine children's verbalizations in order to obtain access into the thought processes involved in
reasoning and learning, and more specifically the thought processes involved
in analogical reasoning (Crisafi & Brown, 1986; Gentner, 1977).

Goswami (1998) has argued that experience with solving analogies and
thinking about relational similarities affects analogical reasoning ability.
Specifically, the use of analogies in teaching and learning should be critical in
promoting proficiency in analogical reasoning. Further, researchers have
also found durable effects of training children to reason analogically, which
provides evidence that instruction can facilitate the development of analogical reasoning (Alexander, Willson, White, & Fuqua, 1987; Alexander et al.,
1989; Pate, Alexander, & Kulkowich, 1989). Alexander, White, and Daugherty (1997), for example, posited that the processes of mathematical reasoning correspond closely to the component processes of analogical reasoning. Both domains involve the processes of perceiving the basic attributes of
objects (encoding), relating symbols to their abstract concepts (inferring/
mapping), and recognizing patterns among symbols (applying). In addition,
Alexander et al. (1989) found strong evidence of the relationship between
young children's mathematical and analogical reasoning ability.

As noted in previous chapters of this book, Sternberg (1977) articulated
the componential theory of analogical reasoning to describe the specific processes involved in solving conventional analogy problems (i.e., A:B::C:D).
Four particular components were identified in which the relational similari-

ties between terms are identified and underlying higher order relations established. Within this theory, the relational similarity between the first two terms of an analogy (i.e., A and B terms) or the relational similarity between the last two terms of an analogy (i.e., C and D terms) is referred to as a lower order relation. The relational similarity that bridges the first two terms (A and B terms) to the last two terms (C and D terms) in an analogy is referred to as the higher order relation. The recognition and use of higher order relations is viewed as a more sophisticated reasoning strategy than the recognition and use of lower order relations. Specifically, children who are more proficient analogical reasoners attend more frequently to higher order relations when solving analogy problems than less proficient analogical reasoners (Alexander et al., 1987; White et al., 1998).

Whereas previous research has not focused extensively on the effects of classroom contexts on cognitive development, there has recently been a shift in educational psychology to consider the role of classroom contexts on learning. Turner and Meyer (2000) highlight some compelling rationales for examining the effects of classroom contexts, which include classroom discourse, on cognitive development. First, learner psychological reactions to the instructional context will influence what is learned and how learning is developed. Secondly, there are differences in learning and instruction across content areas. Finally, considering the effects that the classroom context may have on the cognitive, social, affective, and motivational components of learning will provide findings that are more contextualized. Therefore, findings can be more meaningful to educators because they represent realistic contexts. Turner and Meyer (2000) claimed that contextualized findings elucidate the how and why of student–teacher interactions.

One goal of this chapter is to elucidate the role that classroom discourse plays on the development of analogical reasoning. In addition to the supporting role of classroom discourse, we believe that the active participation of children in the classroom discourse is crucial to their cognitive development. Therefore, the focus of this chapter is twofold. First, we set out to describe the mathematical and analogical discourse in the classroom contexts as it unfolds over a three-year period. Second, we compare the qualitative differences of the active classroom discourse between children who performed above or below average on mathematical and analogical reasoning measures. Overall, we hypothesized that the quality of mathematical and analogical discourse would change over time, and that the classroom context, as it includes the content as well as the exchange of discourse between teacher and students, should facilitate mathematical and analogical development. In addition, we posited that children who performed better in mathematical and analogical reasoning tests would also engage more actively in the classroom discourse.

To achieve our goals, we observed the classroom discourse for three years, from kindergarten through to the end of second grade. During that period, we focused on the utterances of individual students and student–teacher interactions that pertained to mathematical and analogical reasoning. Our purpose was to explore the following questions:

- How does classroom discourse pertaining to mathematical and analogical reasoning evolve from kindergarten to second grade?
- What general discourse patterns, evidenced in these early childhood classrooms, are related to mathematical and analogical reasoning?
- How do the patterns in classroom discourse mirror children's mathematical and reasoning development?

STUDY COMPONENTS

The Children

Twelve of 29 children were selected for in-depth case studies based on the level of mathematical and analogical reasoning that they demonstrated early in our three-year longitudinal study (as explained in chaps. 2 and 3). Selection was made to ensure differences in children's initial level of reasoning development. The 12 children, who attended two public schools in the mid-Atlantic region of the United States, were tested once every semester and observed six times during each school year, as they progressed from kindergarten to second grade. Among the children (6 females and 6 males), 1 boy and 1 girl left before the end of the first year of the study. Therefore, only data from the remaining 10 children are considered in this analysis.

The Reasoning Measures

The Test of Analogical Reasoning for Children (TARC; Alexander et al., 1987) was used to measure children's analogical reasoning. In Year 1, this measure uses attribute blocks to present children with geometric analogical problems of the form A:B::C:?. In Years 2 and 3, analogies were subsequently presented in pictorial, geometric, and linguistic forms. The Mathematical Reasoning Test for Young Students (MRTYS; English & Alexander, 1997) was structured around basic mathematical skills validated in the literature, including sorting, classifying, patterning, and number sense. As with the TARC, the content of the MRTYS was graduated in difficulty to correspond with the children's increased mathematical ability. (For a more detailed description, see Alexander & Buehl, chap. 2, this volume.) Standard scores were used for these measures.

The Data Source

The inquiry team observed and recorded the children's speech in their classrooms, along with the responses and exchanges from teachers or classmates. These data were collected during varying points in the school day, as a way to explore the occasions of reasoning discourse in general. We subsequently coded the exchanges related to mathematical reasoning representing informal or formal knowledge. The discourse related to analogical reasoning was coded on the basis of lower or higher order relational similarity. In addition, dependability of the coding was established by inviting two doctoral students to reexamine and question the coding until consensus was achieved. The coded classroom interchanges were summarized based on the concepts and activities involved in the discourse to reflect the qualitative differences of the observed incidences.

CHANGES IN DISCOURSE PATTERNS

The first goal of this study was to examine the evolution of classroom discourse as it pertains to the mathematical and analogical reasoning abilities of children in kindergarten through second grade. Overall, the observed children were exposed to numerous resources in their classrooms. For instance, each observed classroom was assigned one teacher, one assistant teacher, and sometimes a student teacher or a parent assistant to interact with students. Various activities full of educational materials were also available for students to explore. To summarize our findings within limited space, daily routines in the classrooms are briefly described and examples of classroom discourse are discussed for each grade.

Kindergarten

On a typical day of kindergarten, the students often had free playtime before group circle time. During circle time, the students often sat on the mat in front of the teacher, and the teachers would sometimes write on the board to introduce words and grammar, such as "We had pizza for lunch," or read books to invite a discussion on a relevant topic. The teachers might also introduce some patterns and ask volunteers to complete the patterns. After circle time, the students often were divided into small groups to work on center activities, arranged by their teachers to extend group discussion. Typical center activities included math, artwork, observations, dramatic play, a discovery area, and games. For example, the dramatic play center could be set up as a science lab, and the discovery area could include geoboards and patterns for the children to engage with on a given day.

We found that in the kindergarten year, the classroom discourse was less structured. Informal mathematical knowledge, and to a lesser degree, analogical reasoning appeared frequently in the teachers' guidance and students' conversation. For example, during morning circle time, one teacher asked her students to observe the shapes of different parts of a plant. The names of the shapes (e.g., oval, curve, and circle) were mentioned throughout the morning and incorporated into various classroom activities (e.g., drawing leaves and observing seeds they planted). Thus, in this initial year, the discourse largely took the form of enculturation.

We also found that teachers purposefully designed classroom contexts that provided students opportunities to associate mathematical knowledge with abstract formal concepts early in the kindergarten year. In the following scenario, the teacher invites students to associate their experience with measuring to the formal concept of measurement.

Teacher: I have a number of objects here that all have something in common. What do these things have in common?

Class: Numbers. They measure. They can help you with cooking.

Teacher: But, does the watch help you with cooking? Would a measuring tape help you with cooking? How can I use a measuring tape? Would this be good for measuring things that are round? Okay, what would I measure with this (referring to a measuring cup)?

Class: [multiple responses] Flour. Sugar. Cinnamon. Salt. Vegetables.

Teacher: What would I measure with this (referring to a measuring spoon)? Pants? Someone's head?

Class: Could use it for plants.

Teacher: Sometimes we could use a measuring spoon to measure plant food. What would I measure with a timer?

Class: Time.

Teacher: I could measure time with this. You could use it to see how long it takes to get ready for bed. [She demonstrates and explains how to use the timer by setting it for 10 seconds and then lets the alarm go off.]

Teacher: What would I measure with a scale?

Class: How much things weigh.

Teacher: What kind of things could I measure?

Class: Food.

Teacher: Today we're going to do some measurements on the computer. You start to measure at the beginning with a zero. What stamp do you want to use to measure the green line? [She demonstrates how to move the stamp next to each other to measure the line.]

Does any one want to estimate? Estimate the number of stamps it will take to measure the green line on the screen?

Class: 9.

Teacher: 9 is a good estimate.

After the demonstration, the teacher asks the children to work in pairs. The class then spends about 20–25 minutes measuring different lines using stamps provided in the software.

In this case, the teacher first utilized familiar objects (e.g., measuring cups, measuring spoons, or timer) to invite students to reflect on the common function of those objects. The function of each tool was then discussed followed by hands-on measuring activities on the computer. In this way, children gradually conceptualized their understanding about measurement by reflecting on the classroom discourse and by also measuring objects they were less familiar with.

In another case, by operating on concrete objects, the classroom context provided students with opportunities to associate their basic mathematical knowledge with abstract formal concepts. For example, the teachers began relating the codified number system (e.g., 1, 2, 3) to the number–word system (e.g., one, two, three). In a daily routine, one teacher asked children to make tally marks to record how many days the eggs have been in the incubator and fill out: "The eggs are ＿＿ days old." In this way, the teacher associated students' previous formal mathematical knowledge (e.g., using the number–word system to count concrete objects, tally marks) with the formal codified number system (e.g., counting an abstract idea of days and writing down an Arabic numeral).

In a math game scenario, a teacher asked each child to count out a certain amount in M&Ms (e.g., 9). The child was then asked to decide how many to feed the big duck and how many would go to the little duck. Each child took a turn, and his/her combination needed to be different from the previous students'. In this way, the kindergartners had opportunities to associate counting with their informal mathematical knowledge (e.g., part–whole relationships). Finally, the kindergartners also learned to symbolize patterns, which are also correlated to the component process of applying in analogical reasoning (Alexander et al., 1997). In a daily routine, the students were directed to represent an AABB pattern by creating different sounds through clapping, humming, or the like.

First Grade

Similar to the previous year, the first-grade classrooms consisted of whole-group, small-group, and center activities on a daily basis. Typical center activities included journal writing, math, reading, observations, computer centers, and games. A typical day also began with students engaging in free play-time before group circle in which the teachers would explain and review assignments and activities such as "super heroes" mathematics, journal-writing activities or written addition and subtraction problems. The teachers would initially direct the group circle lessons after which students would be directed toward independent or small-group work at the various centers.

The length of teachers' instructions became longer and subsequently students' free playtime became shorter. Although classroom discourse involving informal mathematical knowledge was still observed across a variety of situations, it was no longer as evident. Children's formal mathematical knowledge also became more abstract. For example, counting observed in the first grade tended to involve abstract objects (e.g., how many days in a week or in a month) and the written system (e.g., Arabic numeral) instead of concrete objects as observed in kindergarten (e.g., M&M).

Teachers' and children's analogical reasoning in the first grade appeared less frequently, which may be a result of less time spent on art and free choice activities. In addition, the quality of analogical discourse also differed from the previous year. In the kindergarten year, analogy was used to associate two familiar objects. For instance, children used markers as swords to fight, made claims that relatively the fruit tasted like grass, and stretched their arms out and pretended they were airplane wings. In first grade, however, the teachers and students were observed using analogies to explain new concepts. For instance, in the following scenario, analogies are used in the discourse to introduce the concept of water cycle.

Teacher:	Do you know what it's called when things are repeated over and over again?
Student 1:	Pattern.
Teacher:	Yes, also cycle, like a water cycle. What are clouds made of? Remember the word *evaporating*?
Student 2:	At my house we take water out of air . . .
Teacher:	Oh, you use a dehumidifier. My parents have one because it's damp in the basement. It sucks water out of the air.
Student 3:	First they are snowflakes and then down and down they become rain.
Teacher:	Yes, remember in the video, the snowflakes came down and down and then became rain. So you said the water could evaporate from the ocean?
Student 4:	From ponds and rain puddles.
Teacher:	Where else?
Student 5:	Mud puddles.

Teacher: What about when your mom hangs your wet swimsuit out to dry?

Student 2: My grandma too.

Teacher: To give you an example of evaporation, line up and squeeze a sponge and put them on the board. I'll do it first.

Student 3: Hey, it's disappearing.

Teacher: Have your seat. Where is the water going?

Student 1: Air.

Student 6: Light, like the sun. Sun sucks water up.

Teacher: Do you think it has to do with how long? If you hang up wet suits in a house with air conditioning on, will it take longer than out in the sun? You should try.

Then, the teacher divides the children into two groups. One works with an assistant teacher to make three different clouds with shaving cream, and the other works on an evaporating experiment with the teacher.

In this case, for children to understand, the teacher uses *pattern* as an analogy for *cycle*. While children actively reflected on their own experiences to explain the word *evaporating* (e.g., use a dehumidifier and witness the disappearance of rain puddles), the teacher also added examples to enhance the children's understanding (e.g., the drying of wet swimsuits) along with more guiding questions (e.g., where does the water go and which one takes longer to dry). We also see that when faced with an abstract concept, children would use analogy to facilitate their understanding (e.g., sun sucks water up).

In another case, one teacher introduced the class to different types of clouds by analogy, such as cirrus looks like a horsetail, cumuli are like sheep, and stratus is like a fog. The structure of a correspondence was described by the teacher to include a greeting (i.e., Dear Sir), body (i.e., content), and feet (i.e., ending). Also, the students were observed applying analogy to describe a phenomenon (e.g., associating water evaporating with how plants suck water), an unfamiliar object (e.g., a phonograph is like a trumpet on a little table), and a new word (e.g., a swollen sky is like being hurt and turns black). However, the recognition of higher order relations was not observed in the discourse of first graders. Thus, it seems that the use and recognition of higher order relational similarities rarely occurred spontaneously in the teachers' and students' classroom discourse.

In first grade, formal mathematical knowledge became a major focus in teacher–student discourse. Students were not only introduced to different ways of counting (e.g., count by twos, threes, and eights) and grouping (e.g., how to group 15 in different ways), but they also learned the symbols for addition (+) and subtraction (−), which corresponds to the component processes of inferring and mapping in analogical reasoning. The following scenario shows us how the teacher challenges the class to count in various ways:

> On the board, a chart displays 12 counters. Also, each child has his/her counters to facilitate their counting.
>
> *Teacher:* Raise your hand if you can tell me how many counters there are.
>
> *Student 1:* 12.
>
> *Teacher:* How did you count them? [The student gets up and shows how she came up with 12.] Did someone else do it a different way?
>
> *Student 2:* There are 5 on top and 5 on the bottom, and then 2 more are 12.
>
> *Teacher:* Oh, so you grouped them? Okay, did someone else come up with a different way?
>
> One student is called on to show how to count by threes. When he gets stuck, other students try to interrupt him.
>
> *Teacher:* Give him a chance.
>
> The student finishes counting by threes. Two students volunteer to show how to count by ones and fours. The discussion goes on and ends when they have finished all of the possible methods of counting to 12.

In this case, the teacher kept on challenging the students until all of the possible methods were discovered by the class. During this process, although children worked on concrete objects to conceptualize abstract concepts (e.g., counting by threes and fours), the objects per se became more abstract as compared to the previous year (e.g., counters vs. M&Ms).

For the first graders, concrete objects such as cubes, pennies, nickels, and dimes were used in mathematical operations. In this year, the students' number concepts also became more abstract. For example, the children learned that one nickel can have an abstract value of five cents, and letters and words can be used to represent an addition problem (e.g., AM = 1 + 13 for A is the first letter and M is the thirteenth letter). In addition, the classroom discourse relating to formal mathematical knowledge involved many game-like activities and daily observations and recordings. (For example, in a math activity, students used dice or dominoes to make a mathematical sentence such as: +, =, and 2 + 1 = 3). During morning circle time, the weather was recorded routinely. Based on the recorded data, the students found out how many sunny days there were for a given time period, how many cloudy days there were, and how many more cloudy days than sunny days there were. In this way, teachers created opportunities for children to integrate their informal mathematical knowledge (e.g., comparison and change) with their formal mathematical knowledge (e.g., counting using symbolic symbols and subtractions).

Second Grade

Although second-grade classrooms also utilized whole-group, small-group and center activities, there was a greater shift toward individual work. The classroom environment became much more structured and therefore, there was a great deal less free playtime and less time allotted for artwork within the classroom. Even though the teachers also utilized the group circle for reading books, facilitating discussions, and introducing new activities, the teachers often introduced assignments to the class while students were seated at their desks.

Little classroom discourse involved informal mathematical knowledge and analogical reasoning. This was probably due to the more structured nature of the classroom interactions. Most of the activities observed in the classroom discourse were directed and guided by the teachers. Therefore, the students spent a lot of time answering the teachers' questions and working independently on mathematics questions that appeared in stories or in worksheets that were created by the teachers. Analogical reasoning was exhibited in the children's off-task play. For example, one child pretended a triangle was a machine gun and made shooting noises while he was required to solve mathematics problems.

The formal mathematical knowledge appearing in the classroom discourse became more complex and abstract. Not only did the numbers discussed become larger (e.g., count by 25s, 50s) and the operations become longer (e.g., $50 + 50 + 200$) but the types of mathematical operations also increased (e.g., the symbol of multiplication, "$\times$", was introduced). Further, the second graders rarely used concrete objects when solving addition, subtraction, multiplying, and division problems. This was surprising, given that appropriate concrete materials can serve as effective analogies for abstract concepts and processes (English & Halford, 1995). Instead, the children were allowed to manipulate concrete objects when working on estimation and measuring. For example, in the following scenario, the teacher encourages the children to use objects in the classroom to learn the concepts of weight, estimation, and measuring.

Teacher: Today we are going to continue talking about weight. We are going to talk about a pound. How much do you think a pound is? Remember when we got on the scale last week and weighed ourselves. Did anyone weigh just one pound?

Class: No.

Teacher: So how much do you think a pound weighs? I'm going to pass around a can that weighs a pound. I want you to feel it, hold it and then pass it around.

Class: [All of the students participate in the activity.]

Teacher: Did everyone get a chance? Now I want you to think of some-
            thing that weighs a pound.

Class: [many answers] A box of crayons. A basket of markers. The box
            of tissues with sunflowers. A jug of water, etc.

Teacher: Now, I want everyone who responded to get the object that they
            talked about and bring them to the circle.

One student brings 23 cubbies filled with crayons, papers, books, workbooks, etc.

Teacher: What do you think we have in our cubbies? Do you think all
            those baskets with all of those things in them weigh a pound?

Class: [respond jointly] No!

Teacher: Let's think about it. Remember our can that weighed a pound.
            Think about how much this can weighed. Think about the bas-
            kets. Does it make sense to bring all these baskets? Remember
            these baskets are filled with things. Should we get these 23
            cubbies on the scale and see if they weigh a pound?

The class decides to weigh the cubbies.

Teacher: Do you think the cubbies will weigh a lot more than a pound or
            a little more than a pound?

The teacher takes note of the students' responses. Some students say a lot
more and some say a little more.

Teacher: There seems to be a discrepancy in the class so I think we should
            weigh the baskets. Ok, let's make some estimates or guesses on
            how much the baskets all weigh. Let's tally the votes.

The teacher gives every student a sticky note and marker and tells them to
write down how many pounds they think the cubbies will weigh altogether. The teacher then groups the children's estimations into a graph.

Teacher: We don't need to put a zero up because remember all objects
            weigh something.

Class: Yes.

Teacher: Let's look at our graph. What can we say about the graph?

Class: Most people believe that it weighs 2 or 3 pounds.

Teacher: Excellent! What else?

Class: It goes from smallest to largest.

Teacher: Yes. That is something you can tell from the graph. What else?

Class: The same amount of people estimated 2 and 3.

Teacher: Yes. Anything else?

Class: If you add the votes for 2 and 6 (pounds) together, you get 6
            (votes).

Teacher: Excellent. Let's see if we made any good predictions or estimates.

The teacher asks two students to weigh the baskets and finds out that they
don't know how to read the scale. The teacher then draws some scales on
the white board and lets the students practice reading the scale. After that,
they continue to weigh other objects.

In this case, the teacher first associated students' informal knowledge
about weights with the standard unit, a pound, and used a concrete object, a
can, as an analogy of the abstract standard unit. The teacher asked the children to feel the weight of the can and compare it with other objects. Although
the use of analogy did not allow the students to precisely capture the idea of a
pound, it made it possible for them to associate their informal comparison
schema with the newly introduced standard weighing unit. Estimations were
made by comparing the object with the standard unit. The concept of a
pound was gradually acquired through repeatedly measuring concrete materials. In addition, the teacher offered the students opportunities to apply their
learned formal mathematical knowledge, such as number order, counting,
and addition to explicate the chart.

GENERAL DISCOURSE PATTERNS

Our second goal was to examine the general discourse patterns related to
mathematical and analogical reasoning evidenced in the early formal years of
schooling. Overall, we found that in classroom discourse, informal mathematical knowledge appeared across a variety of situations and involved various mathematical concepts. The teachers and students spontaneously used
informal mathematical knowledge during free play and in various group activities related to various subjects such as reading, science, and arts. In fact,
we could not identify a situation in which informal mathematical knowledge
did not appear.

In addition, informal mathematical knowledge was used to refer to various concepts including size (e.g., big, bigger, and biggest), length (e.g., long,
longer, and longest), number (e.g., half, two, and third), frequency (e.g., a little, all, most, least, and fewer), direction (e.g., up, down, and bottom), shapes
(e.g., oval, curve, and circle), time (e.g., one second, multiple seconds, one
minute, years, and fastest), and division (e.g., the teacher asks students to divide into two groups). For example, in kindergarten, students were asked to
compare who was tallest or shortest and to grasp an object that was shorter
than the one held by a classmate. In the construction area, one child decided
to build "a bigger house." During dramatic play, one child exclaimed, "my
car is faster than yours." It seems that not only was informal mathematical

discourse a part of the daily language, but teachers also made an effort to create opportunities for the children to become familiar with the informal mathematical concepts.

Some formal mathematical knowledge, such as counting, was used automatically by the students in their daily conversations. For example, while decorating his puppet lion, one student stated "I could only put on one hair at a time." When building a structure in a construction area, one child spontaneously announced, "I need three more green." However, compared to informal mathematical concepts, formal mathematical knowledge less frequently arose spontaneously. Rather, teachers purposefully used the formal mathematical knowledge to introduce mathematical operations, such as counting, recording, measuring, categorizing, and patterning.

For example, in the kindergarten classrooms, a daily routine required the children to go over the calendar (i.e., a codified system for recording dates) and to count how many days they had been in school for that month. In this case, the introduction of the calendar allowed the young children to count abstract objects, such as days, and aided their understanding of abstract concepts, such as what date it would be one week later. Evidence of formal mathematical knowledge in the students' conversations occurred frequently in response to some specific directive from the teacher. For example, as directed by the teacher, the students marked the number of days required for the eggs in the classroom to hatch. In another case, in response to the teacher's request, the children tried to figure out different ways to combine two numbers to make 15.

In contrast to the great variety of situations observed for informal mathematical knowledge, teachers and students tended to use analogical reasoning under specific conditions. In general, they used analogical reasoning to express their sense perceptions (e.g., the touch of pussy willow is like a fly on my nose), to describe art work (e.g., the author saw each color as its own person and each color has its own dance), and to introduce new concepts and skills by relating them to more familiar concepts and skills (e.g., the teacher shows the student how to write 5 by explaining that it looks like the letter "s" but sharper).

The students also frequently demonstrated analogical reasoning in their dramatic play (e.g., one child used his comb as a saw). However, higher order relations were rarely discussed. The observed higher order analogical reasoning in the classroom discourse occurred primarily during science discussion. For example, in observing ants, one child spontaneously proclaimed, "a twig is as heavy to an ant as a car is to us." Reading books about butterflies to the class, the teacher purposefully compared butterflies to moths and used an analogy to explain their similarities and differences (e.g., moth is to cocoon as butterfly is to chrysalis).

CROSS-CHILDREN COMPARISONS

Finally, we attempted to address how the children's discourse patterns mirrored their mathematical and analogical reasoning development. That is, we were interested in how children, with higher or lower performances in structured mathematical and analogical tests, interact differently within their learning environments across the three years. To achieve this goal, we distinguished students who scored higher on the TARC and MRTYS from students who scored lower on the two tests over the three years. We then briefly summarized the portraits of these higher or lower performance children. The characteristics of interest included children's work-related skills and classroom discourse that related to mathematical and analogical reasoning.

Specifically, two children were grouped into the higher performance group. These children (Joan and Sunny, pseudonyms used) were enthusiastic in their learning and displayed reflective thinking during the observations. Three children, Lara, Tiffany, and Chris were grouped into the lower performance group. It should be noted that Lara and Tiffany left at the end of the first grade. These lower performance children exhibited little reflective thinking and displayed either passive learning attitudes or disruptive behaviors that interfered with their learning. In the following sections, detailed descriptions of the children's characteristics are presented for each school year in which they were observed.

The Kindergarten Year

Joan was observed intentionally seating herself closer to the center of the group during circle time and frequently raising her hand to answer the teacher's questions. She also volunteered to read books to the class and insisted on reading the morning message to the group by herself instead of letting the teacher read for her. In respect to mathematical reasoning, Joan was observed successfully continuing a complex pattern and creating a mathematics problem similar to those the teacher had presented the class.

For example, in their daily routine, the teacher asked Joan to add a piece of block in a patterned "tower." The teacher asked, "If our pattern is blue, blue, green, green, green, green, what color does Joan need to put on?" While the rest of the class was arguing whether it was blue or green, Joan successfully fixed the pattern. When the teacher asked children to create questions about the calendar, Joan responded, "How many days of kindergarten are there in May?" which is similar to the type of questions the teacher asked previously ("If we have two days before vacation and two from this week, how many days do we have in April?").

When counting some objects, Joan was observed repeating her counting as a check on her accuracy. For example, during the center time, Joan was observed skipping over to the math center, which was designed for children to practice numbers and counting. The number of that day was 5. She counted out 10 M&Ms from the baseball dispenser. She then counted five in one hand and picked up the others and put them back in the dispenser. Touching each M&M in her hand, she counted them again and softly said "five." She pointed to each M&M and recounted them and then walked to another center eating the candy.

Sunny was attracted to animals and was observed actively seeking information that related to animals. In his conversation with peers, he often made references to sea animals that he learned about from movies. In his pretend play, he would build "homes" for squid to live in or pretend to have two carnivorous dinosaurs fight over food. Sunny, like Joan, was observed rechecking his own work for accuracy. For example, working on an assignment that required students to draw nine objects, Sunny was distracted several times while drawing. He then recounted how many bees he needed to draw. He counted two more times and decided he needed one more.

In terms of analogical reasoning, reflection on the teacher's descriptions of how butterflies get nourishment with their proboscis, Sunny responded, "Like a bee." During activity time, Sunny was observed to associate what he knew with what he observed in his exploration. For example, Sunny got two prisms, looked through them, and said, "Bees really see like this. From a bee's point of view." Later, he said to himself, "If dogs see in black and white, then bees see . . ." It appears that he spontaneously tried to compare the sight of dogs with that of bees. Whereas the two children in the higher performance group exhibited self-regulatory skills by checking the accuracy of their own work, the children in the lower performance group were reliant on their teachers to regulate their learning and performance. The teachers and teaching assistants were often observed reviewing the lower performers' work and cueing them to their errors. For example, when Lara's teacher discovered an error she responded, "You said six. Did you count six? Let's count together. 1-2-3-4-5, you need one more."

In contrast to the children in the high performance group, Lara exhibited very little analogical reasoning and had difficulty staying on task. She tended to get bored before the task was completed. She was observed walking away in the middle of a task while exclaiming, "I'm not going to do it." Lara exhibited difficulty staying on task even with direct guidance from the teacher or teaching assistant.

During a task that required the children to build towers with blocks the teaching assistant (TA) works directly with Lara.

TA asks Lara: "Does it matter how far apart I put these (referring to blocks at the bottom of the tower)?"

Lara responds, "I don't know."

TA begins to build her own tower, "Does it matter if these (pointing to blocks at the top) fall down?"

Lara does not respond.

TA continues to attempt an exchange with no response from Lara.

Chris was relatively dependent on help from others and relied on the opinions of others, as well. He was observed repeatedly asking one peer, "Do you like my painting?" Not getting any response from that peer, he turned to ask another peer the same question, signaling his lack of confidence. When one teaching assistant suggested the children draw what they see on the computer, Chris responded, "I don't want to. I just want to look." Working on another assignment, Chris asked the teaching assistant, "Do I get to play after this?" and complained, "I have been drawing so long."

Tiffany did not exhibit a preference for challenge. In her work, she was observed doing a simple two-color patterning. Her major interest was to make a necklace instead of creating a challenging pattern. Tiffany exhibited a grasp of informal mathematical concepts, such as accurately comparing the length of two objects. Tiffany also displayed some analogical reasoning but only during play, for example, pretending that a tube was a gun and a cane.

Although these children in the lower performance group also displayed some informal counting, none of them was observed repeating their counting to check for accuracy. In addition, any demonstration of their analogical reasoning was observed during free play and generally tended to have only lower order relational similarity (e.g., using a tinker toy as a plane and pretending to fly), and never was related to class discussions.

In summary, the higher and lower performance children displayed different characteristics in their work-related skills and classroom discourse relating to mathematical and analogical reasoning. The higher performance children exhibited complex patterning in their work, active informal counting, and analogical associations in classroom discourse in stark contrast to the lower performance children. The lower performance children rarely exhibited complex patterning, active informal counting, or analogical association in their classroom discourse.

The First Grade Year

Joan, as observed in the previous year, frequently raised her hand to participate in class discussions. In addition, she was observed helping her peers with their assignments. During one observation, she even complained to the teacher that her assignment was easier than the other students' assignments. Joan also displayed reflective thinking. When the teacher asked the class how they knew that 16 was an even number, Joan explained, "Six is an even number, so 16 is an even number" (analogy). Joan also displayed an understanding of the concept of "patterning stem" and was able to articulate the concept clearly. For example, as seen in the following scenario that focused on patterns, Joan demonstrates formal mathematical knowledge and the component process of applying.

> *Teacher:* Today when we did the morning message, some people had trouble with patterns. We did patterns way back in the fall. I want to go over patterns a little. [The teacher drew on the white board a pattern consisting of circle, triangle, circle, and triangle]. Here is my pattern. What is my pattern stem? Come show me. Draw a line under the pattern stem.
>
> Students appear unsure.
>
> *Teacher:* When I say pattern stem, what am I talking about?
>
> *Joan:* [raises her hand and is called on] The part of the pattern that repeats.
>
> *Teacher:* What does *repeat* mean?
>
> *Class:* Over and over again.
>
> *Teacher:* The pattern stem is that part that goes over and over again.
>
> *Teacher:* [draws a pattern of triangle, triangle, circle, triangle, triangle, circle, triangle, triangle, circle using different colors] What is my pattern stem?
>
> *Class:* [many voices] triangle, triangle, and circle.
>
> *Teacher:* The pattern stem of my pattern is . . . triangle, triangle, and circle.
>
> *Teacher:* [holds up a card with a pattern of hexagon, triangle, and diamond] Get out the manipulatives and create this pattern. What is another way we could say the pattern, Joan?
>
> *Joan:* yellow, green, brown, yellow, green, brown.
>
> *Teacher:* Good. Here is another pattern . . .

In this case, examples were given to the class. Students were asked to identify pattern stems (formal mathematical knowledge, component process of applying) and to create their own patterns based on given pattern stems, repeatedly. It seems that Joan not only could articulate the concept of pattern stem, she could also recognize patterns from multiple perspectives (e.g., shapes and colors). During their practices, other students asked Joan if they could use a different color or if their patterns were correct. In one case, Joan instructed a fellow student, "You have to use the exact same color. You should outline your pattern stem."

Sunny was observed frequently assisting peers with their work. Concentrating on his own assignment, Sunny told the other student to "stay with me, and I will answer your question" in response to the student's requests for help. Also, Sunny was consciously aware of his counting strategies and kept on checking his counting results. For example, in a mathematical discussion section, he was observed using private speech, such as "I knew it" or "I get it," after an answer for each problem was stated by the teacher. When solving questions related to their recording data, such as how many more no's (12) compared to yes's (8), he explained to his peers, "You can go like 8, 9, 10, 11, 12. I count above 8. That is how I usually do it." Moreover, before the concept of *negative* was introduced to the class, Sunny spontaneously questioned about the concept. He asked the observer, "Can you take away 3 from 0?" When the observer responded, "Can you?" Sunny said, "If you take 2 away from 0, you would have a negative number."

As observed during the kindergarten year, the lower performance children frequently exhibited off-task behavior although they sometimes were observed working quietly and intensely. For example, Lara was observed leaving her work to play a game and then returned to work. The lower performance children also tended to wait passively for help or new assignments, instead of actively seeking aid or assignments to achieve mastery of concepts. For example, when Chris did not know how to do an assignment, he stopped and waited for the teacher to help him. He did not attempt to try various approaches while waiting for the teacher. Tiffany would passively sit and wait until it was time to move on to the next task when she finished her work.

In terms of mathematical-related discourse, the lower performance children did not demonstrate reflective thinking. The analogical reasoning discourse of these children was only identified in their pretend play and focused on lower order relations, which is similar to the observations obtained the previous year. That is, they recognized the relational similarity between two familiar objects, but did not associate the relational similarity to academic concepts. During circle time, the lower performance children generally listened passively and rarely actively participated in discussions. For example, in a discussion focusing on different ways to count to 12, while the class was actively participating, Chris was looking around the room and distracted by his neighbor and not engaged in the activity. The lower performance children also displayed less adaptive learning skills. For example, in the following description of a math activity, Chris has difficulty maintaining focus on the question.

Chris: Now, Ms. W [teacher assistance] can you read this?

Ms. W: [reads the worksheet] There are 6 red marbles and 2 green. How many are there?

Chris: Four.

Ms. W: Now, listen to what I just said. You can use your fingers.

Chris: [counting on his fingers] eight.

Ms. W: Can you write it out as a math problem? Write it in math language.

Chris writes 6 + 1.

Ms. W dismisses Chris to go to the centers.

It seems that Chris tends to jump quickly to find an answer based on some familiar key words (e.g., 6 and 2) and pays little attention to the meaning of the question (e.g., used subtraction first then switched to addition). He also spent little effort on the assignment (e.g., did not check whether 8 is consistent with 6 + 1). In addition, the teacher seems to hold a lower standard for Chris (e.g., did not correct his writing and dismissed him).

Tiffany exhibited a greater ability to stay on task in the first grade. Although Tiffany displayed some knowledge of formal mathematical knowledge (i.e., pattern recognition), she still exhibited a greater reliance on informal mathematical knowledge compared to her higher performance peers. Tiffany was frequently observed counting on her fingers and using manipulatives. As in kindergarten, Tiffany relied on the teacher and teaching assistants to verbally cue her to errors in her work, and did not demonstrate self-regulatory skills.

In summary, the higher performance children not only did well academically but also began to help their peers. They displayed reflective thinking, formal mathematical knowledge, and the analogical process of applying in classroom discourse. In contrast, the lower performance students tended to be passive learners, relying heavily on the aid of others, and spending more time off-task. They showed little improvement in their analogical reasoning abilities, nor a shift into formal mathematical thinking. Even though the classroom content emphasized the recognition and use of patterns, the lower performance students did not display an understanding for these concepts, particularly when compared to their higher performing peers.

The Second Grade Year

Joan continued to participate actively in class discussions. She also was observed finishing her work quickly and paying close attention to details. In a measuring task, for instance, she set the scale to 0 before weighing the object. Sunny often solved problems and answered questions in multiple ways. For example, in a math activity, the teacher asked students to build 57 with blocks representing tens and ones. Sunny claimed, "I can make a ten out of ones" and built 57 in three different ways: 5 tens and 7 ones, 4 tens and 17 ones, and 3 tens and 27 ones. That is, when others were trying to replace 1 ten with 10 ones, Sunny replaced 2 tens with 20 ones. Sunny also demonstrated the ability to relate or associate symbols with their abstract meanings (associated with the component processes of inferring and mapping). For example, when other students answered a question with two quarters, Sunny remarked that this is the same as a half-dollar. In a classroom discussion focusing on calculating expenses and getting change, Joan and Sunny both displayed an active attitude in the discourse processes.

> *Teacher:* Let's say a soccer ball is on sale and costs a mere 48 cents. An apple costs 26 cents. I can take 26 cents out of my coin jar and then 48 cents, and then I can put them together and add the sum. Can anyone tell me what that is?
>
> Joan, Sunny, and other kids raise their hands.
>
> *Teacher:* You could count it out, or you can add it.
>
> The teacher draws on the overhead 26 cents plus 48 cents and walks through it with the students and comes up with 74 cents.
>
> *Teacher:* Okay, this is what you're going to do. This sheet says, "count your money." You're going to count the total amount . . . Then you're going to purchase items . . . First, you're going to add up the sum of these two items, then you're going to subtract it from the money you do have.
>
> *Other:* What's finding the sum?
>
> *Teacher:* What's finding the sum? Can anyone help him?
>
> *Sunny:* Adding.
>
> Joan gets a worksheet, starts working immediately, and finishes the worksheet in less than five minutes while other students continued to work on the worksheet.

In the prior scenario, the second graders began to solve problems that required multiple steps of processing (e.g., summing up the cost of two items, then subtracting the sum). Although students (e.g., Joan and Sunny) keep on actively reflecting on the discourse processes (e.g., as observed through their raising hands and asking or answering questions), it is the teacher that dominates the discourse processes. The individual child's reflections in the discourse processes thus become difficult to observe.

In contrast, Chris would become bored during a long discussion and begin to engage in off-task play. Chris was observed immediately seeking assistance from the teacher while his partner was still trying to work out a problem himself. Sometimes, when he was not sure how to do the work, Chris would ask other students for the answers instead of asking for minimal assistance and completing the task himself. For example, when working on mathematics problems with his partner, Chris wrote $47 - 10$, then looked to his partner for the answer. When his partner answered "37", Chris questioned, "Are you sure?" then wrote 37 on their worksheet. Chris also experienced difficulty understanding the teacher's instructions for the assignment.

Teacher: [asks the students to start with a number, such as 57, and subtract it with a number rolled from a die] If you roll a 20, then write $57 - 20 = 37$.

Chris: [rolled a 20 on a 39, and wrote $20 - 39 = 29$].

Later, on another day, working on calculating the cost of two items.

Teacher: How much would 30 and 40 be?

Chris: 19.

Teacher: [repeats her question.]

Chris: 10.

Teacher: Do you think $30 + 40$ would be less than either 30 or 40?

Chris: 70.

Teacher: Good.

It seems that Chris was confused about the meaning of the mathematics assignments. He used whatever strategies that came to his mind as in kindergarten. Chris chose the correct one (addition) only when the teacher gave him enough hints to limit the possibility of using other strategies (e.g., subtraction).

Similarly to the previous year, Chris's analogical reasoning discourse was primarily related to his off-task play. For example, when the class was working on an assignment, Chris rolled up a paper towel and held it up to his eye to look through it like a telescope. When most of the class had their hands raised, Chris was watching students with his telescope.

Thus, the difference between the higher and lower performance students became relatively significant. Whereas the higher performance children were trying to master their tasks, the lower performance students were seeking opportunities to play and assistance from peers. Importantly, the higher performance children were demonstrating abilities found to predict mathematical learning and be related to analogical reasoning ability, such as relating symbols to their abstract meanings and recognizing patterns.

Overall these portraits show that, for each school year, child engagement, level of reflection, teacher facilitation, peer interactions, and curriculum arrangements were associated with children's analogical and mathematical reasoning development with great interactions.

CONCLUSIONS AND EDUCATIONAL SIGNIFICANCE

This study offered the opportunity to explore the evolution of classroom discourse and cognitive development over the course of three years. Children's discourse patterns were looked at specifically in relation to their mathematical and analogical reasoning development. Also, this study afforded the occasion to examine the content and nature of discourse processes that arose in these classroom communities and to track changes from the kindergarten year to second grade—a period of active transition from informal to formal mathematical reasoning.

Several conclusions can be derived from this study. First, informal mathematical knowledge was integrated into a variety of situations relating to various concepts. It seems that informal mathematical knowledge, which occurred spontaneously, has become a part of the classroom culture. Instead, formal mathematical knowledge occurred in specific situations, such as when teachers purposefully introduced formal mathematical concepts and when the students responded to specific directives from the teacher. Analogical reasoning was used both spontaneously and for specific purposes, such as associating one concrete object with another. However, there was little direct attention paid to analogical reasoning by the teachers and very little of the observed classroom discourse was related to more complex associations. In general, the analogical reasoning that arose in pretend play and conversations was used to express sensory perceptions, describe art, and introduce new concepts.

Second, as presumed, the classroom activities became more structured and children's discourse became more restricted to academic subjects over the course of the study. In this situation, formal mathematical knowledge gradually dominated most of the classroom discourse. By comparison, analogical reasoning, which tended to occur in less restricted activities (e.g., pretend play and art tasks), was exhibited less frequently over time. However, we documented some qualitative changes of analogical reasoning. In the first grade, contrary to what was observed in kindergarten, the students began to use analogies to associate concrete objects with abstract concepts. The teachers also used concrete materials to serve as analogies to introduce new concepts.

Finally, children who scored higher on the TARC and MRTYS were observed reflecting on what they learned and applying this knowledge to new situations. They were more active in mastering tasks in direct contrast to children who scored lower on the TARC and MRTYS. The analogical reasoning of the lower performance children observed in their classroom discourse often occurred in their off-task play. Therefore, future research focusing on children's naturally occurring analogical reasoning should avoid examining only the frequency of analogical discourse.

REFERENCES

Alexander, P. A., White, C. S., & Daugherty, M. (1997). Children's use of analogical reasoning in early mathematics learning. In L. English (Ed.), *Mathematical reasoning: Analogies, metaphors, and images* (pp. 117–147). Mahwah, NJ: Lawrence Erlbaum Associates.

Alexander, P. A., Willson, V. L., White, C. S., & Fuqua, J. D. (1987). Analogical reasoning in young children. *Journal of Educational Psychology, 79*, 401–408.

Alexander, P. A., Willson, V. L., White, C. S., Fuqua, J. D., Clark, G. D., Wilson, A. F., & Kulikowich, J. M. (1989). Development of analogical reasoning in 4 and 5-year-old children. *Cognitive Development, 4*, 65–88.

Baroody, A. J., & Wilkins, J. L. M. (1999). The development of informal counting, number, and arithmetic skills and concepts. In J. V. Copley (Ed.), *Mathematics in the early years*. Reston, VA: National Council of Teachers of Mathematics; Washington, DC: National Association for the Education of Young Children.

Cobb, P., Boufi, A., McClain, K., & Whitenack, J. (1997). Reflective discourse and collective reflection. *Journal for Research in Mathematics Education, 28*(3), 258–277.

Corwin, R. B. (1995). *Talking mathematics: Supporting children's voices*. Westport, CT: Heinemann.

Crisafi, M. A., & Brown, A. L. (1986). Analogical transfer in very young children: Combining two separately learned solutions to reach a goal. *Child Development, 57*, 953–986.

Dockett, S., & Perry, B. (2000, April). *"Air is a kind of wind": Argumentation and the construction of knowledge*. Paper presented at the annual conference of the Association for the Study of Play, Baltimore.

Dubinsky, E. (1991). Reflective abstraction in advanced mathematical thinking. In D. Tall (Ed.), *Advanced mathematical thinking* (pp. 95–123). Dordrecht, Netherlands: Kluwer.

Duckworth, E. (1996). *"The having of wonderful ideas" and other essays on teaching and learning*. New York: Teachers College Press.

English, L. D., & Alexander, P. A. (1997). *A longitudinal and cross-cultural study of the analogical and mathematical reasoning patterns of young children*. Proposal submitted to the Australian Research Council.

English, L. D., & Halford, G. A. (1995). *Mathematics education: Models and processes*. Mahwah, NJ: Lawrence Erlbaum Associates.

Gelman, R., & Gallistel, C. R. (1978). *The children's understanding of number*. Cambridge, MA: Harvard University Press.

Gentner, D. (1977). Children's performance on a spatial analogies task. *Child Development, 48*, 1034–1039.

Ginsburg, H. P. (1989). *Children's arithmetic: How they learn it and how you teach it* (2nd ed.). Austin, TX: Pro-Ed.

Ginsburg, H. P., Klein, A., & Starkey, P. (1998). The development of children's mathematical thinking: Connecting research with practice. In W. Damon (Series Ed.) & D. Kuhn & R. S. Siegler (Vol. Eds.), *Handbook of child psychology: Vol. 2. Cognition, perception, and language* (5th ed., pp. 401–476). New York: Wiley.

Ginsburg, H. P., Pappas, S., & Seo, K.-H. (2001). Everyday mathematical knowledge: Asking young children what is developmentally appropriate. In S. Golbeck (Ed.), *Psychological perspectives on early childhood education: Reframing dilemmas in research and practice* (pp. 181–219). Mahwah, NJ: Lawrence Erlbaum Associates.

Goswami, U. (1998). Causal reasoning about pairs of relations and analogical reasoning in young children. *British Journal of Developmental Psychology, 16*, 553–569.

Inhelder, B., & Piaget, J. (1964). *The early growth of logic in the child. Classification and seriation* (E. A. Lunzer & D. P. Papert, Trans.). New York: Harper & Row. (Original work published 1959)

Lampert, M. (1998). Investigating teaching practice. In M. Lampert & M. L. Blunk (Eds.), *Talking mathematics in school: Studies of teaching and learning* (pp. 153–162). New York: Cambridge University Press.

Lilburn, P., & Rawson, P. (1994). *Let's talk math: Encouraging children to explore ideas.* Westport, CT: Heinemann.

McClain, K., & Cobb, P. (1998). The role of imagery and discourse in supporting students' mathematical development. In M. Lampert & M. L. Blunk (Eds.), *Talking mathematics in school: Studies of teaching and learning* (pp. 56–81). New York: Cambridge University Press.

Nunes, T. (1993). Learning mathematics: Perspectives from everyday life. In R. B. Davis & C. A. Maher (Eds.), *Schools, mathematics, and the world of reality* (pp. 61–78). Boston: Allyn & Bacon.

O'Connor, M. C. (1998). Language socialization in the mathematics classroom: Discourse practices and mathematical thinking. In M. Lampert & M. L. Blunk (Eds.), *Talking mathematics in school: Studies of teaching and learning* (pp. 17–55). New York: Cambridge University Press.

Pate, P. E., Alexander, P. A., & Kulkowich, J. M. (1989). Assessing the effects of training social studies content and analogical reasoning processes on sixth-graders' domain-specific and strategic knowledge. In D. B. Strahan (Ed.), *Middle school research: Selected studies 1989* (pp. 19–29). Columbus, OH: Research Committee of the National Middle School Association.

Perry, B., & Dockett, S. (1998). Play, argumentation and social constructivism. *Early Childhood Development and Care, 140,* 5–15.

Piaget, J. (1972). *The principles of genetic epistemology.* London: Routledge & Kegan Paul.

Putt, I., Perry, B., Jones, G., Thornton, C., Langrall, C., & Mooney, E. (2000). Primary school students' statistical thinking: A comparison of two Australian states. In J. Bana & A. Chapman (Eds.), *Mathemetics education beyond 2000* (pp. 519–526). Perth, Australia: Mathematics Education Research Group of Australasia.

Resnick, L. B. (1983). A developmental theory of number understanding. In H. P. Ginsburg (Ed.), *The development of mathematical thinking* (pp. 109–151). New York: Academic Press.

Resnick, L. B. (1989). Developing mathematical knowledge. *American Psychologist, 44,* 162–169.

Rittenhouse, P. S. (1998). The teacher's role in mathematical conversation: Stepping in and stepping out. In M. Lampert & M. L. Blunk (Eds.), *Talking mathematics in school: Studies of teaching and learning* (pp. 163–189). New York: Cambridge University Press.

Rogoff, B. (1990). *Apprenticeship in thinking: Cognitive development in social context.* Oxford: Oxford University Press.

Rogoff, B. (1998). Cognition as a collaborative process. In W. Damon (Series Ed.) & D. Kuhn & R. S. Siegler (Vol. Eds.), *Handbook of child psychology: Vol 2. Cognition, perception and language* (5th ed., pp. 679–744). New York: Wiley.

Steffe, L. P., von Glasersfeld, E., Richards, J., & Cobb, P. (1983). *Children's counting types: Philosophy, theory, and application.* New York: Praeger.

Sternberg, R. J. (1977). *Intelligence, information processing, and analogical reasoning: The componential analysis of human abilities.* Hillsdale, NJ: Lawrence Erlbaum Associates.

Tang, E. P., & Ginsberg, H. P. (1999). Mathematical reasoning: A psychological view. In L. V. Stiff (Ed.), *Developing mathematical reasoning K–12* (pp. 45–61). Reston, VA: National Council of Teachers of Mathematics.

Turner, J. C., & Meyer, D. K. (2000). Studying and understanding the instructional contexts of classrooms: Using our past to forge our future. *Educational Psychologist, 35*(2), 69–85.

Van der Veer, R., & Valsiner, J. (1991). *Understanding Vygotsky: A quest for synthesis.* Cambridge, MA: Blackwell.

Vygotsky, L. S. (1978). *Mind and society: The development of higher psychological processes.* Cambridge, MA: Harvard University Press.

White, C. S., Alexander, P. A., & Daugherty, M. (1998). The relationship between young children's analogical reasoning and mathematical learning. *Mathematical Cognition, 4*(2), 103–123.

5

PORTRAYING MATHEMATICAL AND ANALOGICAL REASONING IN THE YOUNG: THREE CASE STUDIES

Debby Deal
Loyola College in Maryland

Shanon Hardy
George Mason University

The foundational research base for this chapter has been presented in other chapters of this book, in particular, chapter 1. The perspective adopted in the present chapter is that analogical and mathematical reasoning are cognitive processes, which are essential to establishing and organizing conceptual knowledge. There remains, however, a lack of research showing specifically *how* young children develop these reasoning abilities. The existing research base is limited to a predominantly quantitative research paradigm based on cognitive learning theories that focus on children's completion of tasks constructed by researchers. These tasks have typically been administered in laboratory contexts rather than in more natural classroom contexts. In our review of the literature, we were not able to locate any investigations that used qualitative methodologies to study the development of analogical and mathematical reasoning by young children in classroom settings. That is, little is known about whether or not analogical and mathematical reasoning are present in day-to-day learning in early childhood classrooms.

Studies situated within the school context show promise for helping researchers better understand how young children develop proficiency in these two important types of reasoning. We chose to use a qualitative methodology to study young children's mathematical and analogical reasoning processes over time to add to the extant literature. The specific research questions that guided this component of our study were the following:

1. How does a small sample of young children develop mathematical and analogical reasoning over time?

2. How does the development of these young children's analogical reasoning parallel their development of mathematical reasoning?

3. How and when do these young children use mathematical and analogical reasoning during classtime?

METHODOLOGY

We selected a case study design because it is best suited to formulating an empirical understanding of how young children develop mathematical and analogical reasoning over time within the context of early childhood education (Yin, 1994). Additionally, we were interested in using our understanding to support and improve instruction. Previous work in this area has contributed largely experimental data regarding cognitive growth and young children's potential ability. We sought to enrich this body of research by providing a more holistic picture of young Australian and American children's development within the school environment. Merriam (1988) suggested that one of the strengths of a case study design is that it "offers a means of investigating complex social units consisting of multiple variables of potential importance in understanding the phenomenon" and is therefore particularly well suited to classroom contexts (p. 32).

As our research questions indicate, we were interested in not only exploring the influence of the classroom environment but also investigating the relationship between children's informal and formal use of mathematical and analogical reasoning in the classroom and their performance on individualized measures. Yin (1994) and Merriam (1988) agree that a case study design does not preclude the use of quantitative data, and we feel that the combination of data affords several benefits. Most importantly, it provides a bridge to the extant experimental literature and allows for triangulation of data within our study.

The purpose of this chapter is twofold:

1. To illustrate how the development of analogical and mathematical reasoning is manifested in three participants, and

2. To look for patterns or themes across the three individual cases.

In the next section, we describe the school sites and classroom teachers, and discuss the selection of participants.

Contexts and Selection of Participants

The contexts and participants of our study have been addressed in chapters 2 and 3. We wish to emphasize that we selected schools in the United States and Australia that served children from similar socioeconomic backgrounds.

Hence, the school populations often included homes with one or two professional parents in middle-class neighborhoods. Shade Tree Elementary and Redfox Crossing Elementary (pseudonyms), the two American schools, were located in a large suburban school district in the mid-Atlantic region of the United States. Generally, both schools reflected a child-centered philosophy in kindergarten and the primary grades. This was exemplified by the children's work that decorated the classroom and hallway walls, and the daily emphasis on student choice in both kindergarten classrooms. Additionally, observations during kindergarten through second grade indicated whole-group, small-group, and center activities occurred regularly. Compton Preschool and Primary (pseudonyms), one of the Australian schools, also embraced a child-centered philosophy that was manifested by the instruction and classroom arrangements. Analogical reasoning was not explicitly taught in any of the participants' classrooms.

Each of the schools housed an extensive variety of mathematics and science manipulatives, social studies materials, and children's literature. Children were observed using manipulatives during teacher-directed lessons and during self-selected activities. Moveable child-sized furniture facilitated the child-centered approach at each school. Computers were available for the participants in both the American and Australian classrooms. The school libraries were inviting to children and contained a large selection of quality children's literature. Identifiable differences among the three schools included demographics, mathematics curriculum, and school culture.

As noted in chapter 3, the study addressed the first three years of the children's schooling. In the United States, this encompassed kindergarten, first, and second grade, while in Australia the participants were in preschool, Year 1, and Year 2.

Demographic and Curricular Differences

Shade Tree Elementary School served students in kindergarten through third grade and housed a special education preschool program. It was unique in the school system because it was the only school that serviced kindergarten through Grade 3 only. The population consisted of primarily middle-class families who held professional positions in the surrounding metropolitan area. The Houghton Mifflin Mathematics series (Bohan, Clark, Kelleher, & Thompson, 1995) was adopted by the school and implemented throughout the study. In addition, teachers were encouraged to develop and use their own instructional materials to supplement the Houghton Mifflin program.

Redfox Crossing Elementary School is located in a middle-class suburban neighborhood. It was an arts and science magnet school for students in kindergarten through sixth grade, and a gifted and talented center for students in third through sixth grades. Redfox Crossing Elementary also serviced students with special needs through partial and full inclusion. Due to its magnet school programs, the school had a culturally and economically diverse student population. The Growing with Mathematics series (1999) was adopted by the school for kindergarten through second grade; however, only the second-grade teacher in the study used it as the core math program. The kindergarten and first-grade teachers participating in the study indicated that their math program was more eclectic in nature and used a variety of teacher-designed and commercial materials.

Compton Preschool was a small facility constructed in the 1980s as one part of a double unit center. The second unit was used by the primary school due to limited preschool enrollments. The building included a playroom, teacher's office, kitchen, and storage room. Outside there was a fenced double play area with two sandpits, a fixed wooden playground structure, and two frames for connecting additional equipment, such as climbing ropes and swings. In addition to the manipulatives commonly found in preschools, Compton Preschool had a variety of large collected and donated materials, such as old adding machines, calculators, radios, dress-up clothes, and fabric. Children were encouraged to explore the materials as well as develop their own ideas in sociodramatic play. At the time of the study, there was not a published curriculum guide for preschools in this area. The teacher used *M3 Mathematics: Mapping Mathematical Meaning* by Pengelly (1992) as her main reference. An emphasis on numeracy and literacy was apparent at both the preschool and primary school.

Compton Primary School was adjacent to the Preschool and slightly older. Portions of it were renovated in 1998. Like the preschool, it was well stocked with manipulatives and it was clear that the focus was on developmentally appropriate practices for young learners. The classroom environment was readily adaptable to individual, small-group, and large-group instruction and, like the preschool, sociodramatic play was encouraged. A variety of published manuals, including *M3 Mathematics* (Pengelly, 1992), *Group Solutions: Cooperative Logic Activities for Grades K–4* (Goodman, 1992), and *Mathematics Curriculum and Teaching Program* (Curriculum Corporation, 1992), were used by some teachers within the school. Other teachers preferred to work mainly with manipulatives or adapt ideas from resource guides. In general, the Australian teachers seemed to use fewer paper and pencil activities than their American counterparts.

School Culture

We posit that there is a strong link between school culture and instruction. Staessens (1993) defined school culture as a socially constructed reality and explained that "members of an organization create their own culture" (p. 111). Visitors to Redfox Crossing Elementary quickly notice an informal, friendly atmosphere in which classes walking through the halls tend to be chatty and in haphazard lines. Although the principal made the critical decisions regarding instructional programs and curriculum, she was not involved in the day-to-day activities of the classroom, which may explain the casual atmosphere. Under her leadership, the goal orientation of the school singularly reflected her vision. For example, in 1998 Redfox Crossing Elementary adopted a multi-age (non-graded) program in kindergarten through second grade that was not supported by many of the primary teachers. During the third and final year of the study, the principal retired after 11 years as site administrator. The assistant principal, supported by both the staff and community, was promoted to principal. Unlike his predecessor, he demonstrated confidence in the teachers' decision-making skills and began building a sense of community within the school.

Both the human interactions and the physical appearance of Shade Tree Elementary School reflected an orderly, professional atmosphere. The principal could be characterized as a strong leader who is involved in daily instructional and curriculum decision making. There was a shared goal orientation in the school that was illustrated by the implementation of multi age (nongraded) kindergarten through second grade classrooms in 1999. In contrast to Redfox Crossing Elementary, teachers at Shade Tree School were committed to this innovation and the principal provided professional development to help teachers understand the theory and strategies for implementation.

The school culture observed at Compton Preschool and Primary was similar to the school culture at Shade Tree Elementary. Teachers had a strong voice in the school and actively contributed to the decision-making process. The school administration was facilitative rather than autocratic. Both the strong teachers' voice and the administrative support might have been due in part to the strong teachers' union found in Queensland, Australia. The union has a good deal of autonomy regarding materials selection and how instruction is delivered. For example, one of the teacher participants opted to use her textbook money on mathematics class resources rather than textbooks. Teachers worked in teams to establish the school mathematics program using the broad state curriculum as guidelines.

Case Study Selection Process

As indicated in chapter 4, 12 of 29 children were originally selected for in-depth case studies but after attrition, 10 case study students remained. We address three of these case studies in this chapter, as described next.

We were interested in following the development of children who initially represented a range of achievement in mathematical and analogical reasoning. We also wanted our case studies to reflect a balance of gender and, by agreement with the schools, did not include children with known language or

learning disabilities. The initial teachers provided information on family stability, socioemotional factors, and expected stability in the school. With these
considerations in mind, we identified three groups of students for case studies
of their mathematical and analogical reasoning development. Specifically, we
selected two students with high mathematical and high analogical reasoning
scores, two students with either high mathematical reasoning and low analogical reasoning or the inverse, and two students with low mathematical and
analogical reasoning scores at each school.

In this chapter, we present the case studies of three of the children, one
from each of Shade Tree Elementary, Redfox Crossing Elementary, and
Compton schools—one student with consistently high mathematical and analogical reasoning scores, one student with consistently low mathematical
and analogical reasoning scores, and one student with inconsistent mathematical and analogical reasoning scores.

Case Study Students

Frannie.   The first participant, Frannie, was a high/high student who maintained that profile throughout the study. She attended Shade Tree Elementary
School. All of Frannie's teachers during the study encouraged creative and
critical thinking and modeled developmentally appropriate practices. Her kindergarten teacher and her first-grade teachers were identified as teachers with a
theoretical orientation; for example, they repeatedly cited their sources of
knowledge and beliefs about mathematics instruction as including mentors,
graduate school courses, students, and teaching experience (as addressed in
chaps. 6 and 7, this volume). Her second-grade teacher, Patricia, was identified
as an experiential teacher, who presented a more limited way of knowing by referring exclusively to prior teaching experience when explaining her instructional choices. Frannie's kindergarten teacher, Margaret, had a master's degree in Early Childhood Education and had been teaching for seven years
when Frannie was in her class. Margaret began teaching after her children were
of school age and taught kindergarten and first grade until 1999, when she
chose to become part of a kindergarten/first-grade, multi-age team with
Frannie's first-grade teacher. She was the Teacher of the Year for the school
district in 1998. Frannie's first-grade teacher, Marilyn, began teaching after her
daughter was in high school. She was in her 13th year of teaching when
Frannie was in her class. She taught first grade for eight years and became the
first part of the K–1 multi-age team with Margaret. She earned a master's degree in education and served as a lead teacher in two areas. Patricia, Frannie's
second-grade teacher, also had a master's degree with an emphasis on teacher
research and served in several leadership roles.

Frannie was a bright, outgoing second grader whose entrance into formal
schooling was delayed for a year due to medical reasons. A week before her

intended kindergarten registration, Frannie had a seizure and results from an EEG confirmed that Frannie had a small lesion in her brain. The doctors diagnosed Frannie with a seizure disorder and explained to Frannie's parents that she might also exhibit symptoms associated with Attention Deficit Hyperactivity Disorder (ADHD). Because of the medical diagnosis, Frannie's young chronological age, and Frannie's intensive food allergies, her parents chose to delay her entrance into kindergarten. Frannie remained in the same preschool she had previously attended for two years and then entered kindergarten at age 6.

In addition to her mother and father, Frannie's family included an older sister who attended a gifted education center school and a younger brother who attended Shade Tree Elementary School. Both parents were active members of the Parent and Teacher Association (PTA), and Frannie's mother was a frequent volunteer at the school. Frannie's mother described her as a happy and outgoing "tomboy." Frannie's interests included all sports, particularly soccer, and writing and dramatizing plays.

Frannie's teachers considered her to be an excellent student. Patricia, her second-grade teacher, described Frannie as "brilliant, outgoing, and sometimes contrary" and considered her writing skills to be particularly superior. She was frequently assigned the task of peer-tutor or teacher assistant because she completed her assignments quickly and accurately.

Reed. The second participant, Reed, was selected because his test scores identified him as low in both mathematical and analogical reasoning throughout the study. Reed's teachers had also applied developmentally appropriate practices and encouraged creativity. Reed had the same teacher, Barbara, for both kindergarten and first grade. Barbara was working on her master's degree during the study and had 22 years of teaching experience including 15 years in her current school district. During that time she taught Head Start for 13 years, kindergarten one year, and kindergarten/first-grade, multi-age one year. Barbara often discussed her lack of confidence to teach reading and math while Reed was in kindergarten and first grade. After the first quarter of first grade, Barbara and her teammate decided to group for mathematics. Barbara taught math to their combined kindergartners and her teammate taught mathematics to their combined first graders, including Reed. Although they maintained the groupings for the remainder of the year, her teammate, a second-year teacher at the time, expressed frustration with this decision. Reed's second-grade teacher, Priscilla, had been teaching for 14 years. She taught second grade at Redfox Crossing Elementary for three years and, in contrast to Barbara, was very confident about her knowledge of the curriculum.

Reed was described by his teachers as a low achiever who was developmentally delayed in the physical and emotional domains. He was easily frustrated and had a tendency to cry, one of several behaviors his teachers repeatedly observed in kindergarten through second grade. Additionally, both his kindergarten/first-grade teacher and his second-grade teacher agreed that he often exhibited learned helplessness.

Academics were consistently a struggle for Reed since entering kindergarten. Barbara, his kindergarten/first-grade teacher stated that "Reed shies away from difficult tasks. He is very timid, not a risk taker." Priscilla confirmed that Reed required substantial reassurance and generally had difficulty across subjects, especially reading and writing.

Reed was not reading on grade level in first grade and received additional support including Title I, a federally (U.S.) supported program for low performing students, and Reading Recovery (Clay, 1993), as well as tutoring during the summer between first and second grade. In first grade, Barbara considered Reed's mathematical abilities to be "very inconsistent." Similarly, Priscilla stated that "he doesn't pick up in math or other subjects . . . but after some repetition he gets the big idea. . . ."

Reed's teachers believed that his parents fostered his dependency and lack of confidence. Reed's mother volunteered at the school regularly and often ate lunch with him. During second grade, she stopped spending as much time with Reed in school, and Priscilla felt this change helped Reed to become more independent. Reed was the youngest of three siblings in a blended family. Both his parents and adolescent siblings helped him with his schoolwork. His teachers felt the additional support at home contributed positively to Reed's academic growth although it did not influence his confidence.

Reed's teachers consistently described him as being well liked and having many friends. He was extremely easy-going and rarely observed in conflict with classmates. He often picked children of high ability for partners during group projects and these relationships appeared to be reciprocal.

Kate. Kate was selected because her scores on the TARC and MRTYS varied with no discernible pattern during the study. In both assessments, Kate's scores ranged from well above the mean to substantially below the mean. Kate's teachers for preschool, Year 1, and Year 2 were all placed within the theoretical cluster (see chap. 7, this volume). All of them integrated the development of literacy and numeracy throughout the day and purposely avoided an abundance of paper and pencil activities. Brenda, Kate's preschool teacher, had a bachelor's degree and 15 years of teaching experience in preschool, Year 1, Year 2, and multiage combinations. Based on her understanding of Helen Pengelly's work (see, e.g., Pengelly, 1992) and her own action research, she was very confident in her ability to diagnose and implement appropriate mathematics based on careful observation of her students. Brenda was actively involved in the children's play activities and regularly asked questions that caused the children to think about literacy and numeracy. For Year 1, Kate was in a Year 1, 2, and 3 multi-age classroom. When the Year 2 and Year 3 children went to religious instruction, Mary, Kate's Year 1 teacher, was able to work with only the small group of Grade 1 children.

Like Brenda, Mary (see chap. 7, this volume) participated in many professional development programs and based her instruction on careful observation of children. Mary had 22 years teaching experience with preschool, Year 1, and multi-aged classes of Year 1, 2, and 3 children. She had an undergraduate and master's degree from an Australian university. For the final year of the study, Kate was in a Year 2 class with Ruth who had 12 years teaching experience. Ruth had a master's degree from an Australian University and had taught preschool, Year 1, and Year 2. She believed it was very important for children to "explore it [the manipulatives] on their own without parameters" and scheduled Friday afternoons as a time for children to complete assigned work and then to enjoy self-selected play with art materials, building supplies, and games. She encouraged the children to talk about their activities with each other.

Kate was a social student who was well liked by her teachers and classmates. Her teachers described her as an enthusiastic student who liked to be busy all the time. For example, she often asked, "Can we do a play?" or "Can we sing a song?" Kate also loved to please and often asked to do jobs in the classroom. She liked to know everything that was going on and often maneuvered to be right next to the teacher. At times, her teachers viewed her eagerness to help and to be physically close as a mechanism to gain attention. Kate's teachers also noted that she sometimes did not fully grasp concepts or listen carefully, although she seemed to compensate for her poor listening skills.

Kate's family included her parents and an older sister. Kate also considered her pets, Tess the dog, Max the cat, and five unnamed fish to be part of her family. Her father was a professional who traveled abroad frequently. Kate explained, "Dad visits lots of places in the world . . . he brings presents home." Her mother worked for a dentist. Kate had many interests including gymnastics, rollerblading, watching TV, and playing with her many friends.

Data Collection

Data collection included classroom observations, formal and informal teacher interviews, student artifacts, and individualized test results. We observed the participants at least three times during each year of the study. Each observation lasted between 60 to 120 minutes. At least half of the observations occurred during designated mathematics instructional periods. Other observations took place during morning meeting, art, science, or language arts. We wanted to explore the influence of various contents and instructional routines on children's and teachers' use of analogical and mathematical reasoning. During the observations, we took detailed field notes that captured the context, chronology, and actual quotes of the participants, as much as possible. Additionally field visits frequently included informal conversations with the participants' teacher, which were noted in memos. These notes were augmented with formal interviews, e-mail conversations, and samples of the children's classwork.

As soon as possible after each visit, field notes were synthesized and typed. Field notes were analyzed on an ongoing basis over the course of the study. We began with predetermined descriptive categories and added emergent categories (Miles & Huberman, 1994). At the descriptive level, we looked for examples of analogical and mathematical reasoning. "During play," "alone/with others," and "number sense" are examples of emergent categories. Once we established categories, we read the field notes multiple times and checked for negative cases and discrepant data (Maxwell, 1996). Additionally, the descriptive categories were checked for inter- and intracoder reliability and achieved a 90% agreement (Miles & Huberman, 1994). As an additional validity check, the teachers of Frannie and Reed read the individual case studies as part of a member check (Maxwell, 1996).

Measures

The Test of Analogical Reasoning for Children (TARC) and the Mathematical Reasoning Test for Young Students (MRTYS) were used as measures of analogical reasoning (see chap. 2, this volume, for a detailed description of each measure and mathematical reasoning).

Cross-Case Analysis

We used a mixed strategy approach, conducting a variables-oriented and a case-oriented analysis (Miles & Huberman, 1994) to identify cross-case themes. As noted, we felt the combination of data would add to our understanding of analogical and mathematical reasoning in these young children. Consequently, we used the variable-oriented analysis to examine relationships between the participants' achievement on the TARC and MRTYS. The case-oriented analysis allowed us to look at specific patterns that were shared by participants.

For the purpose of this study, we examined students' standardized scores on the measures of analogical and mathematical reasoning. This allowed us to explore how each child changed in his or her analogical and mathematical reasoning relative to their peers.

RESULTS AND INTERPRETATIONS

In the following section, we provide descriptions and examples documenting the participants' use of analogical and mathematical reasoning during classroom observations. The descriptive data are interwoven with individualized test data to provide a rich picture of each participant and to view their mathematical and analogical reasoning relative to other students in the study.

Frannie's Analogical Reasoning

Throughout the study, Frannie consistently scored high on the TARC. Her test performance was compatible with her strong academic performance in the classroom. Analysis of Frannie's TARC z scores show a slight decline from the first pretest to posttest (1.223 to 0.4) and then a steady growth for subsequent scores (see Fig. 5.1).

Frannie's score on the third-year pretest (1.191) was the highest of the case study participants. Frannie's eager participation in all classroom activities was apparent throughout the three years of observations. Although Frannie was not frequently observed to spontaneously use verbal analogies, her art and creative writing projects included explicit analogies.

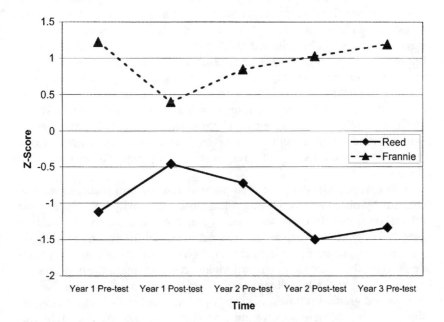

FIG. 5.1. TARC scores for Frannie and Reed (USA).

During a kindergarten observation, Frannie provided an analogical explanation when the teacher asked the children, "What would happen if we do not take care of the world?" Frannie stated that we need to take care of the world or it could look like, "a spill of oil." When the children were instructed to draw a picture in another kindergarten activity, Frannie selected a brown crayon and remarked, "This is soil." She then added black to the picture and exclaimed that the "black is soil and the brown is clay." Frannie continued to draw 11 flowers in the soil creating a red, yellow, blue, and purple pattern. As she added a blue line above the flowers, she informed one of her peers, "This is air." During an art and writing project in second grade, Frannie was observed creating a construction paper person. Rather than using an available pattern for the parts (skirt, top, arms, hair, and head), Frannie created the person by cutting her own paper shapes and then commented to another student, "Allen, this looks like your mom."

Frannie, as previously noted, continued to improve on the TARC despite an infrequent use of verbal analogies during classroom instruction. Her creativity and imagination continued to surface during writing and art projects.

Frannie's Mathematical Reasoning

Frannie's high performance in mathematical reasoning was apparent throughout the three years of the study. Although Frannie's kindergarten pretest score (0.69) on the MRTYS was not the highest score among the American children, she achieved the highest scores of all of the case study children on all remaining MRTYS measures. Her first-year scores increased markedly from 0.69 on the pretest to a 1.634 on the posttest. Frannie's MRTYS responses, as noted by the research team, clearly demonstrated an understanding of patterning and number sense. For example, when asked for clarification of a correct response, Frannie stated, "Because you started a pattern." Additionally, field notes taken during each test administration stated that Frannie had a "fast response" or "spontaneous responses" to most items.

Frannie repeatedly demonstrated her understanding of mathematics concepts during observations. During a kindergarten activity on number order and measurement, Frannie was observed answering correctly all questions posed by the teacher. When asked to explain a stem during a first-grade activity on pattern stems, Frannie stated, "the part of the pattern that repeats." She proceeded to create her own pattern and correctly mark the pattern stem. Frannie also assisted her classmates in finding their pattern stems.

In second grade, Frannie quickly grasped the concepts of regrouping and estimation. In one activity, Frannie's teacher informed the class that they were going to discuss weight. She then passed around a can that weighed a pound and asked each student to try to find something else in the classroom that weighed about a pound. Students were then asked to determine the weight of the cubbies using estimation. The students' estimates ranged from 2 to 60 pounds. Frannie estimated, "I think it weighs about five pounds." The actual weight was seven pounds.

Throughout the study, Frannie responded to questions immediately and was consistently eager to participate in activities that involved mathematics. The observations revealed that Frannie mastered new mathematics skills quickly and was able to apply them in classroom and real-world contexts. She frequently assisted other students during class and was the only case study child who consistently exhibited high z scores on both the TARC and the MRTYS.

Reed's Analogical Reasoning

Reed's performances on the TARC and MRTYS were consistent with classroom observations and his teachers' assessments. Reed's performance scores on the TARC were the lowest among his classmates. This closely paralleled his performance on standardized tests given by the school in first and second grade. Although all his test scores during the study indicated low achievement, there were some instances of minimal improvement (see Fig. 5.1). For example, Reed scored -1.118 on the first TARC pretest in kindergarten and then showed some improvement on the subsequent kindergarten posttest and first-grade pretest. Figure 5.1 also clearly shows a drastic decline on the first-grade posttest followed by a slight improvement on the second-grade pretest.

Our observational data reinforce the TARC assessments. Reed exhibited limited use of analogical reasoning in formal classroom activities. Generally, Reed's use of analogy occurred during unstructured classroom activities and involved manipulative materials. For example, in first grade, Reed and a classmate discussed video games and then Reed spontaneously picked up a shell and placed it to his ear. Reed said to his friend, "This is my ear. It is made out of metal." He continued the analogy by holding the shell to his mouth and talking into it.

We observed Reed using analogies during instruction. One instance occurred during math class in first grade. The teacher asked the class to arrange seven squares of paper into groups of two. After Reed arranged his squares, the teacher asked him to explain his arrangement. Reed responded, "I did like a train." His response indicated his ability to identify similarities between abstract objects and common items. A similar example was observed during an art discussion during which the class was shown pictures of work by Alexander Calder. When asked what a kinetic sculpture reminded him of, Reed replied, "I think it's a merry-go-round, wee."

Reed's weak performance on the TARC seemed to reflect his overall performance in school. His lack of confidence was clear each time he was given the TARC and became a consideration when arranging the testing schedule. Due to the nature of the TARC and MRTYS, we presented it to the participants as games and most of the children were eager to participate. Reed, however, was still hesitant. Prior to his initial pretest in kindergarten, he watched another child take the test and then his teacher stayed with him during part of the test. Reed remained hesitant throughout the study, despite the play-like atmosphere and the research team's frequent visits to the school.

Reed's Mathematical Reasoning

As noted, Reed demonstrated a lag in his mathematical development compared to his classmates. Throughout the study, we observed that Reed repeatedly requested assistance from his peers and learned new concepts at a delayed pace. For example, during second grade, when the rest of the class was counting by tens, he reverted to counting by ones. As illustrated in Fig. 5.2, Reed's initial score on the kindergarten MRTYS was −2.404 using a standard z score significantly lower than his same-age peers and even lower than

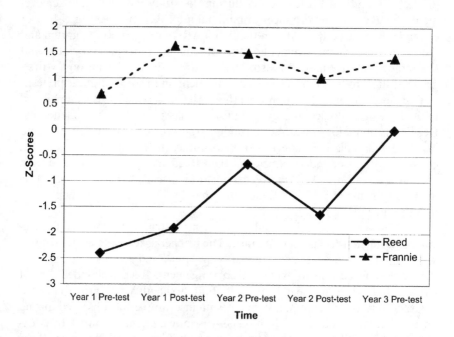

FIG. 5.2.   MRTYS scores for Frannie and Reed (USA).

his performance on the kindergarten TARC pretest. Although Reed showed some improvement over the past two and a half years, he still lagged behind his classmates. Like his TARC scores, his subsequent MRTYS scores increased on the kindergarten posttest (−1.908) and first-grade pretest (−0.657) and then took a sharp decline on his first-grade posttest (−1.635). Also like his TARC scores, Reed showed an improvement on his second-grade MRTYS pretest score (−0.003).

On the MRTYS, Reed exhibited difficulties in a number of mathematical skills, including spatial and measurement concepts, comprehension of patterns, spatial and logical reasoning, and sorting and classifying. Our classroom observations support the findings of the mathematical assessments. Reed demonstrated limited overall mathematical skills and frequently relied on his classmates for assistance during in-class assignments.

His teachers agreed that Reed had difficulty developing number sense and other basic math concepts. Priscilla reported that in second grade, Reed could tell time, understand abstract concepts such as odd and even numbers, and began to add numbers in his head. She described him as weak in computational skills but commented that his parents worked closely with him and that he demonstrated consistent improvements "little by little." Priscilla stated that she saw "that in all his work, it was just little baby steps, but he moved in the right direction." His improvements in math skills may be due to a number of factors such as his parents' consistent support at home, maturation, or the more structured mathematics lessons that are common in second grade.

Over the course of the study, Reed's long-term mathematical reasoning was slightly lower than his analogical reasoning. His score on the MRTYS was the lowest of all the case study children each time it was administered and paralleled his classroom performance in mathematics. It is unclear whether school context, hesitancy to take risks, or immaturity individually or jointly had a significant influence on Reed's success in mathematics. We noted that Reed made significant progress between the kindergarten MRTYS posttest and the first-grade pretest, and then showed a major decline on the first-grade math test. We were anxious to see if this was the beginning of a pattern or whether Reed's second-grade MRTYS posttest continued to reflect marked growth.

Kate's Analogical Reasoning

Kate is a particularly interesting participant because of the inconsistency in her test performance on both the TARC and the MRTYS. Analyses of her test scores and classroom observations posed a puzzling picture regarding Kate's ability to understand and use analogical reasoning. Observational data collected throughout the study provided continuous examples of Kate's use of analogies. Her TARC scores however, followed no discernible pattern and vacillated from significantly below the Australian mean to slightly above the mean over the course of the study (see Fig. 5.3). For example, on the pretest administered during Year 2 of the study, the mean was 27.56 and Kate scored a 30, placing her slightly above the mean. However, on the posttest during Year 2 of the study, Kate scored 22, which showed a decline below both the mean (28) and her pretest score. For Years 1 and 3 of the study, Kate's within-year scores on the TARC improved between pre- and posttesting.

In contrast to her irregular performance on the TARC, classroom observations in preschool through Year 2 indicated that Kate used analogies during mathematics or imaginative play when interacting with manipulative materials and friends, respectively. During preschool, Kate used analogies frequently during sociodramatic play with other children. In one instance, Kate and another girl imagined that they were spiders as they sat in a rope mesh strung between bars in an outdoor playing area. Kate told her playmate, "Oh our web's slippery. I'm a baby red back and you be a baby red back . . . let's go and catch a fly." They continued their play by chasing and holding another child whom they identified as "my fly." Another time, Kate used a long narrow shell to bore into a cup of sand and explained that it was "a screwing nail." Kate continued to use analogies during Year 1 and Year 2. In addition to imaginative play, analogies were sometimes observed during

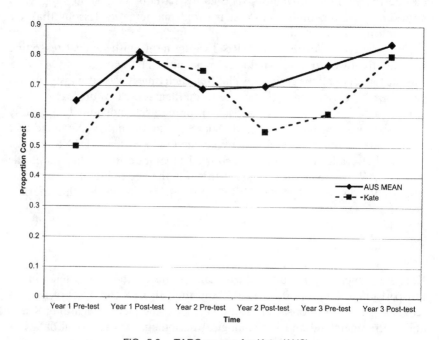

FIG. 5.3.   TARC scores for Kate (AUS).

structured activities, such as building boats using multilink blocks. In this session, Mary worked with Kate and three other Year 1 students to develop math and science concepts. When the teacher inquired why Kate's boat floated, Kate responded that she did not know and then proceeded to tell her friend, "Yours looks like an eel." The girls pursued this idea and finally agreed that both their boats had "baby eels."

The incongruity between the TARC and observational data raises questions regarding Kate's performance on the TARC. It is not clear why there was an inconsistency between the test data and Kate's spontaneous use of analogies. It may reflect Kate's developmental level, or it may suggest a lack of transfer between analogies, which came naturally to Kate, and the less familiar and sometimes more abstract relationships found on the TARC. In other words, when Kate initiated the action and chose the descriptors in a comfortable setting with familiar manipulatives and people she trusted, she might have been able to identify analogical relationships successfully even though she was not able to successfully identify the traditional A:B::C:D relationships on the TARC.

Kate's Mathematical Reasoning

During the study, Kate's mathematical reasoning development was also continuously observed in the classroom. As with her performance on the TARC, she was inconsistent on the MRTYS. Similar to her TARC scores, Kate's initial Year 1 mathematics assessment raw score was 68, which placed her well above the Australian mean of 50.04. She demonstrated mild growth during Year 1 and remained above the Australian mean on the Year 1 posttest (see Fig. 5.4). In contrast, Kate's pretests during Years 2 and 3 of the study placed her below the Australian mean, and it was not until her final posttest during Year 3 that she once again scored above the Australian mean.

Kate's performance on the subtests again displayed irregular periods of gain and regression. For example, Kate achieved a perfect score on the matching section of the Year 1 pretest, but on the Year 1 posttest her raw score was 11/16. Throughout the study, Kate's results on other within-year subtests, such as patterning and spatial and logical reasoning, showed similar fluctuations. Her most consistent areas of achievement were seen in measurement and number sense.

Interestingly, Kate was observed using measurement and number sense frequently during instructional and imaginative play periods. In one spontaneous and brief episode in Year 1, Kate opted to not play another game of Mancala, an African counting game, and instead retrieved a number scale and placed the numbers one and two on opposite sides. She told her friend, "That's not level, is it?" and changed the one to a two. She then noted,

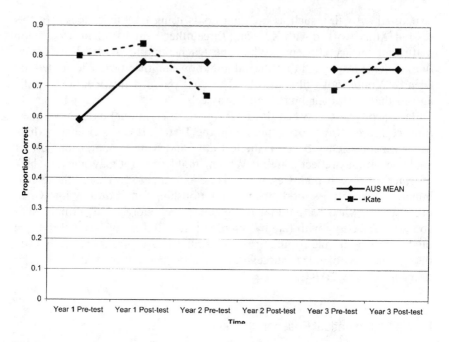

FIG. 5.4.   MRTYS scores for Kate (AUS).

"That's level. It's equal. I'm going to get the bigger numbers. Eight is my lucky number, so is six but six isn't there. [Puts eight and eight on the scale] Look it's level. It's equal." Just as quickly as Kate initiated this activity, she ended it and moved on to another activity with her friend.

Observations also showed that Kate appropriately used numbers in multiple contexts beginning in preschool. She counted manipulatives correctly during instruction and play and applied her understanding of numbers when completing pictures and math tasks. As part of a lengthy sociodramatic play session in preschool, Kate self-corrected herself saying, "My baby is going to turn zero, I mean he's going to turn one this year. He was just born." During the second year of the study, Kate again showed her grasp of numbers while playing a game with Year 2 and Year 3 children. In the game she had 41 points and then received 25 more points. The other children were anxious to tell the total score, but her teacher asked the children to allow Kate to work it out. Thinking aloud, Kate said, "Five and one more, six. Four and two more, six." Kate recorded 66 and a Year 2 student questioned it, but Kate was confident she was correct and stated, "No, it's right." At the end of the game, she demonstrated her knowledge of ordinal numbers when she announced that she came in second and Gregory came in first. Her teacher asked her how she knew this, and she promptly explained, "He got more than me."

Although Kate's performance on spatial and logical reasoning was inconsistent, her classroom observations indicated that she could successfully apply these skills. In addition, she was observed to correctly use and respond to mathematics terms such as *least*, *most*, *under* and *in*. Kate's ability to think analytically about a situation and decide a practical course of action was noticed during a math and science lesson when Kate was in Year 1. After hearing the directions, Kate explained to her teacher that she and a classmate were "working together as a team and that way we don't have to use as many of the blocks." Observations also showed that Kate could translate story problems into number sentences and correctly compute the problems.

Similar to her long-term analogical reasoning performance, Kate's mathematics profile is inconsistent. Her scores on the MRTYS indicate an unpredictable pattern of conceptual development in mathematics. However, her classroom use of mathematics concepts and verbal expression of her understanding of the concepts indicate a more typical pattern of conceptual growth.

A CROSS-CASE ANALYSIS: SUMMARY COMMENTS

Our individual cases were selected because each represented a distinct profile on the TARC and MRTYS. Whereas Frannie exemplified the successful student, Reed portrayed a consistently weak student. In contrast to Frannie and Reed, Kate offered an anomalous picture of development. Careful analysis of the observational and individualized test data has yielded a comprehensive picture illustrating how three diverse children developed and used analogical and mathematical reasoning in their first three years of schooling. For each of the three children, development of their analogical reasoning appeared to mirror development of their mathematical reasoning even though they did not receive explicit instruction in analogical reasoning.

Use of analogical reasoning in the classroom varied among the participants. Kate appeared to generate spontaneous verbal analogies frequently during teacher-directed and unstructured activities. Reed and Frannie were observed to use spontaneous verbal analogies infrequently. For Reed, this supported his weak performances on all TARC tests. Frannie, who consistently performed well on the TARC, was the only participant to use analogies in her writing. This demonstrated her ability to consciously apply analogies to clarify and enhance ideas and may relate to her ability to do well on the TARC.

Frannie and Kate both used mathematical concepts appropriately during structured and unstructured classroom activities. Again, this validated Frannie's performance on the MRTYS. Kate's MRTYS scores, like her TARC scores, frequently exceeded the mean. Reed did not appear to use mathematical concepts during unstructured activities, which may reflect his delayed understanding of basic concepts, such as number sense. His classroom performance closely reflected his MRTYS scores.

Formal and informal contacts with the participants' teachers and frequent visits to the schools expanded our understanding of contextual and personal factors that may potentially influence young children's natural development of mathematical and analogical reasoning. Our data suggest that teacher experience, mathematics curriculum, and school culture may be significant school-based factors. Development may also be influenced by personal attributes, such as family support, peer relationships, ability, and personality. Analysis across cases indicated that there were no contextual or personal attributes shared by all three participants; however, similarities were noted among subsets of the participants. For example, Reed's kindergarten and first-grade teachers was not familiar with the reading and mathematics expectations or curriculum at kindergarten and first grade. In contrast, Priscilla was very knowledgeable and comfortable with the second-grade curriculum, including the Growing with Mathematics Program (1999), which was adopted but not widely used by the kindergarten through second-grade faculty at Redfox Crossing Elementary. The lack of implementation of the mathematics program reflected the school culture, which did not exhibit a shared goal orientation.

Frannie and Kate's school experiences during the study were much different than Reed's experience. Each of their teachers was experienced in their respective grade levels and comfortable with the school's mathematics programs. A shared goal orientation was manifested by the school culture at Shade Tree Elementary and Compton Preschool and Primary. In both settings, a positive team spirit among faculty, staff, community, and administrators was apparent.

Interestingly, all three participants shared several personal attributes, including healthy friendships. Frannie, Reed, and Kate all had supportive families who valued school success and helped with schoolwork although Reed's family did not appear to encourage independence. Additionally, their teachers' perceptions of the children's abilities matched their performance. Frannie's teachers saw her as very bright, and her performance reinforced their perception. Reed's teachers considered his cognitive ability to be low, and, like Frannie, his performance supported this perception.

Finally, the teachers of the three participants described the personality of each child with very different adjectives. Frannie and Reed were characterized by dichotomous terms. Frannie's teachers considered her to be a risk taker, confident, and outgoing, whereas Reed's teachers said he was shy, lacked confidence, and was not a risk taker. In addition, he cried often and was immature. Kate's teachers described her as a student who loved to please and be helpful but also needed a lot of attention.

In summary, we found that there appeared to be a connection between the development of mathematical and analogical reasoning in three diverse young children, even when analogical reasoning was not explicitly taught.

Frannie's and Reed's high and low MRTYS and TARC scores also appeared to reflect their classroom use of analogies and mathematical concepts. School context, prior experiences, and personal attributes may also contribute to or inhibit individual development. A combination of these influences may explain the incongruities across Kate's TARC and MRTYS scores as well as her ability to appropriately use analogical and mathematical reasoning in class.

EDUCATIONAL IMPLICATIONS

As noted previously, the existing literature on analogical and mathematical reasoning in young children has been predominantly explored through a quantitative research paradigm. The purpose of this study was to augment the extant literature by contributing rich descriptive data regarding the development of mathematical and analogical reasoning in young children. Therefore, we want to be certain that our conclusions reflect the nature of the data and do not suggest unsubstantiated correlational results. Although we note similarities between our findings and previous related research, we emphasize that our findings are not conclusive and need to lead to future research that uses multiple methodologies to answer new questions that emerged from our data. For example, our data revealed that Frannie was consistently successful at both analogical and mathematical reasoning, whereas Reed was consistently unsuccessful in both types of reasoning. In contrast, Kate's development was inconsistent over the course of the study. What factors contribute to the development of analogical and mathematical reasoning in young children and account for performance differences between learners? How are these factors mediated through experiences in the child's environment, such as the home, community, and school? With these limitations and questions in mind, we provide the following implications.

Earlier studies (Alexander et al., 1989; White & Caropreso, 1989) have indicated that with explicit instruction young children are capable of developing analogical reasoning competence. In this study, the participants did not receive any direct teaching related to analogical reasoning. However, their analogical reasoning development progressed in parallel with their mathematical reasoning. These findings mirror prior research that indicated linkages between mathematical reasoning and analogical reasoning (Alexander, White, & Daugherty, 1997). Specifically, the findings of Alexander et al. (1997) suggested a link between language development, general knowledge, and analogical and mathematical reasoning. This outcome raises additional questions for further research. For example, how would young children's mathematical reasoning be influenced by explicit teaching of analogies? How does teachers' knowledge of mathematical and analogical reasoning influence student learning?

124   DEAL AND HARDY

Equally significant are the implications for practice. Our data confirmed the
assertion of the National Council of Teachers of Mathematics' *Principles and
Standards for School Mathematics*, namely, that communication/language is a
critical aspect of mathematics. It is important to listen to how children talk
about their mathematical experiences and observe their spontaneous use of
mathematical concepts. During observations, Frannie's frequent and spontaneous use of mathematical terms and reasoning contrasted sharply with Reed's
very limited use of quantitative terms and reasoning. Informal observations by
teachers can supplement more formal assessment data and offer a window into
children's understanding of mathematical concepts.

Additionally, administering the MRTYS showed us that children's mathematics skills could easily be overgeneralized and create an inaccurate assessment. For example, during both the kindergarten pre- and post-MRTYS,
Frannie obtained one of the highest scores; however, she scored poorly on the
sorting subtest, earning a raw score of 8 out of 15 on the pretest and 9 out of
15 on the posttest. In other words, children who are perceived to be strong in
mathematics may have conceptual "gaps" in their development and may be
missing key concepts. Left undiagnosed, these students may experience difficulty with more complex mathematical concepts as they advance in school.

It is also critical to assess specific mathematical concepts when children
like Kate perform inconsistently. Throughout the study, Kate's number recognition and number sense performance varied. On some tests, such as the
Year 1 number recognition posttest, she answered all of the questions correctly; yet, on the Year 2 pretest on number sense, her raw score was a 22 out
of 34. For students like Kate, careful, consistent monitoring of performance
during instruction and detailed summative assessment are necessary to identify and address gaps in conceptual development so that continuous progress
can occur. Such data make a clear case for carefully assessing specific mathematical skills and concepts of all learners and providing appropriate differentiated classroom instruction.

REFERENCES

Alexander, P. A., White, C. S., & Daugherty, M. (1997). Analogical reasoning and early mathe-
   matics learning. In L. English (Ed.), *Mathematical Reasoning: Analogies, Metaphors, and Im-
   ages* (pp. 117–147). Mahwah, NJ: Lawrence Erlbaum Associates.
Alexander, P. A., Willson, V. L., White, C. S., Fuqua, J. D., Clark, G. D., & Wilson, A. F.,
   Kulikowich, J. M. (1989). Development of analogical reasoning processes. *Cognitive Devel-
   opment, 4*, 65–88.
Bohan, H., Clark, G., Kelleher, H. J., & Thompson, C. S. (1995). *Houghton Mifflin mathematics.*
   Boston: Houghton Mifflin.
Clay, M. M. (1993). *Reading Recovery: A guidebook for teachers in training.* Portsmouth, NH:
   Heinemann.

Curriculum Corporation. (1992). *Mathematics Curriculum and Teaching Program.* Carlton South, Victoria, Australia: Author.

English, L. D., & Halford, G. S. (1995). *Mathematics education: Models and processes.* Mahwah, NJ: Lawrence Erlbaum Associates.

Goodman, J. M. (1992). *Group solutions: Cooperative logic activities for grades K–4.* Berkeley, CA: Lawrence Hall of Science.

Maxwell, J. (1996). *Qualitative research design: An interactive approach.* Thousand Oaks, CA: Sage.

Merriam, S. (1988). *Case study research in education: A qualitative approach.* San Francisco: Jossey-Bass.

Miles, M., & Huberman, A. M. (1994). *Qualitative data analysis: An expanded sourcebook.* Thousand Oaks, CA: Sage.

National Council of Teachers of Mathematics. (2000). *Principles and standards for school mathematics.* Reston, VA: Author.

Pengelly, H. (1992). *M3 Mathematics: Mapping mathematical meaning.* Lisarow, Australia: Scholastic.

Staessens, K. (1993). Identification and description of professional culture in innovating schools. *Qualitative Studies in Education, 6*(2), 111–128.

White, C. S., & Caropreso, E. J. (1989). Training in analogical reasoning processes: Effects on low socioeconomic status preschool children. *Journal of Educational Research, 83*(2), 112–118.

Wright Group. (1999). *Growing with mathematics.* New York: Author/McGraw-Hill.

Yin, R. (1994). *Case study research: Design and methods* (2nd ed.). Thousand Oaks, CA: Sage.

6

TEACHERS' KNOWLEDGE, BELIEFS, AND PRACTICES AND MATHEMATICAL AND ANALOGICAL REASONING

C. Stephen White
George Mason University

Debby Deal
Loyola College in Maryland

Carla Baker Deniz
George Mason University

This chapter and chapter 7 focus on the teachers of the participants discussed previously. In this chapter, we present interview data related to the teachers' beliefs, knowledge, and practices and discuss how these teachers view the teaching of early mathematics and reasoning to young children. The chapter includes a theoretical overview, a description of the methodology used to collect and analyze the interview data, a presentation of the findings, and a cross-case analysis. In chapter 7 we provide in-depth case studies of three teachers who are representative of the interview data.

THEORETICAL OVERVIEW

In the past 20 years, there has been an increased interest in the association between teachers' beliefs, knowledge, and practices (Fang, 1996; Kagan, 1992; Pajares, 1992). This interest is based on the contention that the knowledge and beliefs that teachers hold can significantly influence their perceptions and judgments, which, in turn, affect the way classroom communities are established and how and what children come to learn (Fang, 1996; Fennema & Franke, 1992; Kagan, 1992; Pajares, 1992; Schoenfeld, in press). Current interest in the relationship between teachers' beliefs and their knowledge and practice represents a shift from a focus on teacher behaviors and children's achievements to a focus on the thinking and planning that may precede teacher action and may be mitigated by context (Fang, 1996; Schoenfeld, in press; Wilcox-Herzog, 2002). According to Schoenfeld (in press) "teachers' decision making is a complex function of their knowledge, goals, and beliefs. The work is premised on the assumption that context matters" (p. 8). However, the evidence to date on the extent to which teachers' beliefs influence classroom interaction and instruction is inconclusive (Deal, 2000; Fang, 1996; Wilcox-Herzog, 2002).

Within the literature, a range of definitions is associated with teacher beliefs and knowledge. To define teacher beliefs, we have selected Fang's (1996) description: "teachers' theories and beliefs represent the rich story of general knowledge of objects, people, events, and their characteristic relationships that teachers have that affects their planning and their interactive thoughts and decision, as well as their classroom behavior" (p. 49). To define teachers' knowledge we draw from the work of Fennema and Franke (1992), who distinguish between three types of knowledge specific to mathematics teaching and learning. Knowledge of mathematics includes knowledge of the concepts, procedures, and problem-solving processes within the domain in which the teachers teach, as well as in related content domains. Pedagogical knowledge includes knowledge of teaching procedures, such as effective strategies for planning classroom routines, behavior management techniques, classroom organizational procedures, and motivational techniques. Knowledge of learners' cognitions in mathematics includes knowledge of how students think and learn and, in particular, how this occurs within specific mathematics content.

The literature on teachers' beliefs, knowledge, and practices in early childhood and mathematics education vary in regard to the ages and grades of children the teachers teach and the specific aspects studied. The majority of studies on teachers' beliefs, knowledge, and practices in early childhood education focus on teachers of younger children (typically from birth to age 8) and their beliefs and knowledge related to specified practices that are referred to as developmentally appropriate practices (DAP). In mathematics education, studies have generally focused on teachers in elementary, middle, and secondary schools and the relationship between mathematical knowledge and practices. We drew from literature in both early childhood and mathematics education because the participants in this study were teachers of young children aged 5–7. In our overview of the literature, we will first review teachers' beliefs, knowledge, and practices in early childhood education and then address mathematics education.

Teachers' Beliefs, Knowledge, and Practices and Early Childhood Education

In the field of early childhood education, the study of teachers' beliefs, knowledge, and practices has relied primarily on quantitative methodologies and focused on practices with young children often labeled as DAP based on the

National Association for the Education of Young Children (NAEYC) developmentally appropriate guidelines (Bredekamp & Copple, 1997). Practices typically associated with DAP include providing a child-interest centered curriculum based on play rather than "skills," teachers who act in the capacity of facilitators rather than directors, and a focus on individual rather than age-normed development (Wilcox-Herzog, 2002). The particular focus in these early childhood studies has been on teachers' pedagogical knowledge as defined by Fang (1996) as the thinking and planning that may precede teacher action.

For the most part, this area of research has differentiated beliefs, knowledge, and assessments of practice using distinctions between DAP (child-centered) and teacher-directed didactic, or academically directed instruction and learning (Bryant, Clifford, & Peisner, 1991; Charlesworth et al., 1993; Stipek & Byler, 1997; Vartuli, 1999; Wilcox-Herzog, 2002). Typically, researchers interested in the relationship between beliefs and practices for early childhood educators assess whether teachers who espouse developmentally appropriate practice actually implement a curriculum that involves the cluster of practices associated with DAP (Vartuli, 1999; Wilcox-Herzog, 2002). Many of these studies have been designed to develop belief and practice self-report and/ or observational instruments consistent with DAP as a basis for determining beliefs and actual classroom practices (Vartuli, 1999). These studies have included subjects who are teachers in early care and education settings, kindergarten classrooms, the primary grades, and teachers from all three age levels.

A number of the studies that have examined early childhood teachers' beliefs about appropriate practices have specifically focused on the consistency between teachers' beliefs and actions or practices. These studies have demonstrated mixed results in relation to consistency between teachers' beliefs and actions or practices (Wilcox-Herzog, 2002). Vartuli (1999) and Stipek and Byler (1997) both found that the beliefs of preschool, kindergarten, and first-grade teachers were consistent with the teachers' practices. Stipek and Byler (1997) found that preschool, kindergarten, and first-grade teachers had a coherent set of beliefs that mapped on to theoretical frameworks seen in both the early childhood and cognitive development literatures. In Vartuli's (1999) study, beliefs were found to be more developmentally appropriate than practices, and teachers who felt the most control over planning and implementing instruction had the highest ratings on beliefs and practices. In both studies, grade-level variation in teacher practices did occur; as grade level increased, the level of self-reported developmentally appropriate beliefs and practice decreased. Overall, there was more congruence between practices and beliefs found with Head Start and kindergarten teachers when compared to primary grade teachers (Stipek & Byler, 1997; Vartuli, 1999).

Whereas some researchers have found that teachers who espouse child-centered beliefs are more likely to behave in child-centered ways with the children in their care, (Charlesworth, Hart, Burts, & Hernandez, 1990; Stipek &

Byler, 1997; Vartuli, 1999), others have found no relationship (Charlesworth et al., 1993; Hatch & Freeman, 1988; Kontos & Dunn, 1993; Wilcox-Herzog, 2002). Wilcox-Herzog found that in a group of preschool teachers, there was no relationship between teachers' beliefs and their actions. These findings are consistent with previous research that found inconsistencies between teachers' beliefs and their actions (Charlesworth et al., 1993; Fang, 1996; Hatch & Freeman, 1988; Kagan, 1992; Kontos & Dunn, 1993; Pajares, 1992). According to Marcon (1999), when discrepancies between beliefs and practices exist, teachers' beliefs tend to be more developmental than their practices (e.g., Charlesworth et al., 1993). Although it is commonly thought that teachers' beliefs may be related to their interactions with children, the evidence to date is inconclusive (Wilcox-Herzog, 2002).

Teachers' Beliefs, Knowledge, and Practices and Mathematics

In mathematics, attention to teachers' knowledge, beliefs, and practices has included studies that examined the role of problem solving in mathematics (Anderson, 1996; Carpenter, Fennema, Peterson, & Carey, 1988; Fennema et al., 1996; Franke, Carpenter, Levi, & Fennema, 2001); the relationship between teacher's mathematical knowledge and practices (Brown, Askew, Rhodes, William, & Johnson, 1996; Carpenter et al., 1988; Schoenfeld, 1998; Schwartz & Riedesel, 1994); teacher use of concrete materials in teaching mathematics (Perry, Howard, & Conroy, 1996; Sherman & Richardson, 1995); and the relationship between culture, teacher conceptions about mathematics, and student achievement (Philoppou & Christou, 1996). The beliefs of novice teachers have also been examined. These studies have focused on the relationship between beliefs and practices (Borko & Livingston, 1989; Borko et al., 1992; Raymond, 1993) and beliefs, knowledge, and practices (Borko & Livingston, 1989; Borko et al., 1992). Studies of teachers' beliefs and mathematics have employed both quantitative and qualitative research methodologies.

Similar to Fang's (1996) review of the literature on teachers' beliefs in general, these studies demonstrate varying results regarding the relationship between beliefs, knowledge, and practices in mathematics. For example, Thompson (1984) found that teachers' beliefs, views, and preferences about mathematics and its teaching played a significant role in shaping the teachers' characteristic patterns of instructional behavior, whereas Raymond (1993) noted that practices are not always consistent with beliefs. Borko et al. (1992) examined a novice mathematics teacher's emergent knowledge, beliefs, thinking, and actions in order to understand why the teacher's lesson on fractions was not successful. Borko et al. suggest that, because the teacher's own beliefs about mathematics teaching were derived from her own experiences as a student in mathematics classrooms, in her teaching methods courses, and as a student teacher, the teacher's conceptual understanding of fractions was limited. The results of these studies demonstrate inconsistencies between teacher beliefs and their practices in areas such as problem solving and the use of concrete materials. This inconsistency may be due to the teacher's ability to actually implement specific beliefs.

Several studies have focused on the relationship between teacher knowledge of mathematics and practices (Borko et al., 1992; Buzeika, 1996; Carpenter et al., 1988; Franke et al., 2001; Schwarz & Riedesel, 1994; Thompson, 1984). Schoenfeld (1998) points out that teacher response reflects teacher knowledge as well as teacher goals for individual learners. Schwarz & Riedesel (1994) found a moderate positive correlation between teacher practice and beliefs and a low positive correlation between the teachers' own understanding of mathematics concepts and their teaching practices. In contrast, Carpenter et al. (1988) found that although teachers could identify distinctions between mathematics problems and the strategies students use in solving problems, the teachers could not organize their knowledge into a relationship between the problems, students' solutions, and problem difficulty. The results of these studies indicate that there are inconsistencies between teachers' knowledge and their practices. Changes in teachers' beliefs and in their practices could explain this variance in the relationship between teacher beliefs and practices.

Change in teachers' beliefs and practices in mathematics has been studied by Borko, Davinroy, Bliem, and Cumbo (2000); Buzieka (1996); Fennema et al. (1996); Franke et al. (2001); and Wood, Cobb, and Yackel (1991). Fennema et al. (1996) found that there was a dynamic relationship between teachers' practices and changes in their beliefs. They also found that teachers varied in the way their beliefs changed. Some teachers changed rapidly and made instructional changes rapidly. In some cases, teachers' beliefs changed before instruction; in other cases, teachers' beliefs changed after instruction. The results of these studies indicate that changes in teachers' beliefs may be related to actual practice and to developing an understanding of children's mathematical thinking. However, understanding teacher change requires careful scrutiny to determine the catalyst for change and how the teacher responded (Schoenfeld, in press).

Research specific to primary grade (kindergarten through Grade 3) teachers' beliefs about mathematical instruction has included beliefs about the importance of mathematics instruction and social-emotional development; the relationship between teachers' beliefs, teachers' knowledge, and their students' achievement; and beliefs about teacher and student roles and how those beliefs change. Kowalski, Pretti-Frontczak, and Johnson (2001) found that teachers believed that social-emotional skills are significantly more important for preschoolers to learn than early mathematics skills. Peterson, Fennema, Carpenter, and Loef (1989) found significant positive relationships between first-grade teachers' beliefs, teachers' knowledge, and students' achievement in mathematics. They noted, however, that teachers vary widely in their pedagogical content beliefs and their pedagogical content knowledge about mathematics. Again, this variation could be explained by the ongoing professional development of the teachers and their changes in beliefs and knowledge. In a case study designed to examine the changes in teachers' beliefs during the course of a year, Wood et al. (1991) found that teachers' beliefs about their own role, their students' role, and nature of mathematics changed. The teachers' beliefs moved from transmitting information to teaching their students to be thinkers and independent constructors of mathematical concepts and operations. These findings indicate that professional development may have a significant influence on primary-grade teachers' knowledge, beliefs, and practice.

The findings of studies in both early childhood and mathematics education indicate that that there are inconsistencies between teachers' beliefs and practices. In both fields of study, the inconsistencies are often linked to control over planning and implementing instruction that reflects specific beliefs. The correlational nature of many of these studies may limit our understanding of the relationships between knowledge, beliefs, and practices (Schoenfeld, in press). To gain a more complete picture of the complexity of this relationship, Schoenfeld (in press) suggests that researchers seek more analytical explanations. In studies focused on mathematics, changes in teachers' beliefs may be related to actual practice and to developing an understanding of children's mathematical thinking. Our review of the literature did not reveal previous research on teachers' beliefs and practices in relation to knowledge of mathematics content and reasoning in early childhood classrooms.

METHODS

The purpose of this study was to explore Australian and American teachers' beliefs and knowledge about analogical and mathematical reasoning in young children. We wanted to learn what they understood about these topics, how they came to know it, and how they applied what they knew. The detailed descriptions and multiple perspectives we desired led us to a qualitative interview study (Weiss, 1994). We began with a set of prestructured or core questions that we adapted to elicit rich descriptions, explanations, and examples from each participant. The core questions can be found in the appendix.

Participants and Data Collection

The participants discussed in this chapter were the classroom teachers of the students in the longitudinal study on the development of analogical and mathematical reasoning in young children. Prior to beginning the study, potential classroom teachers in two American and two Australian classrooms were selected by the building principals based on their willingness to participate and were invited to participate in the study by the principal and re-

TABLE 6.1
Teachers' Years of Experience and Educational Background

Name	Grade Level	B.A.	Cert.	M.Ed.	Yrs Teaching	Grade Levels Taught
Margaret	K	Y	Y	Y	10	K, K–1, 1
Barbara	K, 1st Grade	Y	Y	N	15	Head Start, K, K–1, 3, 4
Marilyn	1st Grade	Y	Y	Y	13	K–1, 1
Beverly	1st Grade	Y	Y	N	8	3GT, K, K–1–2, 1–2, 1
Laura	1st Grade	Y	Y	Y	11	K, 1
Patricia	2nd Grade	Y	Y	Y	8	2, 4
Lynette	2nd Grade	Y	Y	Y	3	1–2, 2
Priscilla	2nd Grade	Y	Y	N	14	2, 5–6
Betty	Year 1	Y	N	N	13	Pre, 1, 2, 3, 4, 5
Brenda	Year 1	Y	N	N	15	Pre, 1, Pre–1–2, Pre–1–2–3
Marla	Year 2	Y	N	Y	7	Pre–1, 1, 2, 5–6–7
Deborah	Year 2	N	N	N	9	Pre, 1, 2, 3, 5, 6, 7
Mary	Year 2	Y	N	Y	22	Pre, 1, 1–2–3
Donna	Year 2	Y	N	N	15	1, 2, 3–4–5, 3, 4, 5
Edith	Year 2		N	N	28	1, 2, 3, 1–2–3
Fiona	Year 3	Y	Y	N	28	1, 2, 4, 5, 6
Charlotte	Year 3		Y	N	20	1–2–3, 2, 3, 4, 5
Martha	Year 3		N	N	14	1–2–3, 2, 3, 4, 5, 6, 7
Ruth	Year 3	Y	N	Y	12	Pre, 2, 3

searchers. As discussed in chapter 6, the student participants were the members of these kindergarten and first-year classes. All teachers and students opted to participate in the study. In both the United States and Australia, the school principals placed the student participants in two to three different classrooms for the second and third years. Over the course of the study, a total of 19 teachers, 11 Australian and 8 American, were interviewed. One American teacher, Barbara, was interviewed twice in consecutive years because she was both the kindergarten and first-grade teacher for several of the children. As shown in Table 6.1, the participants represented a wide range of teaching experience and educational backgrounds.

Toward the end of the academic school year, a structured interview that lasted between 30 and 60 minutes was conducted with each classroom teacher who taught one or more of the original case study student participants. Interviews were conducted in the school setting, either during the school day or immediately after school, and were audiotaped and later transcribed verbatim.

Data Analysis

Our data analysis process involved three sets of readings, which ultimately resulted in a cross-case comparison based on families, or clusters "that share certain patterns of configurations" (Miles & Huberman, 1994, p. 174). In this study, the clusters represented the teachers who shared similar orientations toward teaching. Memos and discussions among the research team through-out the data analysis process helped us to make sense of the data and to con-tinuously be alert for discrepant evidence or negative cases.

In our first set of readings, we looked for references in the transcripts to several descriptive predetermined categories: analogical reasoning, mathe-matical reasoning, children's competence at analogical and mathematical reasoning, and the importance of connections between the home and school. The data on analogical and mathematical reasoning contributed to our un-derstanding of the teachers' content knowledge. The data related to chil-dren's competence and home connections reflected teachers' spoken beliefs about children's learning and to a lesser degree provided some evidence of their classroom practices. We used the Nud*ist Vivo ("Nud*ist Vivo," 1998–1999) qualitative software program to facilitate extracting and synthe-sizing the like data across participants.

Once the data were entered, we began the second set of readings and sought to identify emergent categories (Maxwell, 1996; Miles & Huberman, 1994). Several important categories, such as risk taking, personal role models and mentors, how children learn, and connections between math and lan-guage, emerged from the data as recurrent themes. We began to notice what appeared to be groups of participants who shared a similar knowledge base and beliefs. For example, we noted that the participants who referred to role models or mentors also described useful connections between mathematics and language. Next, we looked at the relationship between what the partici-pants said in reference to our initial descriptive codes and what they said in reference to the emergent codes and again found distinctive patterns. For ex-ample, the participants who appeared to have limited content knowledge in-dicated that children were not very competent at mathematical and analogi-cal reasoning, and did not mention personal role models or mentors. These apparent patterns generated a third reading of the data.

The third set of readings involved revisiting the intact transcripts and be-ing particularly attentive to holistic patterns or themes. This reading resulted in a tentative theory that grouped the participants in families or clusters based on three orientations to teaching: theoretical, experience-based, and in-tuitive. Using both the descriptive and the emergent categories, a matrix was developed which allowed us to test the theory and explore the relationship be-tween the three teaching orientations and each participant's knowledge, stated beliefs, and self-described practices. We found that the data supported clustering the participants into the three orientations toward teaching. We also recognized that we needed to merge some of our categories and read the transcripts for a fourth time in an effort to refine our coding system.

We began the fourth reading with a lengthy list that included both our de-scriptive and emergent categories. Ultimately, our individual readings and team discussions allowed us to subsume our previously established descrip-tive and emergent categories under three main categories: knowledge (i.e., content and pedagogical), beliefs, and practices. Once we completed this task, we reread the transcripts to again check our teaching orientations theory and to check if we had classified each participant in the appropriate cluster. As a result of this reading, we moved two participants to different teaching orientation clusters. Once we were satisfied that sufficient evidence supported our theory regarding teaching orientations and that each participant was accurately classified, we generated concept maps for each teaching orientation in an attempt to further delineate and illustrate the characteristics of the theoretical, experience-based, and intuitive participants.

Teacher Cluster Descriptions

The initial unifying concept for each group was how they came to know and believe. For example, only the teachers in the theoretical group repeatedly cited multiple sources of knowledge including mentors, graduate school courses, students, and teaching experience. The experiential group presented a more limited way of knowing by referring exclusively to prior teaching experience when explaining their instructional choices. The intuitive group did not attribute their instructional decisions or responses to people or events. Instead, they often prefaced their responses with "I think" or "I feel" but did not continue to explain why. Once the clusters were formed, other common characteristics emerged within each cluster.

Each of the teachers in the theoretical cluster clearly articulated a depth of knowledge and recognized the interactions between mathematics and language development. Their beliefs about children appeared to be internally consistent and reflected a developmental perspective. That is, they described children as being very competent, learning from adults and peers, and already possessing a great deal of knowledge when they entered school. The range of knowledge and beliefs they espoused further characterized the experiential teachers. Within the cluster, responses sometimes spanned a continuum, sometimes resembled the theoretical teachers, and sometimes resembled the intuitive teachers. For example, the experiential teachers expressed varying views on children's competence but consistently valued and encouraged risk taking like the theoretical teachers. The responses of the intuitive teachers were brief and often included generic explanations and expressions such as "learning should be fun" without further elaboration. They saw children as competent and often considered the home to be a negative influence.

RESULTS

General Knowledge

Knowledge of Mathematics and Analogical Reasoning. The participants in the theoretical group appeared to have substantial knowledge of mathematical reasoning. They were confident when discussing concepts, procedures, and processes of mathematical reasoning and often provided class-room examples to support their explanations. They conceptualized it as an active process that involves concepts, strategies, and attitudes. For example, Mary described mathematical reasoning as "being able to think mathemati-cally, looking at the whole picture of something, and looking at different parts of it. . . . the processes that are involved and the skills and thinking about problems and strategies that they use." Participants identified number sense, recognizing relationships, sorting and classifying, patterning, and esti-mating as key concepts for young learners. They emphasized that learners need to be able to apply concepts to new and different situations and identi-fied strategies that enabled learners to integrate new and old learning. Mari-lyn suggested that mathematical reasoning involved "having a plan, having some idea of how you are going to get from here to there." Other participants in the group reiterated the importance of learners planning, verbalizing, and justifying their thinking. Additionally, they were clear that mathematical rea-soning is not "numbers and facts" or "rote learning." Successful learners were viewed as "independent thinkers" and "risk takers," an attribute that permeated many of the teachers' responses.

When speaking about analogical reasoning, the participants were less con-fidant but still demonstrated basic conceptual knowledge and again cited some classroom examples. In general, they related analogical reasoning to finding connections, patterns, or relationships. Lynette noted that analogical reasoning is "even connected with linguistics . . . it has to do with the ability for a child to find a pattern or a parallel between, oftentimes words, but I've seen it done before with pictures and numbers." Some of the participants sit-uated the ability to reason analogically in childrens' prior experiences and noted that a child's reasoning might vary greatly from their own due to differ-ences in schemata. For example, Marla discussed teaching on an aboriginal reserve and observing that "their reasoning was totally different to other chil-dren that I have taught, and it was all based upon situations close to them, what they have experienced in their life."

The experiential teachers described a variety of processes associated with mathematical reasoning but, unlike the theoretical teachers, they did not ad-dress concepts or attitudes. In general, they did not include examples, and their responses were briefer than those of the theoretical teachers. Of the three groups, the experiential teachers showed the greatest variation in their re-sponses; some appeared knowledgeable whereas others simply "guessed" when defining mathematical reasoning. For example, Priscilla said, "I'm just going to guess. What I think it is and what it means to me is math sense." Priscilla was one of three experiential teachers who expressed a lack of confidence and offered vague responses such as "math is everywhere." In contrast, other expe-riential teachers responded readily and described many of the same processes that the theoretical teachers included. Charlotte said, "It is logical thinking. It is a lateral sort of thinking. You don't definitely have an answer. . . . it can be open-ended. It is problem solving." This subgroup of experiential teachers associated mathematical reasoning with using strategies, proceeding logically and sequentially, recognizing patterns, and making connections.

In terms of analogical reasoning, the experiential teachers' knowledge was much more limited than that of the theoretical teachers and more closely resembled the intuitive responses. Although some of the experiential teachers had heard the term, none were confident in defining it, as exemplified by Charlotte's comment, "Yes, I have heard the word . . . no, I can't tell you what sort it is." However, after stating they were not familiar with the term, three of the teachers guessed, defining analogical reasoning as "comparing," "making connections," and "to break it up in its parts, to use the building blocks to do it."

All of the intuitive teachers characterized mathematical reasoning in general terms with reference to descriptors such as logic and problem solving. Their answers were very brief, void of examples, and included less elaboration than the experiential teachers. They did not appear to base their responses on either theory or experience and, in many instances, prefaced their answers by saying, "I think," "I perceive," or "I feel." Donna even stated:

> To say that I'm talking about mathematical reasoning, or am consciously doing, I would have to say that it wouldn't be at the forefront of my thinking and yet I think that basically it is going in the right direction because I think they're getting some success but to have to sit down and actually analyze what it is called and why I'm doing it, I don't know. It is sort of innate.

Their definition of mathematical reasoning did not include concepts, procedures, or attitudes. Instead, they used broad descriptors such as "common sense," "using mathematics in wider contexts," "the skills children use . . . to figure out things we give them," and "the approach a child takes to figure out a math problem."

None of the intuitive teachers were familiar with the term *analogical reasoning*. Only Laura chose to guess at the meaning. She said, "My thought is it has to do with the stages of development in the brain as to how children would reason at a certain age."

Pedagogical Knowledge. The theoretical teachers discussed pedagogy in terms of how they conceptualized their role and how they organized and motivated learning in their classrooms. Most of the theoretical teachers described their role as a guide who helped children pursue their inquiries and make sense of their discoveries. In general, they communicated through their responses a picture of themselves as facilitators, although most of the theoretical teachers did not use the term. Comments such as Ruth's are representative of the group.

> I think my job critically is to offer challenges and let them discover rather than say, here are the blocks, here is the problem, use the blocks in this way and solve it. I'd much rather say here is the problem, here are the blocks, show me how you do it. What ways can you come up with?

Asking open-ended questions to "to make them think for themselves" and modeling the problem-solving process were also identified as important aspects of the teacher's role.

The theoretical teachers reported organizing learning around enjoyable divergent, real-world problems noting that students "have to have a reason for doing it . . . it has to be meaningful." Part of making learning meaningful involved recognizing and teaching to different forms of intelligence. For example, Lynette said, ". . . if they are more bodily kinesthetic I am going to use songs and dance . . ." They sought to create risk-free environments where students were comfortable to explore. As Edith said, ". . . trying to explain to them that whatever they say it's not failure. That they can try to think and they can come up with their own solution and no one else is to ridicule or laugh . . ." They also stressed the need for children to become autonomous and reflective. Marla was "always getting them to question what they've done, why they've done it and how they've actually gone about it, and is there any other possible way they could have gone about it." They recognized that learning was optimized by recognizing students' individual learning needs and therefore talked about using a combination of whole-group, small-group, and individual instruction; peer tutoring; and differentiated instruction.

The experiential teachers' knowledge about pedagogy appeared to be more consistent than their knowledge about mathematical and analogical reasoning. Their description of their role, classroom organization, and motivation closely aligned them with the theoretical teachers. As the experiential teachers described their knowledge of pedagogy, three themes emerged: their role, open-ended opportunities, and hands-on materials.

Like the theoretical teachers, they portrayed their role as a facilitator with five of the teachers explicitly describing their roles as a facilitator or a "guide on the side." They considered providing children with opportunities to explore and express themselves an important part of this role. For example, Patricia stated:

> I see my role as being a facilitator. I give kids lots of opportunities within the classroom to explore and to talk about and if they come up with, I'm a firm believer that if they come up with an alternate way of looking at something . . . go for it . . . what do you think and it may not necessarily be along my lines . . . but it's still of value and I go, . . . that's great . . . I didn't think about that.

Fiona added that modeling, and working collaboratively before attempting independent tasks was also essential. She noted that the importance of organizing the classroom and "giving them plenty of opportunities to explore, making sure that they have got the materials available . . . lots of number games and things like that, just plenty of resources." The use of hands-on materials was associated with motivation and interest. Fiona explained, "We use concrete materials . . . it's pretty important . . . that they can actually see, feel, touch what the task is they are involved in." Patricia and Deborah also discussed the importance of children taking risks and related this to both their classroom activities and classroom organization.

The intuitive teachers' pedagogical knowledge was also illustrated through their interpretation of role, classroom organization, and motivation. Their ideas were not supported by examples from their experience or theoretical knowledge. The intuitive teachers did not have a common vision of their role but shared similar ideas related to classroom organization and motivation. Beverly saw her role as changing over time. "It goes from something that is very teacher centered, teacher directed, and being involved with them in role playing and activities to something that is very much like an outsider looking in and doing observations of them." Donna and Laura emphasized the need for "real world connections." Donna explained her role as "providing what's missing and then giving it real terms." She emphasized the importance of helping children see how they could apply school learning to their daily lives. Similarly, Laura wanted "children to understand why they are learning math." She tried to build relevance by connecting her lessons to other thematic units in her classroom. The intuitive teachers discussed wanting their classrooms to be fun but, unlike the theoretical and experiential teachers, they did not mention the importance of a risk-free environment. All of the intuitive teachers agreed that activities that used hands-on concrete materials were motivational. For example, Beverly stated, "[Young children] have to be actively involved to really understand what they are supposed to be doing in order . . . to be able to take what the teachers give them and then apply it." Absent from the intuitive teachers' comments were remarks about using open-ended questions to motivate children, encouraging children to ask questions, and helping children to become reflective.

Knowledge of Learner's Cognitions. The theoretical teachers displayed an in-depth understanding of how children learn mathematics, often crediting their knowledge to specific mentors or graduate school experiences. They emphasized the importance of children learning and understanding the process of mathematics rather than memorizing algorithms. For example, Marilyn explained, "I make them go through the process and the kids get impatient with me also but I will say I didn't ask you for the answer, but I asked you what do we know about the problem." Additionally, the theoretical teachers recognized the importance of progressing conceptually from concrete to abstract and providing learners opportunities to explore, debrief, risk-take, and consider multiple solutions. Ruth's teaching goals included "risk-taking, analyzing what they are doing, looking at what they are doing, and talking it through with people so that they can work through for themselves what steps they need to take."

The participants situated children's learning within the social contexts of both family and school and stressed the need for relevance. For example, Edith said, "I think they have to see a reason for doing it too. It has to be meaningful to them." They noted that children learn in different ways and described using grouping and differentiated assignments to meet individual needs. In addition to learning from mentors, the theoretical teachers extended their understandings of learner's cognitions by watching their students and asking their students about the problem-solving process. For example, Edith often asked her students, "How did you get that, or how did you think that, even though it may be wrong but you see their reasoning, you can see the trend of their thinking." The theoretical teachers' focus on process was also manifested by their efforts to connect classroom activities to real-life experiences so that "it becomes something that is useful and needed every single day."

The comments made by the experiential teachers in regard to learners' cognitions lacked a theoretical base but were supported by anecdotes from their teaching experiences. Frequently their responses began by saying, "I think . . ." and then proceeded to describe classroom experiences or individual learners. This pattern is illustrated by Charlotte's comment about how children learn:

> I think just by inquiring, they (the students) suddenly start to see possibilities
> and then it evolves from there, particularly if they are in a group situation where
> one child will say something and someone else will feed on that and then they
> can take it however far they want to.

Like the theoretical teachers, the experiential teachers described learning opportunities that emphasized process over product, although they did not explicitly refer to process. Rather, they focused their comments on the benefit of hands-on experiences with manipulative materials. For the experiential teachers, using manipulative materials achieved an additional learning component they valued, "making it fun." They also sought to identify connections between abstract concepts and real-life experiences in order to motivate learners' cognitive development. For example, after noting that her students were having difficulty with the concept "how many in all," Priscilla asked, "Well, if I said, 'I have 11 girls and 11 boys, how many are there in all? What would we do to find that answer?" She believed that using a relevant context enabled their students to comprehend the concept.

Risk taking was another aspect considered important to children's learning. More than half of the experiential teachers mentioned risk taking and, like Fiona, felt it was "something you're trying to promote all the time." Additionally, the experiential teachers identified other components of cognition named by the theoretical teachers, such as multiple solutions, grouping, collaboration, and differentiated instruction. Most of these teachers indicated that talking about mathematics contributed to concept development although they did not appear to solicit information from the students themselves as a means to learn more about learner cognition.

The responses of the intuitive teachers regarding how children learn mirrored their responses to content and pedagogical knowledge. That is, these teachers used the reference "I perceive" or "I feel" when explaining how young children learn. Their responses did not include detailed answers and referred neither to learning theory nor to their teaching experiences. Their conceptualization of learner's cognitions was much more limited than the other two orientations. For example, all three of the intuitive teachers used terms such as *hands-on experiences, use of manipulatives,* and *active involvement* when describing how children learn, but they did not mention differentiated instruction, grouping, risk taking, or debriefing as influences on learner's cognitions. Donna's comment about how children learn is representative of the group. She said, "[Children learn] through a great deal of experiences and hands-on—experience, I guess, and I wouldn't say necessarily in-school experiences." Similarly, Beverly stated, "They have to be actively involved in it to really understand what they are supposed to be doing." Her comment indicates a connection between hands-on learning and concept development; however, she did not offer further elaboration or illustrate her point with an example.

General Beliefs

Children's Competence. The teachers with a theoretical orientation believed that young children exhibited a range of abilities but overall were very competent even "quite brilliant" at mathematical reasoning. Margaret's response, "I think young children can do anything that we give them the freedom to do," aptly reflected the comments of the other participants. They manifested a social constructivist interpretation of child development and agreed that children come to school with a great deal of knowledge and diverse approaches to problem solving. As Brenda said, "I think [they are] more competent than what past research like Piaget type stuff has indicated. Some years I find that that description of their thinking has been irrelevant to the sort of thinking that they really do." Lynette noted that young children's reasoning ability and language development might not develop in parallel so "they may not be able to put it into usable terms but they have a clear idea of what they are doing." Teachers, parents, and school experiences were all identified as variables which can influence learners' development. There was some disagreement among the eight participants regarding the results of this influence. Most viewed these influences as positive and agreed with Edith who believed that, rather than learning by rote, there is "greater competency because they are questioned and asked to think about things today." However, three of the participants offered a cautionary note. They believed that school could unfortunately narrow children's mathematical thinking in pursuit of the "right answer."

The variance in the experiential teachers' beliefs was again illustrated by their views on children's competence. With the exception of Betty, the experiential teachers considered children competent in varying degrees. Deborah, Barbara, and Charlotte believed children were "quite competent," and their beliefs closely aligned with the theoretical teachers' beliefs. For example, Deborah said, "I think young kids are equipped before they come to school with the ability to think and if we give them the opportunity . . ." Martha, Fiona, Patricia, and Priscilla represented the middle of the continuum. They believed that children exhibit a range of competence and attributed the variation to children's age, ability, and experience. Patricia explained, "Some children are more competent than others based on exposure and based on the language the parents use at home, based on the kinds of things—games they play at home . . . there's a big difference, you can see that in the classroom." Betty, whose beliefs on competence were very similar to the intuitive teachers, discussed another perspective. She said, "I find that they don't really reason as much as perhaps . . . what I experienced a couple of years ago." She was concerned that they were "too institutionalized" and "don't take risks."

None of the intuitive teachers believed that young children were very competent. According to these teachers, young children only understand mathematics concepts at a concrete level. Donna stated, "I believe there is a select few [who are competent]. I don't think as a general rule they're very good at it." Laura and Beverly echoed this sentiment. The intuitive teachers also noted that only some children successfully understood more abstract concepts, such as patterning and estimating. Their comments were generalized, and they did not use their teaching experience as a reference point.

Home Connections.   Like their positive beliefs about childrens' competence, the theoretical participants were equally convinced that what the home environment yields is important. When specifically asked about this relationship, they responded with explicative language such as "immense," "huge," and "a lot." They commonly identified language development and practical knowledge as positive results of home involvement. In addition to these shared beliefs, two additional perspectives on home connections emerged from the data. Five of the participants focused mainly on spontaneous, fun learning in concert with family activities, such as playing board games, shopping, or sorting laundry. They believed that parents often reinforce skills learned at school intuitively. Similarly, children intuitively apply what they have learned at school. Margaret explained that her students' parents often tell her that their children applied classroom-developed rules for thinking skills like sorting at home. She observed that "their out-of-school experiences help them refine and extend their mathematical reasoning abilities." For a smaller group of theoretical teachers, home connections were teacher driven by newsletters and homework. For example, Mary assigned math homework that reinforced classwork and helped educate parents by explaining that "maths is much more than just sums on the grid pad." Mary also started a math backpack program in which there "are definitely no number things . . . so parents and children both write in the journal what they've enjoyed most and what they'd recommend for the next group."

Experiential teachers also believed that home experiences influence children's development; however, they disagreed as to the potential impact the home may generate. For example, half of the experiential teachers saw the home as a positive part of their students' learning. Charlotte's comments were reflective of this group. She remarked, "I think the home plays a big part . . . you can see the parents that talk to their children in here." In contrast, three of the experiential teachers viewed the home as either a potential non-influence or a negative influence. These teachers shared Deborah's belief that "unless parents spend time and talk to their kids and just involve them in what they're doing, they can end up really missing out." Similarly, Barbara noted, "I don't know if as teachers we can assume that things will be done at home." Patricia believed that the home connections can "contribute to their successes in school" but she is concerned that "you see more and more kids losing those . . . not coming in with those skills."

The intuitive teachers also believed that experiences at home can influence children's mathematical learning. When discussing home connections, they provided examples and offered more elaboration than when discussing other topics. For example, Beverly explained that time and money were two concepts that were often enriched at home. She said, "You can definitely tell the kids who are very time oriented at home and who have definite schedules at home that look at the clock and say, 'Oh, when the hand gets to the top of this hour or when it gets to this time, it's dark outside.' " Laura talked about children developing number sense through home experiences, such as setting the table and purchasing a "happy meal." She said, "I think a lot of their experiences determine their basic understanding of a general concept." Donna also thought the home could contribute to children's mathematical development but cautioned that many children come to school without practical mathematics experience and that it is difficult for teachers to compensate for the absence of home experiences.

Math Language Connections. The theoretical teachers explicitly recognized and discussed a positive connection between mathematics and language development. Their comments suggested a link between mathematical reasoning and four aspects of literacy: listening, speaking, reading, and writing. Numerous comments related to the value of "mathematical discourse," mathematics-related literature, writing about mathematics, and verbally modeling the problem-solving process were included in the data collected from the theoretical teachers. Their beliefs regarding the importance of the mathematics–language connection were manifested in their practices and will be discussed in the following section.

All of the experiential teachers, except Priscilla, discussed a relationship between mathematics and language, and most agreed that language was an inherent aspect of mathematics. They did not describe the mathematics–language connection in as much depth as the theoretical teachers and referred to reading and writing in a limited way. That is, they believed that language aids in the development of mathematical abilities. For example, Barbara stated, "the more language abilities that the child has . . . this helps support that competence." Martha believed that talking was just as important as manipulating real objects. She tried to stimulate her students' mathematical thinking through questions or games because this enabled the learners to "hear what the others kids reason, all that sort of verbalizing is just as important as working with it."

Fiona and Charlotte perceived a different relationship between mathematics and language. They believed that children were strong in either one or the other. Fiona explained, "Some children might be really strongly language orientated, but with maths, I had one last year like that. So strong in the languages, but the maths she didn't even want to know about anything to do with number." Charlotte made a similar observation using her own childhood experiences to explain her thinking.

The intuitive teachers did not indicate that there was a connection between language and mathematics; in fact, Donna was the only intuitive teacher to even mention language. When discussing children's experiences in day care, she commented, "There's a lot of language . . . there's not a lot of maths goes on there." Like Fiona and Charlotte, she did not recognize the potential for mathematics learning through language experiences.

Practice

An emphasis on process rather than product and regular opportunities for open-ended problem solving dominated the practices of the theoretical teachers. They stressed the importance of presenting children with problems that had more than one possible solution and problems that could be solved using multiple strategies. Marla encouraged her students to "question what they've done, why they've done it, and how they've actually gone about it, and is there any other possible way they could have gone about it." Similarly, after sharing answers, Edith often asked her children to discuss which answer they thought was the best. This problem-solving focus supported the teachers' desire to establish a risk-free and interesting learning environment where children had easy access to a variety of manipulative materials. For some of the teachers, it also combined with their belief that children have multiple intelligences that need to be addressed. The theoretical teachers saw the problem-solving focus as compatible with practices such as differentiated instruction, scaffolding, and flexible grouping. They also found that both spontaneous and prompted language opportunities, such as debriefing, facilitated problem solving during mathematics.

Recognizing and addressing individual needs through flexible grouping was a consistent pattern with the theoretical teachers. For example, Margaret explained, "I try to make the mathematical things open-ended so everyone can find their place in the experience. I do some large group things, but most of the math is done in small groups or one on one." Some, like Marla, Margaret, and Lynette, advocated a daily math routine that included options for grouping, exploring, and cooperative work. Additionally, the theoretical teachers described instructional practices that adapted to students' needs. Brenda noted, "A lot of scaffolding . . . comes into play there where the degree of scaffolding I give that child is different from what I might give another child with the same activity."

The theoretical teachers wanted their students to "not just do it [problem solving] in maths but to apply it throughout the classroom" and to recognize real-life applications for the mathematics they learned in school. Edith used real money and real events to teach her children about money and time because "they have to see a reason for doing . . . it has to be meaningful to them." Given this philosophy toward mathematics learning, talking about mathematics and other mathematics–language connections were consistent elements of instruction. The teachers described using talk during mathematics in a variety of forms such as "saying what they've learned," talking "about the strategies out loud," "modeling how to talk," "shar[ing] ideas and challeng[ing] each other." Ruth often had her students "pair up with somebody I know can talk it through with them at their level." Ruth's comments demonstrated how interconnected math and language were to problem solving in her classroom. Talk included not only asking questions but expecting students to ask questions as well. The theoretical teachers also described using reading and writing activities that supported mathematics learning. For example, Lynette reported that she "read a lot of literature" and used "writing, picture drawing, story telling" and audiotaping to help motivate her students in mathematics.

The experiential teachers also highlighted process over product and spoke frequently about using open-ended problems. They differed from the theoretical teachers because they were not as consistent or specific in asking their students to verbalize about the problem-solving process. However, they encouraged multiple strategies and were receptive to diverse responses. Patricia provided her students with "lots of opportunities within the classroom to explore and to talk about (problems) and if they come up with . . . an alternate way of looking at something . . . go for it . . ." For a few of the experiential teachers, the priority on process was compatible with designing and implementing lessons that encourage students to "at least try." Deborah told her students, "If they get it wrong, that's fine, that's how you learn things." Most of the experiential teachers did not use the term *risk taking* in their comments although for some, like Barbara, the classroom environment clearly encouraged children to speak freely. For example, she recounted the following experience: "Amanda pointed out a pattern the other day but I didn't see it—she was looking up and down and I was going across—I just couldn't see it and she had to explain it to me."

A variety of approaches to flexible grouping were part of the experiential teachers' instructional practices. Six of the teachers commented on grouping strategies while describing classroom activities. They discussed the need for whole- and small-group instruction as well as individual coaching, at times. Martha said, "You have to do whole-group work where some of it is going to appear hard to some of them and very easy to others, but then you can pull them out into groups and work like that." Priscilla also used flexible groups and adapted the size of the group as necessary. Sometimes she put them in pairs to "stimulate each other." Fiona encouraged students who were capable to work on their own, which allowed her time to work with children who needed additional instruction.

The experiential teachers used a range of motivational strategies and manipulative materials such as classroom stores and mathematics-related games and puzzles. Betty described using counting manipulatives "in the shop" and told of "other sorts of set up areas that they tend to move in and out of." Charlotte gave an example of the children using blocks and bears and then encouraging the children, especially those who were not confident at problem solving, to talk about solving the problems as a relevance, ownership, or fun. The experiential teachers did not explicitly make the connections between these strategies and children's conceptual development as did the theoretical teachers. As mentioned earlier, although some experiential teachers provided an "opportunity (for students) to express themselves" during mathematics, most of the group did not explicitly use language as a tool for learning mathematics.

The intuitive teachers described their instructional practices in terms of the provision of activities and experiences in their classrooms. When describing particular activities, the intuitive teachers focused primarily on the process aspect of the experiences in general terms. For example, these teachers explained that mathematics instruction should focus on hands-on experiences that are based on children's prior knowledge and the "real world." The intuitive teachers referred to the motivational aspects of the activities they provided by emphasizing that the activities needed to be fun and relevant. Like the experiential teachers, the intuitive teachers did not make connections between activities using manipulative materials and conceptual development.

The intuitive teachers described the importance of the teacher acting as a facilitator who provides concrete materials but does not really provide any direct instruction. As Laura stated, "I do not rely on paper–pencil activities too much." In contrast to the theoretical and experiential teachers, the intuitive teachers did not identify open-ended problems as a specific component of the activities they provide. All three of the intuitive teachers provided examples of teaching concepts through thematic units, such as using stores in the classroom where "children create the products, how much the products would cost, and determine what was an appropriate price so they would know how much money . . . they would need." The descriptions of thematic units provided by the intuitive teachers focused primarily on the children's developing and reinforcing skills through their involvement with certain materials. For example, Beverly stated, "We have set up mock stores and giving them money, we have just been working on that and having them go up to the person to buy, like these objects and having them use the skills that they have learned to try to figure our what amounts they need to use, the price is written in print, and then having them use the skills that they have received to pay the storekeeper." Unlike the theoretical and experiential teachers, the intuitive teachers made no explicit reference to language as a tool for learning mathematics.

In terms of recognizing and addressing individual needs, the intuitive teachers focused on differences in ability. Unlike the theoretical and experiential teachers, the intuitive teachers did not specifically mention flexible grouping practices. Rather, all three of the teachers indicated that providing concrete materials in real-life settings was a strategy for addressing individual differences. For example, Donna stated, "I guess I attempt to cater to those that don't have the same level by providing them with, as I have said before, lots of concrete and making it real-life experience that obviously the others have gained along the way but these guys, the other guys haven't, that they're lacking." In addition, Beverly described the use of ability groups in a multiage classroom as a way to address individual differences.

Cross-Case Analysis

The cross-case analysis will serve as the conclusions for this chapter. A more detailed discussion of the conclusions and implications of the beliefs, knowledge, and practices of these teachers will be provided at the end of chapter 7, "Case Studies of Teacher Beliefs, Knowledge, and Practices." Through indepth interviews with numerous teachers in Australia and the United States, we were able to construct a picture of the interaction between knowledge, beliefs, and practices of teachers from different orientations. All of the teachers attempted to create learning environments in which children were valued and learning was meaningful. Although the teachers appeared to share common goals, a cross-case analysis revealed distinct differences between the three orientations. These three orientations appeared to influence how classroom learning was organized, materials were selected, teaching strategies were selected and implemented, and learning expectations were defined and applied.

The theoretical teachers' content and pedagogical knowledge were manifested in both their beliefs and practices. For example, these teachers advocated learning experiences that emphasized problem-solving processes and conceptual understanding. Moreover, the theoretical teachers sought to develop risk takers and independent thinkers through language-rich mathematics instruction. They described their role as facilitators who helped children derive meaning from relevant, open-ended learning opportunities. Frequently, the theoretical teachers acknowledged the influence of mentors and professional development experiences as well their own experiences. They believed that young children are very competent and benefited from differentiated instruction and clear connections between the home and school experiences. Theoretically oriented teachers spontaneously identified the critical role that language plays in learning mathematics concepts.

The beliefs, knowledge, and practices of the experiential teachers were not as consistent as the theoretical and intuitive teachers and often overlapped across these orientations. Their knowledge base was not as clearly articulated and they did not elaborate as the theoretical teachers had. These teachers regularly referred to their own experiences when describing their beliefs and instructional practices. Similar to the theoretical teachers, the experiential teachers saw their role as facilitators who encouraged children to take risks and solve problems independently. The experiential teachers' beliefs about children's competence varied significantly. Although they all acknowledged the influence of home–school connections, some teachers saw the home as a potential positive influence, whereas some described it as a potential negative influence. Many of the experiential teachers agreed with the theoretical teachers that language influences mathematics learning; however, the experiential teachers referred to the influence of language in a much more limited way. The experiential teachers were concerned with motivation and discussed a variety of teaching strategies and grouping practices but, unlike the theoretical teachers, they were not able to clearly articulate how their practice facilitated conceptual development.

When discussing their beliefs and practices, the intuitive teachers did not explicitly refer to mentors, professional development experiences, or their own teaching experiences. Their responses to questions about content and pedagogy were brief and often included jargon. The intuitive teachers indicated that young children learn through experiences that are fun, meaningful, and involve hands-on materials. The intuitive teachers provided a contrast with the theoretical and experiential teachers in several important ways. For example, the intuitive teachers did not mention the need for children to take risks or the need for teachers to differentiate instruction to meet individual needs. The intuitive teachers did not feel that young children were competent in understanding early mathematics concepts, and they did not recognize any connections between the language and mathematics learning. The three intuitive teachers addressed motivation through organizing the classroom with meaningful hands-on materials with no clear reference to concepts, procedures, or attitudes related to mathematics learning. There were also a few similarities with the other orientations. Like the theoretical group, the intuitive teachers thought the home could be a positive influence on children's mathematical learning. Additionally, like the theoretical and experiential teachers, they viewed their role as a facilitator; however, they did not see the need for direct instruction. This may relate to their lack of attention to conceptual development and their emphasis on learning being "fun."

REFERENCES

Anderson, J. (1996). Some teachers' beliefs and perceptions of problem solving. In P. Clarkson (Ed.), *Technology in Mathematics Education, 19th Annual Conference* (pp. 29–37). Melbourne, Australia: Mathematics Education Research Group of Australia.

Borko, H., Davinroy, K., Bliem, C., & Cumbo, K. (2000). Exploring and supporting teacher change: Two third grade teachers' experiences in a mathematics and literacy staff development project. *The Elementary School Journal, 100*(4), 273–306.

Borko, H., Eisenhart, M., Brown, C., Underhill, R., Jones, D., & Agard, P. (1992). Learning to teach hard mathematics: Do novice teachers and their instructors give up too easily? *Journal for Research in Mathematics Education, 23*(3), 194–222.

Borko, H., & Livingston, C. (1989). Cognition and improvisation: Differences in mathematics instruction by expert and novice teachers. *American Educational Research Journal, 26*(4), 473–498.

Bredekamp, S., & Copple, C. (1997). *Developmentally appropriate practice in early childhood programs serving children from birth through age 8* (Rev. ed.). Washington, DC: National Association for the Education of Young Children.

Brown, M., Askew, M., Rhodes, V., William, D., & Johnson, D. (1996). Effective teachers of numeracy in UK primary schools: Teachers content knowledge and pupils' learning. In P. Clarkson (Ed.), *Technology in Mathematics Education, 19th Annual Conference* (pp. 121–128). Melbourne, Australia: Mathematics Education Research Group of Australia.

Bryant, D. M., Clifford, R. M., & Peisner, E. S. (1991). Best practices for beginners: Developmental appropriateness in kindergarten. *American Educational Research Journal, 28*(4), 783–803.

Buzeika, A. (1996). Teacher's beliefs and practice: The chicken or the egg? In P. Clarkson (Ed.), *Technology in Mathematics Education, 19th Annual Conference* (pp. 121–128). Melbourne, Australia: Mathematics Education Research Group of Australia.

Carpenter, T., Fennema, E., Peterson, P., & Carey, D. (1988). Teachers' pedagogical content knowledge of students' problem solving in elementary arithmetic. *Journal for Research in Mathematics Education, 19*(5), 385–401.

Charlesworth, R., Hart, C. H., Burts, D. C., & Hernandez, S. (1990). *Kindergarten teachers' beliefs and practices* (Report No. PS018 757). Boston: American Educational Research Association. (ERIC Document Reproduction Service No. 318 571)

Charlesworth, R., Hart, C. H., Burts, D. C., Thomasson, R. H., Mosley, J., & Fleege, P. O. (1993). Measuring the developmental appropriateness of kindergarten teachers' beliefs and practices. *Early Childhood Research Quarterly, 8*, 255–276.

Deal, D. (2000). *Literacy events during science instruction in a fifth grade classroom: Listening to teacher and student voices.* Unpublished doctoral dissertation, George Mason University, Fairfax, Virginia.

Fang, Z. (1996). A review of research on teacher beliefs and practices. *Educational Research, 38*(1), 47–65.

Fennema, E., Carpenter, T., Franke, M., Levi, L., Jacobs, V., & Empson, S. (1996). A longitudinal study of learning to use children's thinking in mathematics instruction. *Journal for Research in Mathematics Education, 27*(4), 403–434.

Fennema, E., & Franke, M. L. (1992). Teachers' knowledge and its impact. In D. A. Grows (Ed.), *Handbook of research on mathematics teaching and learning* (pp. 147–164). New York: Macmillan.

Franke, M. L., Carpenter, T. P., Levi, L., & Fennema, E. (2001). Capturing teachers' generative change: A follow-up study of professional development in mathematics. *American Educational Research Journal, 38*(3), 653–690.

Hatch, J. A., & Freeman, E. B. (1988). Kindergarten philosophies and practices: Perspectives of teachers, principals, and supervisors. *Early Childhood Research Quarterly, 3*, 151–166.

Kagan, D. (1992). Implications of research on teacher belief. *Educational Psychologist, 27*(1), 65–90.

Kontos, S., & Dunn, L. (1993). Caregiver practices and beliefs in child care varying in developmental appropriateness and quality. *Advances in Early Education and Day Care, 5*, 53–74.

Kowalski, K., Pretti-Frontczak, K., & Johnson, L. (2001). Preschool teachers' beliefs concerning the importance of various developmental skills and abilities. *Journal of Research in Childhood Education, 16*(1), 5–14.

Marcon, R. A. (1999). Differential impact of preschool models on development and early learning of inner-city children: A three cohort study. *Developmental Psychology, 35*(2), 358–375.

Maxwell, J. A. (1996). *Qualitative research design.* Thousand Oaks, CA: Sage.

Miles, M. B., & Huberman, A. M. (1994). *Qualitative data analysis: An expanded sourcebook.* Thousand Oaks, CA: Sage.

Pajares, M. F. (1992). Teachers' beliefs and educational research: Cleaning up a messy construct. *Review of Educational Research, 62*(5), 307–332.

Perry, B., Howard, P., & Conroy, J. (1996). Teacher beliefs about the learning and teaching of mathematics. In P. Clarkson (Ed.), *Technology in Mathematics Education, 19th Annual Conference* (pp. 453–460). Melbourne, Australia: Mathematics Education Research Group of Australia.

Peterson, P., Fennema, E., Carpenter, T., & Loef, M. (1989). Teachers' pedagogical content beliefs in mathematics. *Cognition and Instruction, 6*(1), 1–40.

Philippou, G., & Christou, C. (1996). A study of teachers' conceptions about mathematics. In P. Clarkson (Ed.), *Technology in Mathematics Education, 19th Annual Conference* (pp. 9–15). Melbourne, Australia: Mathematics Education Research Group of Australia.

Raymond, A. (1993). *Unraveling the relationships between beginning elementary teachers' mathematics beliefs and teacher practices.* Paper presented at the 15th annual meeting of the North American Chapter of the International Group for the Psychology of Mathematics Education, Monterey, CA.

Schoenfeld, A. H. (1998). Toward a theory of teaching in context. *Issues in Education, 4*(1), 1–94.

Schoenfeld, A. H. (in press). How can we examine the connections between teachers' world views and their educational practices? *Issues in Education.*

Schwartz, J., & Riedesel, C. (1994). *The relationship between teachers' knowledge and beliefs and the teaching of elementary mathematics.* Paper presented at the 1994 Annual Meeting of the American Association of Colleges of Teacher Education, Chicago, IL.

Sherman, H., & Richardson, L. (1995). Elementary school teachers' beliefs and practices related to teaching mathematics with manipulatives. *Educational Research Quarterly, 18*(4), 27–36.

Stipek, D. J., & Byler, P. (1997). Early childhood education teachers: Do they practice what they preach? *Early Childhood Research Quarterly, 12*, 305–325.

Thompson, A. (1984). The relationship of teachers' conceptions of mathematics and mathematics teaching to instructional practice. *Educational Studies in Mathematics, 15*, 105–127.

Vartuli, S. (1999). How early childhood teacher beliefs vary across grade level. *Early Childhood Research Quarterly, 14*(4), 489–514.

Weiss, R. S. (1994). *Learning from strangers: The art and method of qualitative interview studies.* New York: The Free Press.

Wilcox-Herzog, A. (2002). Is there a link between teacher beliefs and behaviors? *Early Education & Development, 13*(1), 82–106.

Wood, T., Cobb, P., & Yackel, E. (1991). Change in teaching mathematics: A case study. *American Educational Research Journal, 28*(3), 587–616.

APPENDIX

Teacher Interview Questions

1. What does *mathematical reasoning* mean to you?
2. Are you familiar with the term, *analogical reasoning*? What does the term mean to you?
3. How competent at mathematical and analogical reasoning do you consider young children to be?
4. How did you acquire your understanding of mathematical reasoning?
5. How did you acquire your understanding of analogical reasoning?
6. How do you perceive your role in developing the children's mathematical reasoning?
7. How do you attempt to stimulate your children's mathematical reasoning?
8. What differences in reasoning ability do you see in your children?
9. How do you attempt to address these differences?
10. What kinds of mathematical reasoning abilities do you think your children will need to be successful in first and second grade?
11. Do you take these future reasoning needs of your children into account? If so, how do you do it?
12. In what ways do you think the children's out-of-school experiences contribute to the growth of their mathematics reasoning?

7

CASE STUDIES OF TEACHER BELIEFS, KNOWLEDGE, AND PRACTICES

C. Stephen White
George Mason University

Debby Deal
Loyola College in Maryland

This chapter presents three case studies that illustrate in more depth the three orientations described in chapter 6. We present a detailed case study of Mary, a theoretical teacher, Patricia, an experiential teacher, and Donna, an intuitive teacher in order to elaborate further on their knowledge, beliefs, and practice. We believe that the individual portraits presented here add relevance to the conclusions and implications we present at the end of this chapter for both chapters 6 and 7.

THE THEORETICAL TEACHER

When entering Mary's classroom, it is clear that this is a place where the developmental needs and interests of young children have been given a top priority. The physical environment, teacher-to-student, and student-to-student interactions offer evidence that developmentally appropriate practices provide a framework for the instruction and organization that characterize Mary's classroom. Visitors will most likely see Year 1, 2, and 3 students actively involved in a variety of activities that support mathematics and literacy learning. Mary may be providing instruction or support for individuals, small groups, or the whole class at one of the child-friendly centers she designed for the room. A survey of the room shows that it is full of child-size furniture and well-provisioned commercial and teacher-made manipulative materials for mathematics, literacy, art, science, and drama.

Mary has been teaching for 22 years and has taught preschool, Year 1, and multi-aged classes of Year 1, 2 and 3 children. She has undergraduate and master's degrees from an Australian university. Mary's frequent references to mentors and professional development courses along with her solid knowledge of content and pedagogy and her belief in children's competence clearly placed her in the theoretical orientation group.

Knowledge

Knowledge of Mathematics and Analogical Reasoning. Mary was very clear about what mathematics is and what it is not. She described mathematics as "the processes that are involved and the skills and thinking about problems and strategies." Mary further elaborated that mathematical reasoning involves thinking mathematically, that is, seeing not only the whole problem but also its constituent parts and being able to chunk and synthesize the data. It is not, according to Mary, "rote learning, knowing number facts." Mary sees her job as not just educating students but also educating parents so that they will "see that maths is not about just numbers on the group page." She wants parents to gain a better understanding of the nature of mathematics so that they will be able to support their children's work in meaningful ways.

Mary's knowledge of analogical reasoning paralleled her knowledge of mathematics and elicited a detailed response. She began her explanation by saying, "being able to make an analogy when you're reasoning, being able to think about—again chunk those pieces in your mind. . . ." She proceeded to elaborate using "heffa-lumpies," imaginary creatures, as an example. The task was to look at a variety of creatures and determine which were heffa-lumpies and which were not. In order to be successful, Mary explained that students must be "able to pick up those differences and similarities in lots of different tracking movements that my brain would make and coming back to the defining terms and those attributes that are key to being a heffa-lumpy."

Problems like the heffa-lumpy were regularly included in Mary's teaching plans and led her to observe that students might be "having difficulties in numbers and yet with analogical reasoning they're quite brilliant!" She noted with amazement that other teachers often do not devote time to teaching analogical reasoning and "when I talk about this with other teachers I'm talking a foreign language." Mary attributed her understanding of analogies to a "great semester with a wonderful lecturer and lots of reading . . . and applying it to what kids show me they know about it." Crediting learning to mentors and students was a unique quality associated with the theoretical teachers and reflected by their beliefs and practices.

Pedagogical Knowledge. Mary's strong pedagogical knowledge is visible in her classroom and heard explicitly in her conversations. She related motivation to the environment and planned her classroom carefully to facilitate a "community of mathematical discourse." She described her goal in this way:

> I think the environment has got to stimulate it [learning], in that you provide in the environment, and there are key underlying issues that I want kids to know . . . I want them to have this environment in maths—there was an assignment I did once that said a community of mathematical discourse where everybody would talk mathematically to each other and share ideas and challenge each other and that is something that I really have tried hard. I have really had to overcome this real fear from kids that they have got to have the right answer . . . sometimes you've got to get it wrong to get it right, and that's so important.

She purposefully designed learning areas that were child sized and conducive to small- and whole-group instruction. Throughout the year, Mary balanced fixed areas within the room with flexibility to adapt to meet the needs of the students. For example, for whole-class instruction and discussion there was always a large carpeted area and for small-group instruction there was a hexagonal table and chair arrangement especially selected to encourage discussion. Additionally, throughout the year Mary maintained a "problem of the week" area and an estimating area. Portable shelves were filled with manipulative materials including beans, buttons, counters, seeds, Legos, and colored pasta. There was a variety of materials for displaying children's work as well as an overhead projector, chalkboard, white board, flannel board, easel, and magnetic board for instructional purposes. Mary frequently used the easel or the overhead projector during lessons.

Mary's view of her role as a facilitator and challenger was consistent with her decisions about the classroom environment. She described herself as "more of a catalyst, more a challenger, and it is certainly not like I've got the jug of knowledge here, not at all." She considered it her responsibility to know her student's strengths and weaknesses and support their development. Mary noted that "you really have to sit down with kids and find out what they already know and that is a huge challenge" considering the number of students and wide range of developmental levels. However, her use of flexible grouping and her emphasis on children becoming independent learners allowed her the opportunity to talk with children individually. She made an effort to "pose challenging, open-ended questions" which provided her with valuable assessment data. She remarked that the students' responses often surprised her, as their answers revealed that they knew a great deal about the specific task or a related task.

Knowledge of Learner's Cognitions. Mary's understanding of how children think and learn mathematics complimented her mathematical and pedagogical knowledge. As a multi-age teacher, Mary focused on the developmental levels of her students rather than their chronological placements. She considered this vital to meeting the needs of each student who might be incorrectly assessed and instructed inappropriately. For example, Mary described Connor who "amazes me with what he can think of mathematically. He just can't sit still long enough to show you and so he could easily be seen as not being good at maths." Mary described a base-10 experience where Connor and two classmates discovered that using 14 dice helped them to quickly reach the thousands. When she asked how they computed the large sums, the boys responded, "We're finding it's easier if we just estimate first and then use a calculator." Mary commented that their strategy was "brilliant." She proceeded to then give another example and explain that for this student "even thinking out loud what he is doing is an important part." Mary said that she frequently used open-ended tasks and cooperative problem solving during mathematics instruction. She explained that by having open-ended tasks that let students work on different levels, they are able to be successful and develop the strategies and skills necessary to progress. Cooperative problem solving provided opportunities for students to work in multi-age and multi-level groups so that "they help the other kids." Additionally, Mary opted to not use a textbook already purchased by the school because "I do not believe children learn maths by just filling in the sheets." The following year she used the textbook money to purchase mathematics resource materials.

Beliefs

Children's Competence.   As noted earlier, Mary considered young children to be very competent, even "quite brilliant" at mathematical and analogical reasoning. She was concerned that traditional schooling practices did not appreciate or give priority to developing reasoning skills and frequently stifled children's development. For example, Mary commented:

> There seems to be a huge emphasis in primary schools still on the way we were taught mathematics and I think preschoolers tend to show quite brilliant reasoning skills as well because they can think in divergent ways and think of a lot of attributes at the same time.

Mary used several students as examples to support her beliefs. She described a patterning activity in which Trevor collected all the manipulative boxes rather than just a few items as Mary had expected. As the boxes vanished from the shelf, Mary was "horrified" but then she realized he was building a "repeated pattern of boxes in a maze shape . . . more like a concentric shape" and that although he had deviated from the original task, he was demonstrating incredible spatial awareness. Mary valued his problem-solving ability and knew that by not restricting his construction to a couple of items or giving him a worksheet, both she and Trevor benefited. She was adamant that her role was to "allow them the scope to show me what they know; and also to look at a wide range of different strategies . . . because I'm constantly amazed at what they already know about problem solving."

Home Connections. Mary believed that the interaction between home and school was critical to children's intellectual growth and their attitudes toward mathematics. She worked to educate the parents of her students because she recognized how children's attitudes toward mathematics can influence their learning and that children often reflect their parents' attitudes. That is, if parents have a negative attitude toward mathematics, due to their own childhood experiences, or do not see mathematics as relevant, they may pass these attitudes on to their children. Mary worked with parents throughout the year to expand their understanding of mathematics so that they could more effectively help their children. She used some instances, like a school open house and informal conversations, to explicitly expand parents' conception of the nature of mathematics. She also used homework as a more indirect parent education tool.

Mary purposefully planned homework that offered parents a model of the mathematics children did during class time in the hope that it would prompt them to interact with their children in mathematically challenging ways. For example, she described a homework assignment where the children were assigned a game "where you had to actually think about whether it was better who started first, whether that helped in the winning and the competition, and to experiment with who starts first." She wanted parents to recognize that the emphasis was on the process rather than the product. Mary initiated the "maths backpack" program and used it as another opportunity to educate both the children and the parents. In it, Mary put strategy games and analogical reasoning tasks, but there were "definitely no number things . . . I want to show them a whole wide variety . . ." The maths backpack rotated among the children for a two-night period, and Mary reported that they were always anxious for their turn.

Math Language Connections. Literacy was an integral aspect of mathematics learning, in Mary's view, and another belief shared by teachers with a theoretical orientation. Mary observed that reflective writing was a major focus in the curriculum and considered verbalizing a precursor to effective writing. She said, "You can't write before you can think in terms of talking about it." She emphasized repeatedly how important it was for children learning mathematics strategies to talk through the process. Mary also articulated that part of her role was to model the process. She explained it this way: "So when we do strategy games in the classroom. . . . we've talked about [it] and I've modeled that, how you've got to talk out loud what you're thinking." As a result of the frequent modeling and practice, Mary noticed that her students had become less competitive and more metacognitive. Mary reinforced literacy skills through several classroom programs, as well. She explained that the maths backpack always contained a journal for children and their parents to record what they liked best and what they recommended for the next parent–child team. Additionally, mathematics–language connections were reinforced through an e-mail project with another multi-age class. The project, which resulted from a seminar, involved an exchange of challenging mathematics problems between Mary's class and another multi-age class.

Practice

Mary's beliefs about children's competence, home–school interactions, and mathematics–literacy connections appeared to be reflected in her practice. For example, she considered children very competent at mathematical and analogical reasoning and included both as regular components in her mathematics instruction. Students were scaffolded from one level to the next through modeling, practice, cooperative work, and extensive feedback from Mary. She sought to develop a classroom environment where students were comfortable taking risks when problem solving. During math instruction, she frequently posed open-ended questions and tasks; when students responded with divergent answers, she was encouraging and supportive. The emphasis was on understanding the process of mathematics and being able to apply it outside the classroom, which reflected her knowledge of mathematics and pedagogy. Despite her belief in children's abilities, Mary admitted that occasionally her students still surprised her. Referencing Vivian, she said, "She comes out with really amazing things that I sometimes think, I've got her in a box of where I think she is at and then she says something else and I think . . . I didn't even realize she knew that." As shown by her observation of Vivian, Mary's eagerness to listen to her students allowed her to notice changes in their knowledge and attitudes and then propel the learning forward. Rather than following a curriculum guide, Mary used informal formative assessment to guide her planning of mathematics lessons.

Mary was proactive and purposeful about interaction with parents. Programs such as the maths backpack used literacy as a tool to learn mathematics and expand parents' and students' understanding of mathematics. Reflecting her belief that home connections significantly contributed to children's mathematics learning, she carefully planned and introduced the maths backpack program so that parents would understand the goals and purpose. Mary also tried to address the issue of girls and mathematics through a puppet, Penny Problem Solver. She explained, "I have deliberately made it a girl for a lot of gender equity reasons with maths." The puppet was used to introduce mathematics problems, "some of which don't have immediate answers." Mary's comments and use of Penny Problem Solver was again consistent with the theoretical teachers pattern of drawing on their professional knowledge to aid in instructional decisions and practice.

THE EXPERIENTIAL TEACHER

Patricia's classroom gives one the sense of a warm, caring environment. The front of the classroom contains an open area that is used for large group activities with a chair facing the area. As Patricia sits in that chair, she has the blackboard on her right and an easel on her left. The children in her class gather on the floor in this area to hear Patricia read stories, explain the activity of the day, and participate in whole-group activities. There are four large tables arranged in the room where the children sit in groups of six during individual work time. There is an abundance of manipulative materials used for mathematics instruction placed on shelves throughout the sides of the classroom. One student often goes to gather specific materials, such as crayons, pennies, rulers, or unifix cubes, from around the room to share with others at their table.

Patricia has been teaching for eight years. She has taught fourth grade and is currently teaching second grade. She has a Master's in Education from an American university. Patricia's exclusive referrals to prior teaching experience when explaining her instructional choices and her beliefs about the importance of risk taking placed her in the experiential orientation group. In many instances, Patricia's beliefs were similar to the beliefs of the theoretical teachers.

Knowledge

Knowledge of Mathematics and Analogical Reasoning. When asked what she thought mathematical reasoning was, Patricia responded "logical thinking with some kind of sequential thought." She compared "sequential thought" to blocks that build on each other. She stated that children need to learn the "components" in order to have the foundation to think sequentially. Patricia noted that mathematical reasoning involves knowing "one-more, one-less kind of ideas, concepts . . . skills . . . strategies . . ." and being able to apply those strategies to real-life experiences. She added that it also involves "making connections between concepts" and "transferring the skills and concepts . . . if they know one plus two equals three, well . . . you already know two plus one equals three."

Unlike her knowledge of mathematical reasoning, Patricia stated that she had "never heard of analogical reasoning." Despite this, she ventured a guess: "I would say that it is comparisons between objects and why you decided they were similar or different." When she responded to questions about mathematical and analogical reasoning, Patricia did not refer to theories related to mathematical reasoning.

Pedagogical Knowledge. Patricia's pedagogical knowledge is apparent in how she organizes her classroom for instruction and in her conversations. She sees herself as a "facilitator" who gives her students "lots of opportunities . . . to explore and to talk about" mathematical concepts. Patricia often allowed for and encouraged alternative explanations and ideas on how to solve different mathematical problems. Many of the activities she uses in her classroom are hands-on and she likes to convey to the children that "it's a game" whenever they work with math problems. In addition, she noted that she wants the children to have ownership over the activities they engage in.

For children who are having more difficulty with the concepts, she stated that she tries to "provide as many strategies for those kids . . . and make sure . . . that I give them extra time . . . more people working with them individually to kinda strengthen that foundation." Flexible grouping is also something Patricia advocated in her classroom: "I try to get them out in small groups as well you know, to work with other adults in the building to do problem-solving activities. I also think heterogeneous groups are important." Patricia's overall goal for the students is for them to "be able to apply those concepts and what they've learned" in the real world. She routinely provides open-ended activities that can be varied according to the children's responses as she guides them through particular problems.

Knowledge of Learners' Cognitions. As an experiential teacher, Patricia did not demonstrate a theoretical understanding of how children learn mathematics. Rather, she used anecdotes from her teaching experiences and her own learning experiences to explain how children learn. When referring to her own learning about mathematical reasoning, Patricia described learning through playing board games with family members at home. In addition, she noted that she remembered herself struggling in mathematics and that everything "suddenly clicked" for her. For the children that are struggling in her classroom, Patricia observed that ". . . those building blocks need to be in place before the light bulb turns on. . . . having someone work with you and take the time to find out where you're coming from and where you need to go . . . and strategies to help you get there." Drawing again on her experiences, she noted that mathematics are part of day-to-day experiences and emphasized that it is important to make "math a part of everyday life so it's not a separate entity." She tried to do this in her classroom through relevant activities and appropriate manipulatives. Like Mary, Patricia also acknowledged the value of children taking risks and making mistakes during problem solving. She explained:

I'm a firm believer that if they come up with an alternate way of looking at something I'm like, you know, go for it, you know, what do you think and it may not necessarily be along my lines . . . it's still of value and I go 'well, that's great, and, you know, I didn't think about that'.

Similar to the other experiential teachers, Patricia stated that learning mathematics should be fun and described using hands-on activities and manipulative materials to engage her students. She observed that her students were motivated by "hands on. Lots of hands on. Especially in second grade, you know I always tell them 'It's a game!' and then, for some reason, even though it's not, you know, they're really excited . . ." Again, drawing on her experience, she discussed her emphasis on collaboration between children as a way to enhance learning. She explained:

Pairing kids with their peers is a biggie because sometimes I could sit there and beat a concept to death trying to explain it to a child and they just don't get it, but sometimes if their classmate just mentions it and tells them how to do it they get it like that. So I always use kids.

Patricia's understanding of learners' cognitions was similar to Mary's knowledge of how children learn. The main difference between the two participants in this area was how they came to know.

Beliefs

Children's Competence. Like the other experiential teachers, Patricia considered children's competence in mathematical reasoning to vary. She identified prior experience and language as two potential factors that can influence children's competence. She noted that competence "has a lot to do with experience and . . . exposure." For example, she believed that playing games at home greatly influenced a child's potential ability to reason in mathematics. "I know lots of kids are a little more proficient when they play board games." As noted previously, this belief seemed to result not only from her teaching experience but also from her own learning experiences. To Patricia, language is another key component in determining how competent a child will be at mathematical reasoning. "Some children are more competent than others based on . . . the language the parents use at home." Patricia's beliefs about the importance of the home environment and its impact on children's competence was expanded as she talked further about home connections.

Home Connections. Patricia firmly believed that experiences children have at home can influence their development as learners—both positively and negatively. She believed that home experiences can have a "tremendous" impact on students' mathematical reasoning and described several specific scenarios in which parents and caregivers could support cognitive development by using "real-life experiences." For example, she suggested that when parents go to the grocery store, they can help their children learn how to estimate by having them "try to keep a mental tally of what you have, what they're spending." Additionally, she suggested that parents could use cooking recipes as a teaching opportunity, giving the example "okay if we have . . . eight cookies here and five people, how do you think we're going to be able to make it fair for everyone." Through these and other experiences at home, Patricia believed that parents could help their children learn fractions and the concept of division.

However, Patricia warned that some home experiences could have a negative affect on children's mathematical reasoning abilities.

> I think we kinda got into a loss kinda thing with the video games. I think the kids aren't really spending the time to think about what they're doing and so we're losing those wonderful board games where they have to think about it . . . you see more and more kids losing those, or, you know, not coming with those skills.

Patricia's beliefs about the mixed benefits that can result from home interactions reflected her experiences as a teacher.

Math–Language Connections.   Similar to the other experiential teachers, Patricia saw language as an inherent aspect of mathematics. She believed that language assisted in the development of mathematical abilities. As noted in the home connection section, Patricia felt that children's experiences with language at home had the potential to boost or delay their learning in school. In the classroom, Patricia indicated that teaching children to use language to work through problems was a key aspect of learning mathematics. For example, she stated that she offered "kids lots of opportunities within the classroom to explore and to talk about [math]" with adults and peers. Children often worked in small groups or partners to facilitate them talking about the problems as they solved them. Additionally, Patricia enlisted other adults in the school environment to work with children individually. Reading and comprehending was a further aspect of language that Patricia considered vital to success in mathematics. Patricia explained that she tells her students "first you have to read the problem, you have to understand what the problem is asking you" and then the children have to decide how to solve it. She inferred that an essential part of this process for children is metacognition. That is, Patricia believed they needed to be able to ask themselves "What do I know about this problem?" to successfully solve it.

Practice. Patricia's beliefs about children's competence, home–school interactions, and mathematics–language connections were reflected in her practice. As mentioned previously, Patricia sees herself as a facilitator who implements "lots of hands-on" experiences and strives to communicate that math is fun. In general practice, this belief is demonstrated through regular use of manipulative materials and math games. She tries to motivate her students by giving them "ownership of their work." As mentioned previously, Patricia believed children acquired valuable language and mathematics skills through playing board games at home and in the classroom. For example, during one math lesson she explained, "They made up the cards, they thought of a way to do the game, they did it, and then I . . . walked around to see who was doing what they needed to do and making sure they were understanding the concepts." Patricia, like the other experiential teachers, encouraged multiple solutions and accepted alternative solutions. She provided her students with "lots of opportunities within the classroom to explore (problems) . . . and if they come up with . . . an alternate way of looking at something . . . go for it . . ."

Patricia noted that she tries to address individual needs through a variety of approaches including multiple problem-solving strategies, flexible grouping, and one-on-one tutoring. Her classroom was designed so that children could participate in numerous learning centers focused on different mathematics concepts. Flexible grouping was used to determine which centers children visited. If learners are having difficulty with a concept, Patricia said, "I give them that extra time, and . . . more people working with them individually to kinda strengthen that foundation." When visiting her classroom, we noted that she regularly scheduled parent volunteers to support small-group and individual learning. She discussed placing children in small, carefully selected heterogeneous groups. She explained, "I have a few kids that I believe are having tremendous difficulty in reasoning and stand out and I take great care in pairing those kids up . . . someone's who's very proficient with someone else who may be a little weak." Patricia also sought to meet the needs of children who "are not only *not* having problems but who have a tremendous ability to reason" by asking other adults in the building, such as the teacher of gifted and talented children, to work with these children on more advanced problem solving.

THE INTUITIVE TEACHER

When entering Donna's classroom, one might see individual desks arranged in rows and assume that this is a traditional classroom with the teachers' desk and an easel facing rows of children's desks. However, after several visits it becomes apparent that Donna periodically changes the desk configuration, sometimes by groups and sometimes individually in rows as the unit or theme of study changes. The physical environment is arranged to allow children flexible work options. They can work individually or in small groups at their desks. Large groups meet on a carpet area or in an adjoining smaller room. A variety of mathematics materials, such as games, puzzles, counters, cubes, shapes, and bundling sticks, are neatly arranged on shelves on the sides of the classroom. As a follow-up to a teacher-directed lesson, children work individually on prepared worksheets or in their mathematics workbook. The children also use hands-on materials, such as counters, cubes, or teacher-prepared games and activities. Sometimes, Donna conducts large- and small-group lessons outside on the playground.

Donna has been teaching for 15 years and has taught classes of Year 1, Year 2, Year 3, Year 4, Year 5, and multi-aged classes with children of Year 3, 4, and 5 children. She has an undergraduate degree from an Australian university. Donna's responses were brief, lacking in elaboration, and not supported by examples from experience or theoretical knowledge; therefore, she was placed in the intuitive orientation group.

Knowledge

Knowledge of Mathematics and Analogical Reasoning.   Donna primarily used general descriptors when describing mathematics and mathematical reasoning. Her description of mathematics focused on children's understanding of the concept of number, with reference to the ability to identify numbers and "a basic grasp of number." She did not elaborate or provide examples for what an understanding of number meant. When describing mathematical reasoning, Donna associated the terms *common sense* and *logical reasoning*. Donna indicated that patterning was an important component necessary to understand mathematics. In the one example of her teaching that she provided, she focused on patterning. She said, "I tell you, the kids who can do patterning—just the transfer of that pattern to something else, it was basically those kids whom I believe to be more mathematically responsive, that were able to do that and the others really, really struggled." In terms of her knowledge of analogical reasoning, Donna stated that she was not familiar with the term and did not attempt to make a guess. When asked about her own experiences as a young learner, Donna stated that she did not acquire an understanding of either mathematical or analogical reasoning. Overall, Donna provided few specific examples to clarify her statements with no reference to theory or her many years of teaching experience.

Pedagogical Knowledge.   Donna's pedagogical knowledge is visible in her classroom although it was not explicitly articulated during her interview. Children used a variety of concrete materials during teacher-directed, whole-class mathematics lessons. Donna regularly provides numerous large- and small-group and individual follow-up activities using hands-on materials. After instruction in large and small groups, children worked individually to practice a particular skill that had been taught.

Although Donna did not provide detailed descriptions of the types of experiences she provided, she emphasized that her instructional activities needed to have real-world connections and be concrete. She also indicated that she adapted to "teachable moments" when they presented themselves. Donna did not refer specifically to particular teaching strategies or describe her classroom environment. She described herself as a facilitator and conceptualized this role as providing concrete, real-life experiences in the classroom. Donna felt that it was essential for children to see real-world connections in the experiences she provided. She stated that she feels it is important to "help children see how they could apply school learning to their daily lives." For example, on a day when the children in her classroom had awakened at 5 o'clock in the morning to watch the World Cup soccer game, Donna made use of their interest in the games and used the clock to discuss the time of the game in different parts of the world.

Knowledge of Learners' Cognitions. Donna's responses about how young children learn were similar to her responses concerning content and pedagogical knowledge. That is, her responses were not detailed and seemed to draw on her intuitive understanding rather than theoretical or experiential knowledge. Again, Donna spoke generally about learning and conveyed that children learn through "a great deal of experience and hands on experience, I guess." Similar to the other intuitive teachers, Donna used the reference "I guess" when explaining how young children learn. As mentioned previously, her explanations concentrated on learning through experiences that are concrete and involve materials children can manipulate. Unlike Mary and Patricia, Donna did not mention developmental levels, the use of open-ended tasks, risk taking, or collaboration.

Beliefs

Children's Competence. Generally, Donna did not consider young children to be very competent at mathematical and analogical reasoning. Unlike Patricia and Mary who indicated that young children in general are competent at mathematical reasoning, she stated, "I believe there are a select few. I don't think as a general rule they are very good at it. I don't think they've got very good skills at a young age, with the exception of a few." As discussed in the mathematical knowledge section, Donna used patterning as an example of a concept that differentiates young children's competence. She indicated that those children who were able to replicate a pattern were more "mathe-

matically responsive," whereas children who could not replicate patterns
were less competent. When discussing young children's competence, Donna
did not elaborate beyond the patterning example.

Home Connections.   Donna believed that the connection between home
and school is important and can influence children's mathematical learning.
Compared to her other responses, Donna's answers to questions about home
influences were the most detailed and specific. Like Patricia, she believed that
out-of-school experiences have an "incredibly, absolutely incredible influence" on mathematics and analogical reasoning and "everything else" that
young children learn. Donna also indicated that children's experience in the
home prior to formal schooling influenced their success in school. She felt
that children who did not have relevant experiences related to reasoning and
mathematics at home were "already way behind." Moreover, Donna felt that
teachers could not really compensate for the absence of home experiences.

Although Donna emphasized the importance of home experiences, she did
not discuss specific activities she planned or conducted with parents as Mary
and Patricia had done. Similarly, she did not discuss homework or activities
related to mathematics or reasoning that parents could participate in with
their children. Donna described mathematical experiences that occurred out
of school in general terms, such as "thinking about it at home." Donna did
not describe any type of collaboration or cooperation with parents and families; rather, she implied that any mathematical reasoning experiences that occurred at home were separate from those she provided at school.

Math–Language Connections.   In terms of language, Donna discussed
the importance of language to young children's learning in general but did
not indicate that there were any connections between mathematics and language. For example, when discussing home experiences, Donna indicated
children whose parents talk to them at home have an advantage over those
children who do not have these experiences. She also observed that children
who attend child care benefit from language opportunities but not mathematical opportunities. She stated, "Not a lot of maths goes on . . . anyway
there's a lot of language. . . . from my own experiences there's not a lot of
maths that goes on there." Throughout her comments, Donna made no explicit connection between language and the learning of mathematics.

Practice.   Donna's description of her practice mirrored her pedagogical
knowledge and again seemed to be influenced by her intuitive understanding
of how children learn. However, Donna's practice did not consistently reflect
her stated beliefs. As mentioned previously, she saw herself as a facilitator
who provided a great deal of hands-on experience using concrete examples of
the concepts she is teaching. Moreover, it was noted during most of the observations that the maths lessons were teacher directed and included either

teacher-prepared worksheets or math workbooks. In some instances, children were also observed using hands-on materials in groups and individually. Donna described her practice in general terms with no reference to a professional knowledge base or her previous teaching experience. Donna explained that she addressed individual needs by again mentioning that she provided concrete experiences and "making it real" for those children who were not at higher levels of mathematical reasoning. As previously mentioned, Donna did not discuss her classroom environment nor provide specific information about the instructional techniques that she uses.

CONCLUSIONS AND IMPLICATIONS

As noted in the cross-case analysis in chapter 6, there were distinct differences between the three teacher orientations in the broad areas of knowledge, pedagogy, and learners' cognitions. Similarly, there were variations in the beliefs held by teachers in each orientation about how children learn, connections between the school and home, connections between mathematics and language, and specific instructional practices. While previous research in early childhood and mathematics has examined relationships between teachers' beliefs and knowledge or between teachers' beliefs and their practices, the differences between the three orientations of teachers in this study suggest that there is a relationship between teachers' beliefs, their knowledge, and their practices. Moreover, the findings of this study indicated that teachers' mathematical and pedagogical knowledge influenced their beliefs, which, in turn, influenced their practices. Our findings also demonstrated that there were no apparent relationships between teachers' content and pedagogical knowledge and their years of teaching experience and education. Consequently, future studies need to examine the relationship between different types of teacher knowledge and their beliefs and practices. These studies need to include teachers who teach different ages and grade levels as well as other subject matter content such as literacy, science, and social studies.

The knowledge, beliefs, and practices of the teachers in this study can be placed on a continuum from intuitive to experiential to theoretical. Theoretical teachers explained their knowledge and beliefs by referencing theoretical frameworks, teaching experience, and listening to children. They provided rich examples of practices associated with effective/exemplary teachers. The experiential teachers made decisions based on knowledge that appeared to reflect their experiences as opposed to the multiple sources of knowledge used by the theoretical teachers. In contrast, the intuitive teachers appeared to make instructional decisions more spontaneously. Although the examples of practice the intuitive teachers provided were not necessarily ineffective, these teachers could not clearly articulate any rationale for the decisions they make regarding their instructional practices.

   This intuitive-to-theoretical continuum needs to be considered in future studies that examine the influence of teachers' beliefs and knowledge on practice. For example, in this study it appeared that the theoretical teachers viewed young children as competent and thus provided them with challenging and motivating activities. Future research needs to examine specific questions related to these implications, such as Is there a relationship between the theoretical teachers' content knowledge, their belief that young children are more competent, and their provision of more challenging, conceptually oriented activities? In other words, does more learning occur in the classrooms of theoretical teachers?

   The difference between the teachers in the three orientations also raises questions regarding how the theoretical teachers attained a stronger theoretical framework. Future research efforts need to examine the types of experiences, critical incidents, and motivation that may have influenced these teachers. By obtaining a picture of how these teachers came to be more theoretical, we may be able to determine how teachers can move from an intuitive orientation to a theoretical orientation. Further study of how teachers develop their beliefs and knowledge can provide insight into whether or not their knowledge and beliefs move progressively toward a theoretical orientation as they participate in professional development programs and gain teaching experience. Obtaining a working knowledge of the thoughts and practices of teachers at various stages along the intuitive-to-theoretical continuum may provide those interested in the professional development of novice and experienced teachers with insights into appropriate expectations for teachers at varying stages in their professional development.

   Efforts to influence teacher practices, whether as part of preservice or inservice programs need to consider teachers' beliefs and knowledge. Professional development programs can address differences in teachers' beliefs, knowledge, and practice using a variety of methods, such as encouraging teachers to reflect on their own teaching and decision-making practices and make explicit their own beliefs about the purposes of early childhood education. Professional development programs also need to recognize differences in teachers' knowledge and beliefs and develop meaningful experiences that recognize individual differences in teachers rather than follow a "one size fits all" approach. By considering the relationships between early childhood teachers' beliefs and their content and pedagogical knowledge, future professional development efforts may be able to promote teaching practices that are more theoretically based in both academic content and pedagogy. To address the lack of previous attention in the literature on the relationship between content knowledge and early childhood teachers' practices, it is especially important that future professional development efforts concentrate on preparing these teachers with understanding subject matter content.

8

COMMENTARY: ANALOGICAL REASONING AND MATHEMATICAL DEVELOPMENT

Usha Goswami
Faculty of Education, University of Cambridge

Reasoning by analogy is widely accepted to be a core component of human cognition. Its contribution to cognition has been defined in varying ways. A recent definition of analogical reasoning introduced the concept of "mental leaps." Holyoak and Thagard (1995) refer to the act of forming an analogy as seeing one thing as if it were another, an activity that requires a kind of mental leap between domains. In chapter 1 of this volume, Lyn English defines analogy as "the ability to reason with relational patterns." She notes that analogy involves the detection of patterns, and the identification of the recurrence of patterns in the face of variation in their elements. I will argue that both relational patterns and mental leaps are essential to mathematical activity. So is a third aspect of analogical reasoning, the creative aspect. Analogical thinking has been at the core of some of the greatest discoveries in science. A striking example of this is the analogy that led to Kekule's (1865) theory about the molecular structure of benzene (see Holyoak & Thagard, 1995). In a dream, Kekule had a visual image of a snake biting its own tail. This gave him the idea that the carbon atoms in benzene could be arranged in a ring. The similarity between the snake and the carbon atoms was at a purely structural/relational level—the level of circular arrangement. Recognizing creative abstract similarities such as these is also an important part of mathematical thinking. Put simply, analogy is part of how mathematicians think. Mathematicians themselves recognized this a long time ago (e.g., Polya, 1957).

Analogy is also an important part of how young children think. As English points out, young children reason by analogy from their earliest school

169

experiences. In fact, analogy is probably available from infancy onwards (see Goswami, 1991, 1992, 1996, 2001 for overviews). Most of the studies that support this conclusion about the early availability of analogy define analogical reasoning as similarity-based reasoning. The most important kind of similarity for an analogy is *relational* or *structural* similarity. In many analogies, the objects in the analogy are not perceptually similar at all. Their similarity is at a purely relational or structural level. Kekule's analogy of a snake biting its own tail is a good illustration of this (the relational similarity with the molecules is the abstract relation "circular arrangement"). Frequently, however, objects in the two situations being compared in an analogy bear some perceptual resemblance to each other—they share "surface" similarity. This similarity of appearance can often support the analogical mapping. An example is the invention of Velcro, which followed the observation by Georges de Mestral that burdock burrs stuck to his dog's fur (see Holyoak & Thagard, 1995). The *surface similarity* in the appearance of the small hairs coating burdock burrs and the fuzz on Velcro supports the relational similarity of "effective sticking mechanism." These two factors—relational similarity and surface similarity—both affect analogical reasoning (e.g., Gentner, 1989). However, they seem to do so in the same way for both children and adults (see Goswami, 2002).

INDUCTIVE AND DEDUCTIVE MATHEMATICAL REASONING

Mathematical thinking, however, encompasses more than analogy. Some mathematical concepts are so sophisticated and abstract that they are only understood by a handful of people. Other aspects of mathematical knowledge are essential for everyday life. Activities such as spending money, estimating time, planning journeys, and cooking require a lot of informal mathematics. These kinds of mathematics are more dependent on deductive reasoning, whereas analogy is a form of inductive reasoning, enabling the thinker to go beyond the information given. Both inductive mathematical reasoning (e.g., pattern detection) and deductive mathematical reasoning (e.g., calculation) require some explicit teaching. However, other aspects of children's understanding of the logical concepts underpinning mathematics seem to develop by themselves. They develop from children's everyday experiences within their social and physical environments. This was the aspect of mathematical development that most interested Piaget (see Piaget, 1952), and that interests the researchers in the current study.

Piaget was interested in the reasoning processes underlying children's solutions to mathematical problems. Although his work is not so popular these days, he did produce a coherent theory about how mathematical reasoning develops (see Bryant & Nunes, 2002, for an overview). His theoretical work was heavily influenced by the philosophy of logic. Piaget focused on discovering the formal rules or principles underlying different forms of mathematical reasoning. These formal rules were thought to be domain-general and content-independent, and were assumed to operate in their purest form in totally unfamiliar domains. This led to a plethora of studies investigating whether young children could use formal mathematical rules in unfamiliar contexts, which they typically couldn't.

Analogical reasoning, in contrast, fits within the framework of inductive reasoning rather than deductive reasoning. When there are gaps in our knowledge, we have to reason by induction. Generalizing on the basis of a known example, making an inductive inference from a particular premise or drawing an analogy are all examples of inductive reasoning. These are the kinds of skills of interest in this book. Early studies of inductive reasoning were influenced by a very different branch of philosophy, that of concept formation and induction. Within this framework, it was taken for granted that the existing state of the child's conceptual system in a given domain would have an important effect on the child's reasoning. However, it was assumed that the basis of early induction might be different from the basis of more mature induction. It was believed that younger children might be overinfluenced by perceptual knowledge (their reasoning was assumed to be "perceptually bound"). Because of this, relatively unfamiliar contexts were again used to assess reasoning skills, and in such situations young children usually failed to reason on the basis of relational rather than perceptual similarities until they got older.

The early focus of the mathematics research field on (assumed) content-independent mathematical principles has now been superseded by a growing interest in the range and extent of children's mathematical thinking and the way that it is affected by social and cultural contexts. Traditional approaches to studying mathematical reasoning that focused on uncovering when children became able to reason according to the "laws of mathematics" have been replaced by an interest in the systematic effects of children's existing physical and cultural beliefs on mathematical reasoning. Children's existing beliefs can form coherent theories that explain external reality very well in many situations and so can be quite impervious to change. The shift in research paradigms, to investigating how well children's mathematical knowledge frameworks approximate reality at different points in development, and under which circumstances these approximations change, is a welcome one. It is also the approach that underlies the longitudinal and cross-cultural study of mathematical and analogical development reported in this book.

The studies reported here aim to explore the thinking behind children's mathematical responses, and the extent to which that thinking is analogical. A core assumption is that a basic aspect of mathematical reasoning is the ability to see connections and relationships among mathematical ideas, and to apply this understanding to the solution of new problems. As recognizing relationships among entities and applying those relationships to new problems is core to analogy as well, it seems likely that analogical reasoning and mathematical reasoning will turn out to be related. This was indeed the case in this study. I will comment on the relevant findings in more detail later in this chapter. First, I will consider the three kinds of analogical reasoning outlined in the introduction in terms of their implications for mathematical development.

ANALOGY AND RELATIONAL PATTERNS

Classic investigations of analogical development have focused on the item analogy paradigm A:B::C:D, which can be broadly construed as a measure of the recognition of relational patterns. The relational pattern involved is that between two entities, A and B. To solve the analogy, the same pattern must be applied to a third entity, C, in order to generate the solution entity, D. Examples of relational patterns used with young children include "large red circle (A) is to small blue circle (B) as large red square (C) is to small blue square (D)" (Alexander et al., 1989); "half circle (A) is to half rectangle (B) as quarter circle (C) is to quarter rectangle (D)" (Goswami, 1989); "apple (A) is to cut apple (B) as playdoh (C) is to cut playdoh (D)" (Goswami & Brown, 1989); and "dog (A) is to kennel (B) as bird (C) is to nest (D)" (Goswami & Brown, 1990). These kinds of relational patterns are recognized and solved by children as young as 3 years of age (as some of this material is covered in chap. 1, this volume, I will not describe the experiments in detail here).

The ability to abstract patterns and apply them to new entities does not seem to constitute a hurdle in cognitive development. Indeed, relational patterns are a basic aspect of perceptual as well as cognitive processing. For example, language acquisition relies on pattern detection, and infants are very good at this. Six-month-old infants can recognize and distinguish the phonetic pattern corresponding to the vowel in *pop* and the vowel in *peep*, and can sort new instances of the two vowels produced by novel speakers (these experiments rely on the head-turn paradigm; see Kuhl, 2000). They can also learn the stress and intonation patterns that characterize their mother speaking, even from within the womb, and thus prefer to listen to their mother speaking rather than to an unfamiliar female speaking at birth.

An important question with respect to the development of mathematical reasoning is whether perceptual pattern recognition and conceptual pattern recognition are related. One possibility is that perceptual analogies and conceptual analogies are different aspects of the same fundamental mechanism for recognizing patterns, a mechanism that appears to distinguish us from all other species. A second possibility is that perceptual pattern recognition is much simpler than, and therefore distinct from, conceptual pattern recognition. The latter requires some form of reflection on one's knowledge. Perceptual learning of linguistic patterns in infancy requires the extraction of patterns from sensory input, but drawing an analogy based on, for example, causal relations requires not just the perceptual analysis of the objects in the analogy but also some conceptual knowledge about their properties. It probably also requires some knowledge about causal structure that must be fairly abstract (e.g., knowledge that organizes information about the temporal and causal frameworks of events).

If the latter view is preferred and the ability to detect perceptual relational patterns is thought to be unrelated to the ability to detect conceptual relational patterns, then a second important question arises. Which kind of relational pattern is more important for mathematics? This question has a number of possible answers. For example, it can be argued that perceptual relational patterns lie at the heart of the number system. When children categorize and group objects such as toy dinosaurs in terms of color, they are using perceptual relations that can be expressed via quantification ("four red dinosaurs"). The proposal that children have an innate understanding of number depends on perceptual relations of this sort. For example, studies based on the visual habituation technique appear to show that even young infants can quantify small numbers and perform numerical operations, such as addition and subtraction, with them (e.g., Wynn, 1992). These behaviors seem to depend on the recognition of perceptual relational patterns (the babies seem to be recognizing changes not in how many objects are being shown, but in the total amount of "stuff" in the displays; see Bryant & Nunes, 2002; Clearfield & Mix, 1999). Researchers such as Bryant and Mix do not accept this recognition of perceptual relational patterns as evidence for innate mathematical reasoning. Rather, they argue that in order to recognize and distinguish numbers, children have to be able to transcend perceptual information.

These researchers argue that the recognition of conceptual relational patterns is more important for mathematical development. Children must understand that two sets of objects can have the same number even if they look quite different (five cakes vs. five trees), and that the number in a particular set of objects stays the same even if there are changes in perceptual appearance (15 sailboats in the harbor vs. 15 sailboats out at sea). Children must learn about both cardinal numbers (that all sets with the same number are qualitatively equivalent) and ordinal numbers (that numbers come in an ordered scale of magnitude), and this is conceptual knowledge. On the other hand, if perceptual relational pattern detection and conceptual relational pattern detection are different aspects of the same underlying mechanism, then there should be important developmental continuities between the mathematical "abilities" studied by infancy researchers and those studied later on in young children.

ANALOGY AND MENTAL LEAPS

Another aspect of mathematical reasoning is the ability to see a solution, or to arrive at a solution that seems to appear spontaneously in mind. This aspect of inductive reasoning has been explored in studies of insight. *Insight* refers to the apparently spontaneous solution of a difficult problem without the application of any conscious reasoning strategies. It was first studied in detail by the Gestalt psychologists (e.g., Maier, 1931). A classic insight problem is the following: In the matchbox problem (Duncker, 1945), participants are required to fix a candle to a vertical surface so that it can burn properly. Various tools, such as string and drawing pins (tacks), are provided to assist them. The drawing pins are in a small box. The solution is to empty the box and pin it to the vertical surface, thereby creating a horizontal shelf on which to stand the candle. Many of the adult participants in the matchbox experiment did not think of this solution, because the box was seen only in terms of its function of containing the drawing pins. This impediment to flexible reasoning was described as "functional fixedness."

German and Defeyter (2000) recently carried out some similar experiments with young children. They produced the interesting argument that younger children might actually be less susceptible to functional fixedness than older children because they have a more fluid notion of function. German and Defeyter designed a variant of Duncker's candle problem suitable for children aged from 5 to 7 years. In one experiment, the children were introduced to Bobo, a toy bear with short legs. Bobo wanted to reach his toy down from a shelf. He couldn't jump because of his short legs, and so the children were asked to help him to reach his toy. Various tools were around to help them, including toy blocks, a magnet, a ball, and a car. These toys were all presented inside a small box. Although the toy blocks could be used to build a tower, it was too short for Bobo to reach his toy. The solution was to empty the box and turn it over, and then to build the tower on top of it. In a control condition, the box was given to the children empty.

German and Defeyter found that the 5-year-olds were equally fast at using the box as a support for the tower in the Functional Fixedness condition and the control condition. In contrast, the 6- and 7-year-olds were significantly slower in the Functional Fixedness condition than in the control condition. They were also significantly slower than the younger children, taking on average 120 seconds to think of the box solution compared to 40 seconds for the 5-year-olds. German and Defeyter argued that younger children may be immune to functional fixedness in certain scenarios because they have more flexible notions of object function.

Brown and her colleagues have suggested that inventive flexibility is not related to age, however. Brown (1989) also carried out some functional fixedness studies, set within the privileged developmental domain of biology and natural kinds. Children show special interest in learning about the world around them, and in this domain inductive reasoning is found in many forms. Brown taught 4-year-old children about different mimicry defense mechanisms in real animals. Children in a Fixedness condition learned about one such defense mechanism, visual mimicry of a more dangerous animal. They learned about the capricorn beetle, which reveals wasp-like markings when attacked; the hawkmoth caterpillar, which has underside markings like a poisonous snake; and the crested rat, which can part its hair to show skunk-like markings. Children in a Flexibility group learned about three different mimicry mechanisms. They learned about the hoverfly, which makes a sound like a bee; the opossum, which can freeze and play dead when attacked; and the walkingstick insect, which can change shape to look like a twig or a leaf. Both groups were then tested for their ability to learn a novel mimicry solution, camouflage by color change.

In this test phase of the experiment, the children were told about two novel examples of mimicry. These were Peppered moths, whose natural mixed white/grey coloring had been predominantly white prior to industrialization in Northern England, but some of whom could be grey/black; and Pocket mice, who had been predominantly light-coated rather than red-coated when they had lived in a sandy-floored forest, but who had been forced to move into a forest with reddish soil. The children were asked what had happened to the moths/mice. The correct answer was that over time the moths had evolved to be predominantly grey/black (making them less visible in the polluted air), and the mice had evolved to be predominantly red-coated (making them less visible against the reddish soil). The Fixedness group, who had learned only one mechanism of camouflage (look like something scary), were poor at inventing the new solution (color change), with only 10% inventing this solution. In contrast, the Flexibility group was very good, with 82% inventing this solution. Thus, in Brown's work, 4-year-olds were close to ceiling in terms of inventive flexibility (although this did follow optimal contexts of learning).

If even rather young children can make analogies based on mental leaps of this form, then again interesting questions are raised with respect to mathematical development. Should this form of analogy be seen as available to all children and thus likely to be related to progress in mathematics? Or is it better conceptualized as a form of analogy that is constrained in important ways, for example, by the existing state of the child's conceptual system, the nature of the function to be learned, and the context in which the new function is first encountered? We already know that inductive reasoning, in general, is broadly constrained by the nature of the knowledge to be learned, the existing state of the conceptual system, and the context in which the new concept is first encountered (see Heit, 2000). This analysis implies that if a privileged domain such as biological knowledge is selected, for which a relatively rich conceptual system develops relatively early, and new concepts within this system are introduced in ways that facilitate cognitive flexibility, then analogical insights should be easy to find. Mathematical knowledge does not seem to constitute a privileged domain of this nature. Most of the conceptual systems underlying mathematics must be learned and arguably only become truly rich in professional mathematicians.

In fact, the best way to introduce new concepts in mathematics is one of the biggest hurdles in designing mathematics curricula. Although there is an assumption that concrete analogies are a useful way of teaching mathematical concepts, there is an important difference in these kinds of analogies and the analogies that children make spontaneously about biological kinds and in other rich domains. When familiar conceptual referents are used in mathematics instruction, the teacher's intention is to use existing conceptual knowledge as a basis for teaching new relational knowledge. For example, the teacher may select familiar referents, such as pizzas, pies and boxes of eggs, to teach children about fractions (e.g., that 1/2 a pizza is relationally equivalent to 1/2 a box of eggs; see Singer-Freeman & Goswami, 2001). Fractions are very abstract representations of aspects of relational similarity that are not an intrinsic part of children's existing knowledge about pizzas and eggs. In analogies about new concepts such as mimicry, in contrast, the children have sufficient collateral and background information to work out the relations for themselves. Children's mental leaps in the biological realm are supported by their prior learning about empirical relations in the world and their knowledge of the network of collateral or background information in which these relations are embedded. Children's mental leaps in the mathematical realm, in contrast, may be severely curtailed by their lack of sufficient collateral and background information to work out the relations for themselves. In fact, many mathematical principles have only been discovered by painstaking thought and experimentation, and depend on empirical relations that are completely outside the experience of the vast majority of people. Obviously, such mathematical knowledge must be directly taught to children. The research question then becomes whether children who are better at making mental leaps are also better at learning such mathematical principles.

On the other hand, for some kinds of brains, the abstract systems underlying mathematics are very easy to learn. Mathematics is one area of cognition where child prodigies are more likely to make important discoveries when they are relatively young. If the likelihood of being a mathematical prodigy is related to analogical ability, then one possibility is that these child prodigies are better at making mental leaps than their peers. Another is that they are better at the creative discovery aspect of analogical reasoning.

ANALOGY AND CREATIVITY

Some of the most creative scientific inventions and insights have been based on analogies. Two examples have already been discussed, namely, the invention of Velcro and the discovery of the molecular structure of benzene. There are also a number of mathematical discoveries that have been based on analogies. A classic example is Archimedes' insight about the value of using water displacement to quantify the mass of different substances. Archimedes had been asked to calculate whether base metal had been substituted for gold in an ornate and intricately designed crown that had been commissioned by his king. Archimedes knew the weight per volume of pure gold, but the crown was so ornate that he was unable to measure its volume. Unable to reach a solution, he went home and had a bath. According to the legend, he then cried, "Eureka, I've got it." When he stepped into the bath, he noticed that his body displaced a certain volume of water. This gave him the mathematical solution to his problem: immerse the crown in water and see whether the volume of water that was displaced was equivalent to that displaced by pure gold.

This kind of mathematical solution really does seem to capture a very abstract kind of relational similarity that is not evident to most people as they get into the bath. This brings us back to the role of the underlying structure of conceptual knowledge in successful analogizing. Even creative analogies in mathematics and science are to some extent knowledge based. Although scientific breakthroughs often depend on the right analogy (Gordon, 1979), the scientists who make the breakthroughs seldom have extra information that is unavailable to their colleagues. Instead, the analogy occurs to them and not to their fellow scientists because of the way that their conceptual understanding of their field is structured and because of the richness of their representations. This, in turn, may be correlated with their intelligence. If intelligence is important, then its importance may explain why classical analogy performance—seeing relational patterns—is a good correlate of IQ. Traditionally, classical analogies are staple items on IQ tests. More recently, it has been reported that more efficient visual processing of stimuli in infancy (using a habituation paradigm) is related to performance on a test of classical analogical reasoning at age 12 (e.g., *bread* is to *food* as *water* is to *beverage*; see Sigman, Cohen, Beckwith, Asarnow, & Parmelee, 1991). This type of evidence supports the notion of a continuum between perceptual and conceptual pattern recognition. It also raises some important research questions. If our goal is to find a special relationship between analogical ability and mathematical ability, we must ask how analogical ability is related to intelligence and whether efficient analogizing is a hallmark of intelligence. Intelligence may have to be controlled in order to establish a unique relationship between analogical reasoning and mathematical reasoning.

OVERVIEW OF THE PRESENT STUDY
AND KEY FINDINGS

The Research Questions

The study described in this book was planned as a longitudinal and cross-cultural study of reasoning development from preschool to the end of second grade. The focus of the research was the development of mathematical and analogical reasoning. Analogy was assumed to be a highly general cognitive mechanism of great power that might play a special role in mathematics. As current views of mathematical reasoning highlight the formation of generalizations and the abstraction of ideas and relationships, and as the identification, extension and generalization of patterns are important in analogical reasoning (English, chap. 1, this volume), it seems logical to propose that the two should be related. The ability to see connections and relationships among mathematical ideas and apply this to new problems is basic to mathematical reasoning, and this building of relationships and correspondences involves important analogical reasoning processes. On this analysis, analogy should be central to mathematical progress of any sort.

However, as already discussed, inductive (analogical) reasoning is not the only kind of reasoning that is important for mathematics, as deductive reasoning is also important. Further, as English also notes, even the most basic mathematical analogies present some complexity for young children. If base-10 blocks are used to represent the numbers to 10, children must interpret the relationships inherent in the design of the materials in order to benefit from the analogy. These relationships are transparent to the teacher, who already understands the system. They are not transparent to the learner, particularly as the numerical relationships that they are intended to convey often depend as well on how the blocks are arranged and manipulated. English suggests that young children have difficulties with such analogies because they need to fully understand the structure of the source analog (i.e., the base-10 system). She notes the "analogical paradox" raised by Dunbar (2001), that is, that participants tend to need help in using analogy in formal instructional settings but do not need help in using analogies in naturalistic contexts. However, there is another aspect to their difficulties as well, which was raised earlier in this chapter. The concrete materials are themselves being used to teach the source analog (here, the base-10 system). This is different from drawing a spontaneous analogy about biology, where the child has to go beyond the information given, but has the support of a richly structured pre-existing knowledge base in doing so. In mathematics, the child does not have a richly structured knowledge base that incorporates concepts like the base-10 system. This is what schooling needs to teach them. Hence, the ability to draw analogies per se may be only one of the skills that are required to become a good mathematician.

The Cultural Comparison

The longitudinal study reported in the chapters in this book also compared children from two cultures, American and Australian elementary schools. The question of culture in cognitive development is an important one. Traditional theories of cognitive development were largely culture-general. For example, Piaget's theory of knowledge development assumed that reasoning in all kinds of cognitive domains (e.g., mathematical reasoning, moral reasoning, physical reasoning, logical reasoning) progressed through a series of universal stages that transcended culture and context. In contrast, Vygotsky differed from Piaget in attributing a central role to social context and culture in children's cognition (see Rowe & Wertsch, 2002). Rather than seeing the development of knowledge as transcending culture and context, Vygotsky argued that an understanding of how knowledge develops requires an understanding of the social and historical origins of knowledge and of changes in that knowledge. In the current study, rather few differences with respect to culture are reported. This is not surprising, as children growing up in relatively affluent homes in America and Australia probably experience more cultural similarities than differences. Also, the relatively small sample sizes in both countries mean that the cultural differences that are reported are ambiguous as to their underlying cause. Only 30 children in each country began the study, and only 22 American children and 6 Australian children remained after 3 years. Nevertheless, the principle of examining the development of mathematical and analogical reasoning across different cultures is a very important one, and this study represents a first step in taking potential cultural differences seriously.

The Analogical Assessments

Children in both countries were given a test of analogical reasoning that has been used by Pat Alexander and her colleagues for almost 20 years. This test is the TARC, or Test of Analogical Reasoning in Children. The TARC depends on plastic blocks of different sizes, colors, and shapes that can be used to present analogy problems of the form A:B::C:? ("classical analogies," according to Goswami, 1991). The TARC is a robust measure for tapping one aspect of analogical reasoning, the ability to form higher order relations between entities that are given. It thus corresponds best to a measure of the ability to see relational patterns. As the children got older, they were also tested with other kinds of classical analogies, namely, pictorial, geometrical, and verbal analogies. These, too, had been mostly used in prior work by Alexander and her group, and can be accepted as robust measures of analogical responding. The analogical assessments were administered at the beginning and end of Years 1, 2, and 3.

One question that it is interesting to pursue is whether the assessments of analogical reasoning used in this study went far enough. Classical analogies clearly tap some aspects of analogical reasoning relevant to mathematics, namely, the ability to reason with relational patterns. However, classical analogies only partially capture children's ability to recognize the recurrence of patterns in the face of variation in their elements, as the variation in item analogies is usually highly constrained. Classical analogies are a good measure of children's understanding of the relational similarity constraint, but they may not be a good measure of children's ability to see connections between abstract mathematical ideas. Further, classical analogy problems do not really give any insight into the child's ability to make mental leaps of the kind discussed by Holyoak and Thagard (1995), nor of their ability to generate creative relational solutions to open-ended problems. Hence, in future studies of this nature, it may be useful to widen the assessments of analogical reasoning.

The Mathematical Assessments

Mathematical reasoning was assessed by tests designed to capture children's abilities in quantification, patterning, representation, and translation. The tasks used relied heavily on prior work by Lyn English. For example, to test patterning, children were given concrete objects, such as attribute blocks and toy dinosaurs, and were asked to group them freely, or to create patterns such as ABBA based on the type and color of the dinosaurs. To test quantification, they were given concrete objects to order in terms of length, or counting tasks and number recognition tasks. To test representation and translation, children were asked to construct simple mathematical problems or to give verbal explanations for certain solutions. The mathematical assessments, therefore, covered a broader set of skills than the analogical assessments. The mathematical assessments were also administered at the beginning and end of Years 1, 2, and 3. In fact, these assessments reminded me strongly of Piagetian tasks dependent on the classification, ordering, and counting of concrete entities. Again, it may have been interesting to include some of Piaget's standard tasks, such as conservation, to see whether they, too, were related to analogical ability.

The Main Findings

The main hypothesis being put to test was that there should be a reciprocal relationship between children's abilities to recognize and apply patterns in an analogical manner and their abilities to perceive numerical patterns and form the appropriate abstractions and generalizations for mathematical reasoning. This hypothesis was largely supported. The children's performance in the analogical tests at the different time points and in the mathematical tests at those same time points was significantly correlated at virtually all the measurement points taken. Longitudinal correlations were also largely significant. Analogical reasoning scores usually showed significant correlations with later mathematical reasoning scores, and vice versa. Regression analyses to explore reciprocal relationships showed that analogical reasoning in Year 1 significantly predicted mathematical reasoning in Year 3, accounting for 24% of the variance in the mathematical scores. Mathematical reasoning in Year 1 also significantly predicted analogical reasoning in Year 3, accounting for 57% of the variance in the analogical scores. These are striking relationships.

As the authors note however, their sample size was small (only 22 children yielded sufficient data for the longitudinal analyses). Hence, these relationships must be interpreted with some caution. For example, the analogical reasoning measure at Time 1 (the TARC) explained less of the variability in mathematics scores at Time 3 (24%) than the mathematical reasoning measure at Time 1 for the analogy measure at Time 3 (57%). An interesting possibility is that this imbalance reflects the fact that the TARC involves the recognition of perceptual patterns, whereas the verbal analogies used to measure analogy at Time 3 require the recognition of conceptual patterns. Perhaps there is a stronger connection between conceptual pattern recognition and mathematical reasoning than between perceptual pattern recognition and mathematical reasoning. Larger groups would enable this hypothesis to be tested.

Further, no control measures for IQ were included in the study. This limits the claim that the patterns found between analogy and mathematics reflect a specific relationship. In order to establish a specific relationship between mathematical and analogical reasoning in children, it is really necessary to first take out that proportion of the variance due to general individual differences in ability, using some form of intelligence measure. The omission of measures of general ability also make it difficult to draw strong conclusions from the analyses of "Strong" versus "Weak" analogical reasoners that are reported in chapter 3. The Strong analogical reasoners may simply have been the more intelligent children. Finally, it is difficult to know how much weight to give the cross-cultural differences reported in chapter 3, given that the children were not matched on any variables except age at the beginning of the study. Nevertheless, the fact that the significant findings were all in line with the authors' hypotheses is encouraging.

Individual Differences: The Case Studies

Further key findings from the study relate to the 10 individual case studies that are reported. These 10 children were observed at varying points in the school day, and discourse relating to mathematical or analogical reasoning was recorded. This discourse was subsequently coded as relating to informal versus formal mathematical knowledge, and to lower versus higher order relational similarity. Informal mathematical discourse turned out to be by far the most frequent type of discourse observed. The children's teachers also appeared to be sensitive to this and made an effort to create opportunities for the children to become familiar with informal mathematical concepts. In contrast, analogical reasoning was only used under specific conditions, many of them creative or artistic (e.g., "the touch of the pussy willow is like a fly on my nose"). Again, this implies that analogies are used naturally and spontaneously when they draw on a rich knowledge base. The young children in this study had a rich experience of the natural world and could all imagine what it would feel like to have a fly land on their nose. Perhaps their teachers were aware of this at some level, and hence only introduced instructional analogies in situations where the relations in the analogy were bound to be familiar to the children themselves.

The only spontaneous use of higher order relations by the children occurred in science lessons (e.g., "a twig is as heavy to an ant as a car is to us"). Again, this confirms the importance of a rich knowledge base for spontaneous analogizing. This is Dunbar's (2001) "analogical paradox," that is, that participants do not need help in using analogies in naturalistic contexts even though they may need a lot of help in using analogies in formal instructional settings. The only formal instructional use of analogy observed in the teachers was during biology instruction. For example, one teacher explicitly compared butterflies to moths in order to explain about the similarities and differences between cocoons and chyrsali. The teacher guessed that the children knew enough about butterflies to make this analogy transparent to the children, and they probably did. In mathematics, most children do not have a richly structured knowledge base of this type that can be drawn on in order to understand new mathematical concepts. Even the simple mathematical concepts measured in this study, such as counting and number recognition, take a long time to develop in young children. This is because they are cultural acquisitions—they are not observable in the world of the young child, but are an abstraction of certain kinds of information within that world.

I will illustrate this point with the example of counting. Gelman and Gallistel (1978) suggested that there were at least five important principles that children had to understand in order to count successfully: (a) (the *one-to-one principle*, that each object in a set must be counted once and once only; (b) the *stable order principle*, that the number words must be produced in the conventional order; (c) the *cardinal principle*, that the last number counted represents the value of the set; (d) the *abstraction principle*, that the number in a set does not depend on the qualities of the members in that set (the rules for counting ducks are the same as the rules for counting blocks); and (e) the *order irrelevance principle*, that the order in which the members of a set are counted makes no difference to the total number. Although Gelman and her colleagues were able to show that even preschoolers grasped at least the first three of these principles, the children only demonstrated understanding with relatively small sets. They made quite a lot of errors with larger sets, which were interpreted as arising from a lack of counting skills. For Piaget, on the other hand, young children's counting was a paradigm case of children using words without understanding what they mean. Piaget argued that children did not understand the meaning of number until they understood the cardinal and ordinal principles discussed earlier, namely, that all sets with the same number are qualitatively equivalent and that numbers come in an ordered scale of magnitude. From his experiments on conservation, transitivity, and seriation, Piaget concluded that children did not understand these principles until they were at school. In either case, it is clear that cultural transmission is important for establishing these principles in young children. The principles are not directly observable in the environment. This suggests that the apparent absence of spontaneous analogies in mathematical reasoning could stem from limitations in knowledge rather than limitations in analogy (as Hatano and Sakakibara note in chap. 9, this volume).

In terms of individual differences, the children most likely to exhibit analogical associations in their classroom discourse and in activities, such as complex patterning, were the Strong analogical and mathematical reasoners. As noted earlier, the Strong analogical reasoners and the Strong mathematical reasoners tended to be the same children. Again, this raises the interesting question of the role of general intellectual ability in the individual differences noted by the researchers. Are the stronger reasoners better because they are better at analogy? Or are they better at analogy because, in general, they are better at everything? It is important for future studies to disentangle these possibilities.

QUESTIONS FOR FUTURE RESEARCH

The study reported in this book represents an exciting first step in the exploration of the extent to which the thinking behind children's mathematical reasoning is analogical. It also raises a number of important questions for future research. To my mind, the most important of these are a more detailed investigation of (a) the role of the knowledge base in enabling analogies in mathematics, and (b) the instructional goals of using analogies to teach mathematics. The role of the knowledge base was raised by English in her introductory chapter. She suggested that young children often have difficulties with analogies, such as base-10 blocks for the base-10 system, because they do not fully understand the structure of the source analog. The relationships that the analogy is intended to convey are transparent to the teacher, who already understands the system. They are not transparent to the child. This raises a different analogical paradox: whether it is possible to use analogies to teach mathematics when the best analogies (e.g., concrete representations for base-10 numbers) in themselves require interpretation and understanding. Singer-Freeman and Goswami (2001) also raised this paradox in their work on instructional analogies for fractions teaching. In fractions teaching, popular conceptual referents include slices in a pie, eggs in a box, geometric regions, and the number line (Behr, Lesh, Post, & Silver, 1983; Dickson, Brown, & Gibson, 1984). However, these conceptual referents are only familiar with respect to their identity, not their representational relations. A child might know that cutting a pie into six pieces gives six slices of pie, but the child needs to learn that one slice represents a sixth of the pie, which is thus relationally equivalent to one egg in a box of six eggs. This pre-existing knowledge of pies and eggs is not richly structured in ways that are already relevant to mathematical principles.

There is another aspect to children's difficulties in using analogies in mathematics too, which was also raised earlier in this chapter. Usually, the instructional concrete materials are themselves being used to teach the source analogue (e.g., the base-10 system or concepts such as parts and wholes). This is cognitively quite different from drawing a spontaneous analogy in biology, where the child has the support of a richly structured pre-existing knowledge base. For mathematics, schooling needs to teach children the knowledge base as well as help them to see the connections and relationships among mathematical ideas. Once the knowledge base is rich enough, children can apply this understanding to the solution of new problems, and then individual differences in analogical ability may indeed begin to influence mathematical attainment. However, it does seem possible that the ability to draw analogies may be only one of the skills that are required for a child to become a good mathematician. Whether those children who absorb the culturally acquired rich knowledge base of mathematical relationships particularly quickly and become mathematical prodigies are those who, a priori, had superior abilities to see relational patterns, make mental leaps, and use analogy creatively, is an open-ended question for future research.

REFERENCES

Alexander, P. A., Willson, V. L., White, C. S., Fuqua, J. D., Clark, G. D., Wilson, F., & Kulikowich, J. M. (1989). Development of analogical reasoning in 4- and 5-year-old children. *Cognitive Development, 4*, 65–88.
Behr, M. J., Lesh, R., Post, T. R., & Silver, E. A. (1983). Rational Number Concepts. In R. Lesh & M. Landau (Eds.), *Acquistion of Mathematics Concepts and Processes* (pp. 91–126). New York: Academic Press.

Brown, A. L. (1989). Analogical learning and transfer: What develops? In S. Vosniadou & A. Ortony (Eds.), *Similarity and Analogical Reasoning* (pp. 369–412). Cambridge, England: Cambridge University Press.

Bryant, P., & Nunes, T. (2002). Children's understanding of mathematics. In U. Goswami (Ed.), *Blackwell Handbook of Childhood Cognitive Development* (pp. 412–440). Oxford, England: Blackwell.

Clearfield, M. W., & Mix, K. S. (1999). Number vs contour length in infants' discrimination of small visual sets. *Psychological Science, 10*, 408–411.

Dickson, L., Brown, M., & Gibson, O. (1984). *Children Learning Mathematics: A teacher's guide to recent research.* Oxford, England: Alden Press.

Dunbar, K. (2001). The Analogical Paradox. In D. Gentner, K. J. Holyoak, & B. N. Kokinov (Eds.), *The Analogical Mind: Perspectives from Cognitive Science* (pp. 313–334). Cambridge, MA: MIT Press.

Duncker, K. (1945). On problem solving. *Psychological Monographs, 58* (Whole No. 270). Washington, DC: American Psychological Association.

Gelman, R., & Gallistel, C. R. (1978). *The child's understanding of number.* Cambridge, MA: Harvard University Press.

Gentner, D. (1989). The Mechanisms of Analogical Learning. In S. Vosniadou & A. Ortony (Eds.), *Similarity and Analogical Reasoning* (pp. 199–241). Cambridge, England: Cambridge University Press.

German, T. P., & Defeyter, M. A. (2000). Immunity to 'functional fixedness' in young children. *Psychonomic Bulletin & Review, 7*, 707–712.

Gordon, W. J. J. (1979). Some source material in discovery-by-analogy. *The Journal of Creative Behaviour, 8*, 239–257.

Goswami, U. (1989). Relational complexity and the development of analogical reasoning. *Cognitive Development, 4*, 251–268.

Goswami, U. (1991). Analogical reasoning: What develops? A review of research and theory. *Child Development, 62*, 1–22.

Goswami, U. (1992). *Analogical Reasoning in Children.* Hillsdale, NJ: Lawrence Erlbaum Associates.

Goswami, U. (1996). Analogical Reasoning and Cognitive Development. *Advances in Child Development and Behavior, 26*, 91–138.

Goswami, U. (2001). Analogical reasoning in children. In D. Gentner, K. J. Holyoak, & B. N. Kokinov (Eds.), *The Analogical Mind: Perspectives from Cognitive Science* (pp. 437–470). Cambridge, MA: MIT Press.

Goswami, U. (2002). Inductive and deductive reasoning. In U. Goswami (Ed.), *Blackwell Handbook of Childhood Cognitive Development* (pp. 282–302). Oxford, England: Blackwell.

Goswami, U., & Brown, A. L. (1989). Melting chocolate and melting snowmen: Analogical reasoning and causal relations. *Cognition, 35*, 69–95.

Goswami, U., & Brown, A. L. (1990). Higher-order structure and relational reasoning: Contrasting analogical and thematic relations. *Cognition, 36*, 207–226.

Heit, E. (2000). Properties of Inductive Reasoning. *Psychonomic Bulletin & Review, 7*, 569–592.

Holyoak, K. J., & Thagard, P. (1995). *Mental Leaps.* Cambridge, MA: MIT Press.

Kuhl, P. K. (2000). A new view of language acquisition. *Proceedings of the National Academy of Sciences, 97*, 11850–11857.

Maier, N. R. F. (1931). Reasoning in humans II: The solution of a problem and its appearance in consciousness. *Journal of Comparative Psychology, 12*, 181–194.

Polya, G. (1957). *How to solve it.* Princeton: University Press.

Piaget, J. (1952). *The child's conception of number.* London: Routledge & Kegan Paul.

Rowe, S. M., & Wertsch, J. V. (2002). Vygotsky's Model of Cognitive Development. In U. Goswami (Ed.), *Blackwell Handbook of Childhood Cognitive Development* (pp. 538–554). Oxford, England: Blackwell.

Singer-Freeman, K., & Goswami, U. (2001). Does half a pizza equal half a box of chocolates? Proportional matching in an analogy paradigm. *Cognitive Development, 16*, 811–829.

Sigman, M., Cohen, S. E., Beckwith, L., Asarnow, R., & Parmelee, A. H. (1991). Continuity in cognitive abilities from infancy to 12 years of age. *Cognitive Development, 6*, 47–57.

Wynn, K. (1992). Addition and subtraction by human infants. *Nature, 358*, 749–750.

9

COMMENTARY: TOWARD A COGNITIVE–SOCIOCULTURAL PSYCHOLOGY OF MATHEMATICAL AND ANALOGICAL DEVELOPMENT

Giyoo Hatano
Tomomi Sakakibara
The University of the Air

The study reported in detail in this volume is an extension of Alexander, White, and Daugherty (1997) in the very interesting and innovative book edited by English. The earlier (1997) study with 4- and 5-year-olds revealed that their analogical reasoning ability, assessed by conventional A:B::C:? form items, was significantly correlated with their ability to extend patterns, but not with three other measures of mathematical learning. Age was a significant determinant of mathematical learning but not of analogical reasoning. The present study was a longitudinal one that traced children from preschool to the end of the second grade. The children, from both the United States and Australia, were tested with a new instrument that is allegedly a measure of mathematical reasoning (the Mathematical Reasoning Test for Young Students [MRTYS]) as well as the same classical measure of analogical reasoning (the Test of Analogical Reasoning for Children [TARC]) used in the 1997 study. The children were tested a few times, so the relationships between these two measures could be investigated developmentally. The MRTYS consisted primarily of three components, Attributions and Patterning, Quantification-Relations, and Quantification-Numbers. It covered a wide range of the products of mathematical learning: Some items were concerned with mathematical reasoning, whereas others tapped requisite knowledge, like the meaning of terms used in mathematics.

In addition, the present study examined classroom discourse in relation to these two modes of reasoning. Classroom discourse is generally supposed to enhance, as well as reveal, the development of young children's knowledge and reasoning. For example, both the teachers' "revoicing" of children's utterances (O'Connor & Michaels, 1993) and evaluative comments by other children (Inagaki, Morita, & Hatano, 1999) are expected to widen and deepen the children's understanding of what constitutes good analogies and respectable mathematical ideas. In the present study, the participating children's performances on the TARC and MRTYS were related to the pattern of discourse in their classroom and their own utterances in it.

Moreover, two other chapters (White, Deal, & Deniz, chap. 6, this volume; White & Deal, chap. 7, this volume) discuss teachers' beliefs about mathematical and analogical reasoning. The authors of these chapters classified the participant teachers into three groups in terms of epistemological orientations (theoretical, empirical, and intuitive), and compared their explanations and practices related to these two modes of reasoning. It is important for us to understand teachers' beliefs and practices to improve teacher education so that the students' reasoning can be facilitated in every classroom. We will not discuss these chapters in this commentary, however; rather, we will concentrate here on children's reasoning, which was, we believe, the focus of the present study.

What was in fact found from this extended study? Alexander and Buehl (chap. 2, this volume) claim that their study of the development of analogical and mathematical reasoning "has contributed to current understanding about young children's learning and development on several fronts." More specifically, the authors of the preceding chapters present clear evidence that young children engage in analogical and mathematical reasoning; that these two modes of reasoning can be reliably assessed by TARC and MRTYS, respectively (chap. 2); that both modes of reasoning developed in the three years up to the second grade; that the two measures were correlated significantly; and that mathematical patterning seems to be a strong link between them (chap. 3). In addition, they found that informal mathematical knowledge was often and ubiquitously referred to by children as well as teachers, whereas analogical reasoning was demonstrated in much more limited situations; however, the classroom activities became more structured over the three-year period (chap. 4); and children's scores on the TARC and MRTYS tended to be consistent with their utterances in the classroom (chap. 5).

We too think that the authors' contributions should be appreciated. Empirical data regarding young children's analogical reasoning and mathematical learning are actually scanty. Reliable measures of these reasoning abilities that are entertaining to children are hard to construct. In fact, such measures are urgently needed for investigating individual differences in reasoning abilities and how they develop. Moreover, the development of reasoning should be related to the classroom context in which it functions.

Despite these contributions, we cannot totally be satisfied with these findings, at least as reported in the preceding chapters, partly because we have had an extremely high expectation as the principal investigators of the study are both leading figures in the field. It is true that their research methods were rigorous—the children's reasoning was assessed by the standard psychometric procedures, classroom discourse was observed and coded objectively, and so on. However, many of their findings are not very new, as "it is clear that basic analogical capabilities are present in preschool children" (Holyoak, Gentner, & Kokinov, 2001, p. 15), and a moderate magnitude of correlation is expected to exist almost always between two cognitive measures. The present analyses of the children's discourse with their teachers are not very informative either for our understanding of learning and development. Our honest impression is that the present chapters, though respectable and useful as a first step, suffer from "methodological behaviorism." Subtle, transient, but interesting phenomena are often ignored in the search for methodological rigor.

In this commentary, we will thus look at the issue of analogical reasoning and mathematical learning from a slightly different perspective and methodological stance than those of the authors. First, we examine relationships between analogical reasoning and mathematical reasoning/learning. We strongly believe that dynamic relationships between these two modes of reasoning cannot be clarified just by correlating them. More conceptual investigations as well as theoretically motivated empirical studies are needed. We offer a few comments of a conceptual nature, which are within the scope of this rather short commentary. Second, we propose a knowledge-based approach to the facilitation of analogical reasoning, and present an example of it. We hope that it will at least complement the approach taken in the present study, with the classic A:B::C:? test of analogical reasoning. Third and finally, we describe the informal teaching–learning processes through which mathematical knowledge is acquired and elaborated. We describe a Japanese informal math education, which has some differences from, as well as commonalities with, American and Australian practices, and analyze this educational process a little more "qualitatively" or "speculatively" than the present authors did.

RELATIONSHIPS BETWEEN MATHEMATICAL AND ANALOGICAL REASONING

What are analogical and mathematical reasoning? We have to characterize each of them before we can discuss the relationships between them. For analogical reasoning, there seems to be a good consensus among psychologists and cognitive scientists. For instance, Vosniadou (1989) indicated, "It is generally accepted that the process of reasoning by analogy involves transfer of structural information from a source to a target system" (p. 414). In other words, analogical reasoning can be characterized in terms of the shared process of extending relational information across two analogs differing in content.

The term *mathematical reasoning* is not frequently used in the community of psychologists and cognitive scientists. Although it is a popular term among mathematics educators, there exist numerous interpretations of it (English, chap. 1, this volume). Although it is too restrictive to equate mathematical reasoning to superior computational and analytical skills, it seems too broad to include in it such skills as gathering evidence, making conjectures, and drawing and validating logical conclusions. These skills are certainly used across a variety of domains, and often called by qualified terms depending on the domain they serve (e.g., biological reasoning, economic reasoning). We assume, if there is any commonality among all instances of mathematical reasoning, it is that they all deal with mathematical entities (e.g., numbers, quantities, geometric shapes, abstract patterns, and their relations). In other words, mathematical reasoning can be quite diverse in the processes or modes of reasoning used: Demonstrating a theorem or proposition requires deduction only; in contrast, finding and extending patterns involve induction.

That mathematical reasoning involves a variety of processes is supported by the authors' own data (Buehl and Alexander, chap. 3, this volume; see also Alexander, White, & Daugherty, 1997): The score of the TARC in the first year it was given was positively correlated with two of the third-year MRTYS subscores (Sequencing and Patterning and Story Problems), but not significantly with other subscores. The Sequencing and Patterning subtest required children to find regularities in a given part (order relationships between elements, such as AB, ABC, AABB) and apply them to a following part. Therefore, what is required to score high on this subtest is obviously analogous to the TARC, which required children to find a relation between the first two elements and apply it to a third element to derive the fourth. The contribution of analogical reasoning ability to the Story Problems will be discussed in the next section.

Moreover, MRTYS measures include what might be called mathematical knowledge rather than reasoning, such as recognizing which is the tallest block. Certainly children have to learn mathematical symbols and expressions in the shift from informal to formal mathematics in their early years. Accumulated mathematical knowledge is potentially related to reasoning, because reasoning can generally be defined as a goal-directed and constrained step-by-step transformation of mental representation or knowledge (Hatano & Inagaki, 2000). Mathematical reasoning is not limited to logically valid or highly plausible transformations, but is controlled by mathematical knowledge as well as reasoning rules, and it is often assumed that because even young children possess basic reasoning rules, rich and well-structured mathematical knowledge is *the* critical component of individual differences in mathematical reasoning. Therefore, as Alexander and Buehl implicitly assume, good measures of mathematical knowledge or learning can be used as measures of mathematical reasoning. In this commentary, we will use the terms *mathematical reasoning, mathematical learning,* and *mathematical knowledge,* more or less interchangeably.

Here we would like to offer three points that we believe are important in our understanding of the relationships between analogical reasoning and mathematical reasoning/learning and that may lead to experiments that were not included in the present study. First is the issue of domain-specificity. Analogical reasoning serves as a source of hypotheses about unfamiliar situations, as a source of problem-solving operators and techniques, and as an aid to learning and transfer (Halford, 1993). Therefore, analogical reasoning as a set of domain-general mechanisms can be used in the domain of mathematics, to generate a hypothesis, solve a problem, or learn a new idea. This conceptualization of the relationships is consistent with that by English (chap. 1, this volume); that is, mathematical reasoning involves important analogical reasoning processes.

There is considerable evidence for the effective use of analogies in mathematics. Not a few mathematical ideas are learned or intuitively justified based on analogies. For example, in an everyday situation, some people, asked to calculate the amount of shrimp to be caught to yield 9 kilos of shelled shrimp, when 3 kilos of shelled shrimp are yielded for each 15 kilos they catch, solved the problem by finding the relationship between the two amounts of shelled shrimp and applying that relationship to the known amount of shrimp caught (e.g., "because 9 is three times as much as 3, you have to catch 15×3 (or $15 + 15 + 15$) = 45 kilos"; see Nunes, Schliemann, & Carraher, 1993). This is almost the same inference as the solution required for classic analogy items. In the classroom discussion, a number of students claimed that $1/2 + 1/5 = 2/7$ "cannot be right because when the denominator is the same, they are not added," suggesting that, they believed, "*not adding* for fractions with the same denominator" and "*adding* for fractions with different denominators" are not structurally similar (Hatano, Morita, & Inagaki, in preparation).

The second point is the issue of second-order domain-generality that complicates the relationships between analogical reasoning and mathematical knowledge. Although mathematical knowledge is not about the material world as such, it is nevertheless very useful for solving real-world problems accurately and efficiently (de Corte, Greer, & Verschaffel, 1996). Ordinary adults and children, though often not aware that they are doing so, perform mathematical operations to find solutions for their everyday problems (e.g., divide a "pie" into quarters and take three to change the original recipe for four into that for three).

This is possible because, though mathematics constitutes a domain, almost all knowledge domains can be mapped to mathematics through a process called mathematical modeling. In other words, instead of solving problems within each knowledge domain, people often convert these problems into mathematical expressions and solve them by manipulating the expressions.

Math education programs take this duality into serious consideration—good programs try to enhance the acquisition of mathematical knowledge by asking students to solve practically significant and/or intellectually challenging problems. To put it differently, much mathematical knowledge is acquired by relying on analogies, but once it is learned, this knowledge can serve as the source for solving problems in many other domains through mathematical modeling. These problems are converted into mathematical expressions and equations in the modeling process. A solution for these problems can be obtained by manipulating mathematical symbols and "decoding" the obtained result.

The third issue involves the selection of the source analog in solving, for both analogical and quasi-analogical (where structural relations are mapped only partially) problems. A number of hints from *How to Solve It* (Polya, 1957) are concerned with the attempt to find the identical or a similar problem that has already been solved. In other words, a critical step is whether a problem solver can find a source analog, from which important relationships among constituent elements can be mapped to the target analog. Even when the two analogs are not structurally the same, the recognition of relational or structural similarity between the target and source problems may be beneficial. One can choose a solution path for the target that is structurally similar to the successful solution path for the source.

However, Polya's hints also suggest that identifying a proper source analog to start with is by no means easy. Gick and Holyoak (1980), who did classic experiments on analogical transfer, pointed out that spontaneous analogical transfer across domains seldom occurs, because before two domains are mapped, an appropriate source domain must be selected, and this process is the hardest one in analogy. Different cover stories often mask the shared structural relations between two analogs. Although creative human minds often try to apply to a novel problem seemingly relevant knowledge from another problem solved earlier, finding the applicable knowledge in apparently dissimilar problems appears to be very difficult. Needless to say, rich domain knowledge serves as an effective constraint in searching for an appropriate source analog. If the proper source analog is salient for some reason, it is very easy to establish mapping between the source and the target, which solves, at least partially, the "analogy paradox," that people can use analogies in everyday situations far more easily than predicted from laboratory studies on analogies (Dunbar, 2001).

A KNOWLEDGE-BASED APPROACH TO THE FACILITATION OF ANALOGICAL REASONING

As Goodnow, Miller, and Kessel (1995) indicate, repeated participation in a socioculturally organized practice or activity enables participants to acquire skills and concepts needed to be competent in the practice or activity, even when they do not intend to learn. Thus, when particular forms of reasoning are often involved in the classroom practice, including discursive practice, their use will be enhanced accordingly. However, organizing a practice in which analogies are naturally and frequently used may not be easy. Newcomers' use of analogies will certainly be enhanced if oldtimers rely on them in the practice, but we must face basically the same problem of how to encourage oldtimers to analogize often.

Another approach to such facilitation is to provide exercises that use target reasoning processes. Direct training may be effective for the development of analogical reasoning. For example, White and Alexander (1986) showed that three consecutive training sessions for the component processes of geometric analogy problems in fact enhanced 4-year-olds' performance on the analogy items. Moreover, the trained children referred to higher order relations between terms more often than their control counterparts. However, there are two serious problems with the direct training approach. First, whether such a training effect can be generalized to other situations where analogies are potentially useful (e.g., mathematical word problems that can be solved based on the earlier solution of a structurally similar problem) is yet to be demonstrated. Second, whether this approach can be taken without giving up constructivism as the salient educational philosophy has to be examined.

We would like to propose an alternative idea, that is, to facilitate the use of analogy by enriching children's knowledge base (e.g., inducing their understanding of relationships between the various elements in it). This enriched knowledge base may then serve as the analog source. We fully agree with the conclusion of English (1997) that "children will be unable to reason if their knowledge base is poor" (p. 215), which was somehow not considered seriously in the present study.

Our example is from the domain of naive biology, which is most familiar to us. Moreover, because "Evidence that analogy is an important mechanism for understanding biological principles comes from a series of studies by Inagaki and her colleagues" (Goswami, 2001, p. 455), we will review these studies.

First of all, Inagaki and Hatano (1987, 2002) assume, as Carey (1985) did, that young children's naive biology is personifying; that is, young children almost always predict and explain biological phenomena of nonhuman animals and plants by relying on analogies that draw on knowledge about humans as the source. This does not mean that young children do not possess the knowledge to differentiate nonhuman animals and plants from humans. However, they do not have a rich categorical knowledge, and thus may rely on analogy in inferences with their knowledge about humans as a source analog, because they are intimately familiar with humans while necessarily novices in most other domains.

Personification is ubiquitous in naive biology. It enables young children not only to predict the behaviors of less familiar animals but also to make sense of and offer a good justification for what they have experienced with animals and plants. Young children's person analogy also produces a number of impressive outcomes (Inagaki and Hatano, 2002).

The idea that personification is a person analogy is a radical deviation from the Piagetian interpretation of animism, but is supported by mainstream researchers in studies of analogy (e.g., Gentner & Markman, 1997; Holyoak & Thagard, 1995). Current studies have indicated that even preschool children can aptly use analogy when they have relevant knowledge about the source analog (e.g., Goswami, 1996). The major barrier to young children relying on analogies is that they do not possess rich knowledge about a variety of entities so that they can choose a proper source analog.

Inagaki extended this idea of analogy-based naive biology to include other analogies with familiar living things. Even young children may draw on knowledge established in an enriched source analog. Inagaki (1990) compared the biological knowledge of kindergartners who had actively engaged in raising goldfish for an extended period at home with that of the children of the same age who had never raised an animal. Although these two groups of children did not differ in factual knowledge about mammals in general, the goldfish-raisers had much richer procedural, factual, and conceptual knowledge about goldfish. More interestingly, the goldfish-raisers used the knowledge about goldfish as a source for analogies in predicting the reactions of an unfamiliar "aquatic" animal (i.e., a frog) that they had never raised, and produced reasonable predictions with some explanations for them. For example, one of the raisers answered when asked whether we could keep a baby frog at the same size forever, "No, we can't, because a frog will grow bigger as goldfish grew bigger. My goldfish were small before, but now they are big."

In a more recent study, Inagaki (2001) examined effects of raising mammals, which are much closer to humans than goldfish. Five-year-old children who had raised mammals (hamster-raisers and dog-raisers) for an extended period at home were compared with same-age children who had not raised mammals. Both groups of children were given an inductive projection task consisting of four novel properties, together with questions involving factual/procedural knowledge about either hamsters or dogs (depending on which they had been raising) and factual knowledge about mammals in general. In the induction task, after being taught about either hamsters/dogs or people a novel property (e.g., immunity) and its function, the children were asked whether each of eight other animals, plants, and nonliving things would have the novel property. It was found that the animal-raisers had a greater amount of factual knowledge about hamsters/dogs than nonraisers, though both groups were comparable in factual knowledge about mammals in general. When required to project the novel properties taught about humans to other entities, the raisers extended them to varied animals including grasshoppers, but not to flowers or stones, more often than the nonraisers. When asked to project given novel properties taught about the raised animal (i.e., the hamster or dog) to other entities, the animal-raisers extended them at least to monkeys on the one hand and frogs on the other more often than the nonraisers. Considering that inductive projection is highly similar to analogy (Inagaki & Hatano, 2003), these results strongly suggest that the experience of raising a mammal as a pet also helps children generate spontaneous analogies using the knowledge about the raised animal as the source.

We believe that, in mathematics, too, to be able to rely on analogy, children must have some source analog that is highly familiar and for which they understand well the relationships among entities, properties, and activities, both real-world and mathematical, that are involved in the analog. They have to know not only what relationships exist among real-world objects and actions but also how they are represented mathematically and manipulated. They have to have repeated, rich experience with the mathematized situation before they can readily retrieve it as the source for understanding and solving other word problems.

An example of such familiar analogs in mathematics comes from studies of street vendors in Brazil, which have shown that they acquire "street mathematics" for commercial activities without systematic instruction. Although it is a form of non-school mathematics, its representations are information-rich, and the meanings of the manipulations are readily comprehensible (partly because they are analogous to actual activities dealing with goods or coins and notes). For example, to determine the price for 12 lemons at Cr$ 5.00 each, a 9-year-old child who was an expert street mathematician counted up by 10s (10, 20, 30, 40, 50, 60) while separating out two lemons at a time (Carraher, Carraher, & Schliemann, 1985).

More interestingly, there is some evidence for the transfer of street or everyday mathematics (Nunes et al., 1993). Saxe (1991) also demonstrated that candy-selling children could compare two hypothetical ratios and explain their judgments much more often than nonsellers. They seemed to use their rich knowledge about commercial activities in which they had to judge which way of selling candies is a good bargain for them in the solution of school-like problems.

In contrast, it is highly unlikely that young children could use the situation model just given as the source. It was not easy even for sixth graders to correctly pair the structurally similar source and target, when their surface content was different (English, 1997). It might be interesting to examine the effect of making some problem situation highly familiar and readily symbolized and manipulable through using it repeatedly, because analogical and quasi-analogical transfer is so important in solving mathematical problems, especially those with apparently different cover stories.

HOW IS MATHEMATICAL KNOWLEDGE ACQUIRED
AND ELABORATED IN SOCIAL INTERACTION?

As indicated earlier, one of the merits of the present study is that it paid due attention to classroom discourse as the catalyst for the acquisition of mathematical knowledge. However, how the engagement in discourse makes mathematical knowledge and reasoning more sophisticated is never explained in the earlier chapters.

Moreover, although Chiu and Tron (chap. 4, this volume) indicate that their goal was "to examine the role of classroom discourse in supporting the development of young children's mathematical and analogical reasoning," they did not try to pinpoint the pattern of interaction that facilitated the target child's reasoning or learning. Instead, they observed the changes in the discourse over the three years as the background to the development of children's reasoning.

Let us discuss, in line with this goal, how children's spontaneous quantitative activity is induced and extended by the teacher (Sakakibara, Hatano, & Inagaki, 2001). We started with the question, How can early educators facilitate young children's mathematical learning without relying on formal, didactic teaching? If math is taught formally, it is not surprising that even young children know a lot about it. However, survey reports, as well as our informal observations, strongly suggest that Japanese early educators are rather reluctant to teach mathematics systematically.

Japanese early educators tend to contrast their institutions as enhancing children's social and personality development with elementary schools, which teach academic knowledge and skills. A recent survey by Yamauchi (1994) clearly revealed this tendency. Kindergarten teachers replied to the questionnaire that, instead of teaching numbers and number-related skills systematically, they prepared materials that were likely to induce quantitative activities (e.g., a variety of card games, skipping ropes, score boards to write numerals on, etc.). The teachers enhanced such quantitative activities further by questioning the children or by participating in the children's activities. They also invited children who revealed more advanced understanding to express their ideas to stimulate other children.

How can such an "indirect intervention" approach produce the fairly high performances of Japanese young children on mathematics tests? We interpret this in the following ways (Hatano & Inagaki, 1999). Japanese culture places a high value on the acquisition of mathematical skills and understanding: Using Ginsburg et al.'s (1997) expression, it "favors quantitative activity" (p. 201). As a result, quantitative activities occur fairly often in kindergartens, and when they occur, they attract children's attention. Kindergarten teachers, who have been trained in the traditional child-centered or child development program, tend to take up some of these activities and try to develop them, though they are not particularly interested in, nor do they try to deliberately pursue, children's mathematics learning. The children's mathematical learning is a product of their teachers' unconscious efforts to engage them actively in sustained group activities, which often involve quantitative components.

That quantitative activities occur fairly often in kindergartens was confirmed by Sakakibara's (2002) observation of whole class activities in 14 classrooms. Quantitative behaviors of the teachers and the children were often observed in almost all types of group activities. Among others, "taking attendance" and "classroom gathering" among routine activities, and "singing," "exercising/dancing" and "art work" among instructional activities were the activities in which quantitative behaviors were observed most frequently.

To illustrate how early math education works in the Japanese culture, more specifically, how quantitative activities are taken up and developed by teachers, we present one free-play activity of 3- to 4-year-old children in preschool (Sakakibara et al., 2001). On the day of the observation, there were 13 children and two teachers in the classroom who engaged in paper-folding activities.

Creating objects with sheets of paper, known as *origami*, is a rather common activity among young children in preschool. The observed activity was of a similar kind, but the children used a variety of newspapers and advertising papers instead of the usual origami, which are sheets of square paper, colorful and smaller.

The observed activity got started during the free-play time when one child took a few sheets of newspaper from a shelf. Two other children wanted to have some of the paper the first child had, and the teacher intervened the interaction, saying, "We have plenty. I'll give each one of you a sheet (*ikko* in Japanese). One sheet (*ichimai* in Japanese) each so. . . ." The teacher brought a pile of newspaper and gave one sheet of paper to each child who wished to have one. At the same time, she provided two rolls of scotch tape on the combined tables of two.

As the teacher set up the working tables and the tape, some children started to create paper objects of their own. For example, a few children created and wore paper cloaks by folding two edges of the paper symmetrically into triangles and taping them closed. One child just folded a sheet of newspaper into four saying, "Fold this into half. Fold this into half. Tap, tap, tap. . . ."

The children's activity seemed to be expanded and activated when the teachers had finished with their work and started to participate in the activity by providing slightly more advanced paper objects than those made by the children: "thin long stick" and "paper airplane." The children who were playing with other toys or tools began to gather around the teachers and each of them asked the teachers to make one for him/her. When the child received the objects from the teachers, he/she played with the objects. When the teachers made paper objects for the children, many teacher–child interactions referring to quantity and/or geometry were observed. Such interactions often involved (a) the ordering of the children who wanted the objects (e.g., "Please make the same one as Mai-chan's." "Wait. After making the one for Kou-chan, OK?" the child and the assistant teacher); (b) the quantity of the object (e.g., "Could you go and get me a scotch tape? One," the teacher); and (c) the shape of the objects that the teachers were making (e.g., "I want you to make it slim," the child). It should be noted that, though the teachers did not consciously pursue the teaching of mathematics, the children were exposed to a number of mathematical terms in the activity and expected to become better prepared to use these terms.

By the time a majority of the children in the classroom had received the objects from the teachers, several children had, again, started to create objects of their own. Some of them used the teacher-made objects to create more complicated paper objects. Others created the original objects using new sheets of paper. The teachers looked around the classroom so that they could check each child's activity. The teachers actively offered help when needed, and the children spontaneously asked the teachers for help as well. Through folding paper, the children received a lot of experience in manipulating geometric shapes and finding the relationships between them: For example, a square can be divided into two triangles or rectangles but not into two squares; a triangle can be halved into two triangles but not into two rectangles or squares, and so forth.

Many uses of quantitative as well as geometrical terms were again observed when the teachers helped the children make objects. For example, when the teacher saw the child who was pulling scotch tape hard, she said, "Don't you think you are taking too much? Don't you think it's too long?" In another example, the teacher responded to the child, who showed the teacher a very long paper stick, by saying, "You put them together! Two of them!?" The interaction with the teachers seemed not only to provide the children with many opportunities to experience quantitative and geometrical terms, but also to help the children develop their quantitative or geometrical comprehension. For example, when the child was struggling with a huge sheet of paper trying to make a shape of tied ribbon, the teacher told the child that her paper was far too big and provided a smaller one. Then, another child, who was watching and listening to the conversation, returned her paper to the shelf, got a smaller sheet of paper, and asked the teacher, "My teacher, will the small one be fine—like this one?"

In summary, as far as the informal teaching of mathematics is concerned, Japanese teachers do many other things than offering corrective or expanding feedback to children's utterances, as the survey results by Yamauchi (1994) suggested. They often (a) arrange situations in which children can manipulate materials and explore their ideas, (b) offer novel and challenging tasks so that a number of children will be attracted to and maintain their interest in the activity, and (c) help the children when they cannot independently achieve their aims, through participating in the activity together with the children. Under such guidance by teachers, a group of children often sustains an activity for an extended period of time and elaborates on it gradually. As a result, children can often perform fairly complex tasks successfully and learn a variety of items related to those tasks. To generalize, as asserted here and there in the preceding chapters, we need both cognitive and sociocultural approaches to understand children's acquisition of mathematical and other domains of knowledge.

REFERENCES

Alexander, P. A., White, C. S., & Daugherty, M. (1997). Analogical reasoning and early mathematics learning. In L. D. English (Ed.), *Mathematical reasoning: Analogies, metaphors, and images* (pp. 117–147). Mahwah, NJ: Lawrence Erlbaum Associates.

Carey, S. (1985). *Conceptual change in childhood*. Cambridge, MA: MIT Press.

Carraher, T. N., Carraher, D. W., & Schliemann, A. D. (1985). Mathematics in the streets and in the schools. *British Journal of Developmental Psychology, 3*, 21–29.

De Corte, E., Greer, B., & Verschaffel, L. (1996). Learning and teaching mathematics. In D. Berliner & R. Calfee (Eds.), *Handbook of educational psychology* (pp. 491–549). New York: Macmillan.

Dunbar, K. (2001). The analogical paradox: Why analogy is so easy in naturalistic settings yet so difficult in the psychological laboratory. In D. Gentner, K. J. Holyoak, & B. N. Kokinov (Eds.), *The analogical mind: Perspectives from cognitive science* (pp. 313–334). Cambridge, MA: MIT Press.

English, L. D. (1997). Children's reasoning processes in classifying and solving computational word problems. In L. D. English (Ed.), *Mathematical reasoning: Analogies, metaphors, and images* (pp. 117–147). Mahwah, NJ: Lawrence Erlbaum Associates.

Gentner, D., & Markman, A. B. (1997). Structure-mapping in analogy and similarity. *American Psychologist, 52*, 45–56.

Gick, M. L., & Holyoak, K. J. (1980). Analogical problem solving. *Cognitive Psychology, 12*, 306–355.

Ginsburg, H. P., Choi, Y. E., Lopez, L. S., Netley, R., & Chao-Yuan, C. (1997). Happy birthday to you: Early mathematical thinking of Asian, South American, and U.S. children. In T. Nunes & P. Bryant (Eds.), *Learning and teaching mathematics: An international perspective* (pp. 163–207). Hove, England: Psychology Press.

Goodnow, J., Miller, P., & Kessel, F. (1995). *Cultural practices as contexts for human development*. San Francisco: Jossey-Bass.

Goswami, U. (1996). Analogical reasoning and cognitive development. *Advances in Child Development and Behavior, 26*, 91–138.

Goswami, U. (2001). Analogical reasoning in children. In D. Gentner, K. J. Holyoak, & B. N. Kokinov (Eds.), *The analogical mind: Perspectives from cognitive science* (pp. 437–470). Cambridge, MA: MIT Press.

Halford, G. S. (1993). *Children's understanding: The development of mental models*. Hillsdale, NJ: Lawrence Erlbaum Associates.

Hatano, G., & Inagaki, K. (1999). Early childhood mathematics in Japan. In J. V. Copley (Ed.), *Mathematics in the early years* (pp. 219–226). Reston, VA: National Council of Teachers of Mathematics.

Hatano, G., & Inagaki, K. (2000). Knowledge acquisition and use in higher-order cognition. In K. Pawlik & M. R. Rosenzweig (Eds.), *The international handbook of psychology* (pp. 167–190). London: Sage.

Hatano, G., Morita, E., & Inagaki, K. (in preparation). *The acquisition of evaluative criteria for mathematical arguments by elementary school children.*

Holyoak, K. J., Gentner, D., & Kokinov, B. N. (2001). Introduction: The place of analogy in cognition. In D. Gentner, K. J. Holyoak, & B. N. Kokinov (Eds.), *The analogical mind: Perspectives from cognitive science* (pp. 1–19). Cambridge, MA: MIT Press.

Holyoak, K. J., & Thagard, P. (1995). *Mental leaps: Analogy in creative thought.* Cambridge, MA: MIT Press.

Inagaki, K. (1990). The effects of raising animals on children's biological knowledge. *British Journal of Developmental Psychology, 8,* 119–129.

Inagaki, K. (2001). *Effects of raising mammals on young children's biological inference.* Paper presented at the Society for Research in Child Development meeting, Minneapolis, MN.

Inagaki, K., & Hatano, G. (1987). Young children's spontaneous personification as analogy. *Child Development, 58,* 1013–1020.

Inagaki, K., & Hatano, G. (2002). *Young children's naïve thinking about the biological world.* New York: Psychology Press.

Inagaki, K., & Hatano, G. (2003). Conceptual and linguistic factors in inductive projection: How do young children recognize commonalities between animals and plants? In D. Gentner & S. Goldin-Meadow (Eds.), *Language in mind* (pp. 313–333). Cambridge, MA: MIT Press.

Inagaki, K., Morita, E., & Hatano, G. (1999). Teaching-learning of evaluative criteria for mathematical arguments through classroom discourse: A cross-national study. *Mathematical Thinking and Learning, 1*(2), 93–111.

Nunes, T., Schliemann, A. D., & Carraher, D. W. (1993). *Street mathematics and school mathematics.* Cambridge, England: Cambridge University Press.

O'Connor, M. C., & Michaels, S. (1993). Aligning academic task and participation status through revoicing: Analysis of a classroom discourse strategy. *Anthropology and Education Quarterly, 24*(4), 318–335.

Polya, G. (1957). *How to solve it.* Princeton, NJ: Princeton University Press.

Sakakibara, T. (2002). Young children's learning of quantity in the preschool activities: Receiving the support from the preschool teachers. *Research on Early Childhood Care and Education in Japan, 40*(2), 227–236. [in Japanese]

Sakakibara, T., Hatano, G., & Inagaki, K. (2001). The development of numerical competence among Japanese young children. *Research Bulletin of Graduate School of Social Sciences, Keio University, 52,* 1–5.

Saxe, G. B. (1991). *Culture and cognitive development: Studies in mathematical understanding.* Hillsdale, NJ: Lawrence Erlbaum Associates.

Vosniadou, S. (1989). Analogical reasoning as a mechanism in knowledge acquisition: A developmental perspective. In S. Vosniadou & A. Ortony (Eds.), *Similarity and analogical reasoning* (pp. 413–437). Cambridge, England: Cambridge University Press.

White, C. S., & Alexander, P. A. (1986). Effects of training on four-year-olds' ability to solve geometric analogy problems. *Cognition and Instruction, 3*(3), 261–268.

Yamauchi, A. (1994). *Report of contract research on the development of quantitative thinking abilities during young childhood and teaching methods for them in kindergartens.* Tokyo, Japan: Tokyo Kasei University.

10

PROMOTING THE DEVELOPMENT OF YOUNG CHILDREN'S MATHEMATICAL AND ANALOGICAL REASONING

Lyn D. English
Queensland University of Technology

> *[T]he striking fact is not young children's mathematical incompetence. Instead it is their ability to engage with interesting and serious mathematical questions.*
>
> —Ginsburg, Pappas, and Seo (2001, p. 208)

This concluding chapter begins with a brief overview of the main findings of our study. The remainder of the chapter offers suggestions for fostering the development of mathematical and analogical reasoning in the early school years. I also acknowledge the valuable input from the authors of the commentary chapters (chaps. 8 & 9, this volume).

From observing our young participants as they progressed from preschool through to the end of second grade, we found clear evidence of analogical reasoning and mathematical reasoning in both their play activities and in their more structured learning experiences. Furthermore, we saw improvements in their reasoning over the three years as well as during the course of each grade level. Children who scored higher on our analogical and mathematical reasoning tests were observed to reflect on what they had learned and to apply this knowledge to new situations. These children were more active in mastering tasks, in contrast to children who scored lower on these tests. On the other hand, the lower performing children often displayed analogical reasoning in their off-task play, indicating a need for future research to address not only the frequency of analogical discourse but also the contexts in which it occurs. We also need to broaden our measures of analogical reasoning ability beyond those addressed in this study, as the commentaries have indicated.

As mentioned later, the role of analogical reasoning in mathematical problem solving and in the use of concrete representations needs special attention.

Of particular interest is the relationship we found between analogical and mathematical reasoning, with these reasoning abilities following similar trajectories. Although such a link is not unexpected, given that an ability to detect patterns and relationships is fundamental to both reasoning forms, our study has provided evidence of this important, yet little researched, phenomenon. Furthermore, our study has provided evidence of this relationship within both the informal learning context of the preschool and the more formal learning context of the early school years. Although many questions remain about this relationship, including possible variance due to general individual differences in ability (see chap. 8, this volume) and the impact of children's specific mathematical knowledge (see chap. 9, this volume), it is nevertheless apparent that both forms of reasoning play a key role in young children's learning.

Several other factors contribute to the development of these reasoning abilities, including children's increasing cognitive maturity, their classroom learning experiences, and their informal activities beyond school. Although our study did not investigate all of these factors, our assessments and intensive classroom observations suggest that a key role was played by the teachers' input into the children's learning experiences. In particular, a focus on fostering children's mathematical reasoning was evident in both the Australian and American classrooms. On the other hand, analogical reasoning received considerably less specific attention in the classroom, apart from the use of some concrete materials to convey mathematical ideas (e.g., counters and other materials to represent number) and some analogical references in the teachers' discourse with the children in other topic areas. A more specific focus on analogical reasoning, including an emphasis on identifying patterns and relationships, is an area in need of greater attention in early mathematics programs. As our studies and those of others have shown (e.g., Clements, Sarama, & DiBiase, 2003; Ginsburg, Balfanz, & Greenes, 2000; Ginsburg et al., 2001; Greenes, 1999), young children are capable of and are interested in a variety of challenging mathematical activities that develop these important reasoning processes.

PROVIDING OPTIMAL LEARNING EXPERIENCES

Problem Solving and Mathematical Reasoning

There currently exist several perspectives on the types of learning experiences we should provide young children to develop their mathematical reasoning. These include the "play" approach, where there is generally a lack of structure in children's learning, and also a "drill" approach, where children complete numerous workbooks and practice sheets (Ginsburg et al., 2001). Our study supports the type of mathematics learning that Ginsburg et al. advocate for young children, namely, a "challenge" approach where children engage in significant and intellectually engaging mathematical activities. This perspective reflects the belief that young children "can learn, enjoy learning, do not need to be made ready to learn, and should learn a great deal more challenging mathematics than they do now" (Ginsburg et al., 2001, p. 182; Henningsen & Stein, 1997). We saw numerous instances of children's engagement with challenging mathematical tasks from our earliest observations of their activities in preschool. For example, children would work tirelessly with their wooden blocks of various shapes and sizes to build bridges, castles, road systems, and many other engineering feats. We need to ensure that this enthusiasm for mastering mathematical tasks continues in the more formal years of schooling.

Similar sentiments have been expressed in the recent recommendations from the *2000 National Conference on Standards for Preschool and Kindergarten Mathematics Education* (Clements et al., 2003). These standards recommend that young children be provided with "developmentally appropriate" mathematical experiences that are challenging but attainable by most children of a given age range, that are sufficiently flexible to respond to individual needs, and that are consistent with children's ways of thinking and learning. There has thus been strong support for early childhood curricula that present a conceptually broad, yet cohesively structured, set of mathematical learning experiences (e.g., Ginsburg et al., 2000; Greenes, 1999; Klein & Starkey, in press; National Association for the Education of Young Children, 2002; National Council of Teachers of Mathematics [NCTM], 2000).

The important ideas of number, number sense, spatial reasoning, patterning, logical relations, measurement, early algebra, and data analysis have been cited as key components of young children's mathematical growth (e.g., Clements et al., in press; Greenes, 1999; Klein & Starkey, in press; NCTM, 2000). Learning experiences that center on these components should not only be enjoyable and meaningful, but should also direct and focus children's thinking on the important mathematical ideas (Trafton, Reys, & Wasman, 2001). As Trafton et al. noted, there is a natural connection between a coherent development of mathematical ideas and developing these ideas in an in-depth way. When key ideas are presented in a coherent fashion and children see how they are linked, they are more likely to pursue and persist with the underlying mathematics of an activity.

As many educators have emphasized, learning with understanding is essential for a flexible and adaptive use of knowledge, and provides the basis for mastering new situations (e.g., Carpenter & Lehrer, 1999; Fennema & Romberg, 1999; Hiebert & Carpenter, 1992; Hiebert et al., 1997; Weissglass,

1998). Oftentimes though, children's mathematical learning in the early school years is dominated by the solving of traditional word problems. Although these experiences have an important place in the curriculum, there is the danger that they can lead children to adopt superficial learning practices. Numerous studies have indicated how the stereotyped nature of many word problems can lead children to focus on surface features, usually key words, in determining a solution procedure (e.g., English, 1997; Greer, 1997; Nesher, 1980; Sowder, 1988). As a consequence, children can get the correct answer for the wrong reasons, and without engaging with the mathematical ideas of the problem. For example, the terms, *more* and *altogether*, are usually associated with addition and so some children automatically apply this operation whenever the terms appear in a word problem, irrespective of whether some other operation is called for. Such an approach is not conducive to the development of a strong conceptual understanding of the mathematical relations inherent in the problem. As noted in chapter 1 of this volume, children need to be able to detect the underlying structural features of a mathematical problem and to identify related structures in solving new problems. Problem situations that are couched in children's real-world experiences and that encourage them to talk about and model the situation in their own ways can help shift the focus from surface to structural features.

From the early years of school, children's problem-solving experiences need to move beyond traditional word problems to include a broader range of problem-solving activities that engage children's reasoning processes. Such experiences would also provide "a fertile ground for controversy," where children must rely on their mathematical reasoning processes to justify their ideas and arguments (Artzt, 1999, p. 124). Increasing emphasis is being placed on the importance of developing these processes in the early years. For example, Clements et al. (2003) endorsed the development of both general and specific reasoning processes as important components of high-quality mathematics programs for young learners. General processes include "problem solving, reasoning and proof, communication, connections, and representation," whereas more specific processes encompass "organizing information, patterning, and composing, and habits of mind such as curiosity, imagination, inventiveness, persistence, willingness to experiment, and sensitivity to patterns" (p. 3).

An issue that arises here is whether we should just nurture children's reasoning processes through appropriate learning experiences or whether we should also include some direct instruction. As the chapters of this book have indicated, children develop many processes as a natural part of their cognitive growth (for further discussion on this, see chap. 8, this volume). On the other hand, studies have shown positive gains in young children's reasoning when specific processes are targeted in their learning programs. In a recent intervention study, Klein and Starkey (2003) found that prekindergarten children benefited from a 12-month intervention program that included a strong focus on patterning, along with logical relations, arithmetic and spatial reasoning, and informal measurement. Children from low- and middle-income levels made significant developmental progress in their mathematical reasoning compared to children in the control groups. However, the researchers found that although these children could readily handle pattern duplication, they had some difficulty with pattern extension. A range of patterning activities is needed in the early school years to strengthen and extend children's existing capabilities. The important role of patterning in young children's mathematical and analogical reasoning development has been demonstrated in our study.

In earlier studies, Alexander and her colleagues (Alexander et al., 1989; White & Caropreso, 1989) incorporated explicit instruction in their analogical reasoning work with young children. They found that children were capable of developing greater competence in analogical reasoning through this instruction. In our present study, the children did not receive any instruction related to analogical reasoning, yet their analogical reasoning development progressed in parallel with their mathematical reasoning.

This raises the question of how young children's mathematical reasoning would be influenced by a more focused approach on analogical reasoning. Past studies have indicated the need to address analogical reasoning processes with children to assist them in solving structurally similar problems (e.g., English, 1997, 1999; see also chaps. 1 & 9, this volume). It is recommended that children be given guidance in recognizing and applying related problem structures. However, Hatano and Sakakibara (chap. 9, this volume) queried whether such instruction would be violating a constructivist approach to teaching. While not wishing to debate this issue here, it is nevertheless worth commenting that constructivist theories have been interpreted and applied in various, and at times, conflicting ways. Knowledge construction is only one of many relevant processes in learning and reasoning. Other important processes include differentiating among conditions in which a particular solution would be applicable, filtering out irrelevant information, and integrating previously considered quantities or relationships into current understandings (Lesh, Doerr, Carmona, & Hjarmalson, in press). Guiding children in the processes of analogical reasoning would facilitate knowledge construction as well as the other learning processes.

Another area in which analogical instruction requires greater attention is in the use of mathematical analogs, which were not always used adequately in the classrooms we observed.

Reasoning with Mathematical Analogs

The mathematical analogs used in early childhood programs comprise both unstructured and structured materials. These include colored counters, miscellaneous "junk" items, patterning material, blocks of various colors, shapes, and sizes, linking cubes, and base-ten blocks. For mathematical re-sources to be effective learning materials, children must have access to them. By *access*, I mean both the availability of appropriate mathematical re-sources and the ability to engage cognitively with them.

As mentioned in chapter 1, many of the mathematical materials that chil-dren experience have little mathematical meaning per se but feature inherent relationships and properties that can mirror mathematical concepts and pro-cedures. For children to interpret the intended mathematical meaning, they need to reason analogically. In other words, these resources serve in an ana-logical capacity (English & Halford, 1995), where there is a mapping from one structure, the source (i.e., the physical, pictorial, or diagrammatic item), to another, the target (i.e., the mathematical concept or process). To illustrate how mathematical and analogical reasoning processes are both required in using simple resources, I consider the nature and role of discrete items such as counters (or other simple environmental items). These are unstructured analogs because they do not display in-built numerical relationships (in con-trast to base-ten blocks, which display the place–value relations of our deci-mal number system). We made use of unstructured items in our test of mathe-matical reasoning, as addressed in chapter 2.

These simple analogs display mathematical ideas through the way in which the materials are arranged or manipulated. As indicated in chapter 1, the cardinality of single-digit numbers can be conveyed by arranging coun-ters in sets with a specific number of elements, where there is a simple map-ping from the source (each set of counters) to the target (the number names).

In other instances, the analogical reasoning required in understanding mathematical ideas displayed by counters is not so simple. For example, chil-dren frequently have difficulty in determining fractions of a set of objects (see Fig. 10.1). To interpret this example as "three sevenths of the counters are red," the child must initially conceive of the set as a whole entity to determine the name of the fraction being considered (i.e., seven counters → sevenths).

An added difficulty with this set analog is that the items might not be the same size or shape. Hence the child must see the items of the set as equal parts of a whole, even if the items themselves are unequal. While keeping the whole set in mind, the child must then identify all the red counters (three red coun-ters) and conceive of them as a fraction of the whole set, that is, "three out of seven counters, hence, three sevenths." This part/whole construct can be dif-ficult to perceive with this analog. Ascertaining the whole and the parts re-quires more complex analogical reasoning; that is, it requires more or less si-multaneous mapping processes. Consequently, it is not uncommon for children to treat the red and blue counters as discrete entities and interpret the fraction in terms of a ratio (i.e., three parts to four parts, giving the frac-tion three fourths). Given the complexity of this analog for displaying frac-tions of a set, it is not the most appropriate for introducing fractional ideas.

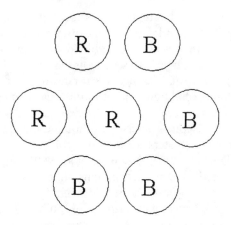

FIG. 10.1. Using counters to represent a fraction of a set. From English and Halford (1995). Reproduced with permission of Lawrence Erlbaum Associates.

When selecting materials to show mathematical ideas, we need to keep in mind that children have to reason analogically in order to interpret and understand what is being conveyed. This requires that the structure of the analog be clearly displayed and explicitly understood by the child. That is, children need to know and understand the objects and relations displayed in the analog. There should also be an absence of ambiguity in the mappings that must be made from the source to the target. When these conditions are not met, the analogs become ends in themselves, rather than a means to an end. The careful selection of analogs for young children's mathematical learning is thus essential. At the same time, children must develop a conceptual knowledge base that enables them to reason appropriately and meaningfully when using these analogs.

INSTRUCTIONAL PRACTICES
IN THE EARLY CHILDHOOD YEARS

The teacher's role in fostering young children's mathematical and analogical reasoning is a crucial one (Clements et al., 2003; Diezmann, Watters, & English, 2001; Greenes, 1999). Young children's reasoning can be enhanced or inhibited by a teacher's actions through her discourse, the type of classroom support she provides, the mathematical activities she implements, and the ways in which she implements them (Diezmann et al., 2001). Our study explored the role of classroom discourse in supporting the development of young children's mathematical and analogical reasoning. By analyzing the children's and teachers' verbal texts (discussions, questionings, etc.), we became aware of the content and nature of the discourse processes that arose in these classroom communities and were able to track changes in these processes from the kindergarten year to second grade—a period of active transition from informal to formal mathematical reasoning.

If we are to maximize children's mathematical reasoning opportunities, we need to establish a classroom culture that encourages discussion, questioning, and debate, that welcomes diversity of thought, that values children's inquiring minds, and that fosters a range of problem-solving and problem-posing activities (Dockett, 2000; Diezmann et al., 2001; English, in press). At the same time, we need to be proactive in introducing young children to important mathematical concepts, skills, and language.

In a recent 10-week teaching experiment in four third-grade classes (7–8-year-olds; Diezmann et al., 2001), teachers were provided with ongoing professional development in supporting the investigatory abilities of young children. Analyses of the observed teacher behaviors revealed three patterns of interaction that fostered children's mathematical reasoning. First, by acting as a role model and providing timely intervention, teachers developed the perception in the classroom that reasoning involves justifiable actions. Second, teachers built on this perception by encouraging children to engage in systematic thinking using appropriate language and strategies (e.g., scaffolding children to make and test conjectures; challenging children's assumptions; encouraging children to present their ideas as a chain of reasoning; p. 293). Third, teachers capitalized on situations and conversations to create opportunities for reasoning. Here, they focused strongly on the mathematics in the situation and used it as a forum for developing the children's reasoning.

The children responded to these teacher actions by repeatedly trying to make sense of their own actions and their discourse, and challenging their peers to do likewise. The children also developed more sophisticated language and strategies as they engaged in the more "formal" reasoning associated with their mathematical investigations (i.e., reasoning as a systematic way of thinking). At the same time, it was imperative that the teachers listened to and observed the children as they engaged in the discursive practices of their classrooms (Artzt, 1999; Ginsburg et al., 2001; Hatano & Inagaki, 1997; NCTM, 2000). Such observations help strengthen the knowledge base on which we can plan developmentally appropriate mathematical experiences.

The need for teachers to build a strong knowledge base, comprising both empirical and theoretical perspectives, has been underscored by many reports in recent years (e.g., Clements et al., 2003; Crawford & Adler, 1996; Ginsburg et al., 2001; Ma, 1999). A thorough understanding of the mathematical content as well as of the ways in which young children develop mathematically, is essential to the design and implementation of rich and intellectually engaging learning experiences. As Ma (1999) stressed in her well-known, cross-cultural study of teachers' mathematical knowledge, teachers need a *"profound* understanding of fundamental mathematics" (italics added; p. 124). Such understanding has "breadth, depth, and thoroughness." Breadth of understanding enables a teacher to connect "topics of similar or less conceptual power," while depth of understanding is a capacity to "connect a topic with those of greater conceptual power." Thoroughness enables one to connect all topics (Ma, 1999, p. 124). It is questionable whether many teachers develop such profound mathematical understanding, but it is clearly a much-needed goal of preservice and in-service teacher development.

In our own study, we explored the teachers' knowledge (content and pedagogical) and their beliefs and practices pertaining to mathematical and analogical reasoning. Although this aspect of our research was not sufficiently extensive to determine if the teachers had a "profound mathematical understanding" of the early childhood curriculum, we nevertheless gained some important insights into their mathematical knowledge and teaching approaches, as we described in chapters 6 and 7 of this volume. For example, on our intuitive-to-theoretical continuum, we saw the theoretical teachers as displaying the most substantial knowledge of mathematical reasoning. Their expressed perceptions and understandings reflect current thinking on young children's mathematical competencies, including the need to provide challenging and motivating learning experiences. Although less confident about analogical reasoning, these teachers did demonstrate a basic understanding relating this reasoning to finding connections, patterns, or relationships. The experience-based teachers described a variety of processes associated with mathematical reasoning but did not address concepts or attitudes, unlike their theoretical counterparts. The experiential teachers also displayed limited knowledge of analogical reasoning, whereas none of the intuitive teachers was familiar with the term. These intuitive teachers characterized mathematical reasoning in very general terms and did not appear to base their responses on either theory or experience.

Our various findings pertaining to the teachers' knowledge and beliefs about mathematics and mathematics education have raised a number of issues in need of attention, as was addressed in chapter 7 of this volume. If future research were to show that more learning takes place in the classrooms of theoretical teachers, then it behooves us to develop more effective ways in which we can help intuitive and experiential teachers become more theoretical in their mathematical knowledge and teaching approaches. Professional development programs, which take into account teachers' existing knowledge, beliefs, and practices about mathematics and mathematics education, would seem better able to address the needs of individual teachers (see Stein, Schwan, Smith, & Silver, 1999). Such development is especially important for early childhood teachers who often lack confidence in their own mathemati-

cal ability (Clements et al., 2003; Perry & Dockett, 2002). The recommenda-
tion of Clements et al. is worth citing in this context:

> Deep knowledge of the mathematics to be taught, together with knowledge of
> how children think and develop those skills and understandings, is critical for
> improving teaching and should be learned in preservice and professional devel-
> opment programs. (p. 4)

CONCLUDING POINTS

The chapters of this book have explored the development of analogical and
mathematical reasoning in 4- to 7-year-old children. Our longitudinal study
traced American and Australian children from their preschool year through
to the end of their second grade. We also addressed the teachers' knowledge,
beliefs, and practices with respect to mathematics, mathematical reasoning,
and analogical reasoning. The study was conducted within the natural classroom and playground contexts, where we were fortunate in being able to observe, first hand, children's spontaneous interactions with their peers, their
teachers, and their environment. We believe that our study has made a significant contribution to the literature on young children's development, especially in our focus on the interrelationships between mathematical and analogical reasoning in both formal and informal learning contexts.

We were also fortunate in securing three eminent researchers to respond to
our study: Usha Goswami (chap. 8) and Giyoo Hatano and Tomomi
Sakakibara (chap. 9). Their collective experiences and rich knowledge bases
have added significantly to our study, of which we are most grateful. In providing critical comment on our study, these authors have identified a number
of issues requiring further research. These include the role of the knowledge
base in enabling analogies and analogical reasoning in the learning of mathematics. As has been emphasized previously in this book, it is imperative that
we analyze the underlying structure of the mathematical knowledge young
children require and provide appropriate learning experiences to facilitate
this development. Such experiences should incorporate appropriate learning
tools that effectively convey the intended mathematical ideas and processes.
The use of meaningful and appropriate language to assist children in working
with these tools is also essential.

In addressing the link between analogical and mathematical reasoning
ability, Goswami stressed the need to consider the role of general intelligence
in this relationship. Future studies need to control for this intelligence factor
in order to explore more fully the relationship between analogical and mathematical reasoning. At the same time, broader measures of analogical reasoning need to be used in future studies, given that the type of analogy we em-

ployed only partially determines children's abilities to recognize the recurrence of patterns in the face of item variation. As Goswami noted, classical analogies may not necessarily be an effective measure of children's abilities to see connections between abstract mathematical ideas. Furthermore, it may be the case that the two forms of classical analogies we used, namely, the perceptual patterns (TARC) and the conceptual patterns (the verbal/pictorial analogies), have different links with mathematical reasoning. As Goswami pointed out, it may be that there is a stronger link between conceptual pattern recognition and mathematical reasoning than between perceptual pattern recognition and mathematical reasoning. This is an important issue that warrants investigation.

Finally, we need to keep in mind the importance of the professional development of teachers. Teachers require both the knowledge base and the opportunities to explore young children's mathematical and analogical reasoning processes. Time to observe children, both collectively and individually, is essential here. Teachers would concur with us that the power of observation in working with young children, or any students for that matter, yields unparalleled insights into their learning. We continue to be fascinated by what we observed during these informative years of young children's development.

REFERENCES

Alexander, P. A., Pate, P. E., Kulikowich, J. M., Farrell, D. M., & Wright, N. L. (1989). Domain-specific and strategic knowledge: Effects of training on students of differing ages or competence levels. *Learning and Individual Differences, 1*, 283–325.

Artzt, A. F. (1999). Mathematical reasoning during small-group problem solving. In L. V. Stiff & F. R. Curcio (Eds.), *Developing mathematical reasoning, K–12* (pp. 115–126). Reston, VA: National Council of Teachers of Mathematics.

Carpenter, T. P., & Lehrer, R. (1999). Teaching and learning mathematics with understanding. In E. Fennema & T. A. Romberg (Eds.), *Mathematics classrooms that promote understanding* (pp. 3–17). Mahwah, NJ: Lawrence Erlbaum Associates.

Clements, D. H., Sarama, J., & DiBiase, A. M. (Eds.). (2003). *Engaging young children in mathematics: Findings of the 2000 National Conference on Standards for Preschool and Kindergarten Mathematics Education*. Mahwah, NJ: Lawrence Erlbaum Associates.

Crawford, K., & Adler, J. (1996). Teachers as researchers in mathematics education. In A. J. Bishop, K. Clements, C.Keitel, J. Kilpatrick, & C. Laborde (Eds.), *International handbook of mathematics education* (Part 2; pp. 1187–1205). Dordrecht, Netherlands: Kluwer.

Diezmann, C. M., Watters, J. M., & English, L. D. (2001). Difficulties confronting young children undertaking investigations. In M. van den Heuvel-Panhuizen (Ed.), *Proceedings of the 25th conference of the International Group for the Psychology of Mathematics Education* (pp. 353–360). Utrecht, Netherlands: Utrecht University.

Dockett, S. (2000). Child-initiated curriculum and images of children. In W. Schiller (Ed.), *Thinking through the arts* (pp. 204–211). Amsterdam: Harwood.

English, L. D. (1997). Children's reasoning processes in classifying and solving computational word problems. In L. D. English (Ed.), *Mathematical reasoning: Analogies, metaphors, and images* (pp. 191–220). Mahwah, NJ: Lawrence Erlbaum Associates.

English, L. D. (1999). Reasoning by analogy in solving comparison problems. In L. D. English (Ed.), *Mathematical reasoning: Nature, form, and development*. East Sussex, UK: Psychology Press.

English, L. D. (in press). Engaging students in problem posing in an inquiry-oriented classroom. In F. Lester (Ed.), *Teaching mathematics through problem solving*. Reston, VA: National Council of Teachers of Mathematics.

English, L. D., & Halford, G. S. (1995). *Mathematics education: Models and processes*. Mahwah, NJ: Lawrence Erlbaum Associates.

Fennema, E., & Romberg, T. A. (Eds.), *Mathematics classrooms that promote understanding* (pp. 3–17). Mahwah, NJ: Lawrence Erlbaum Associates.

Ginsburg, H. P., Balfanz, R., & Greenes, C. (2000). Challenging mathematics for young children. In A. L. Costa (Ed.), *Teaching for intelligence II: A collection of articles* (pp. 245–258). Arlington Heights, IL: Skylight Professional Development.

Ginsburg, H. P., Pappas, S., & Seo, K-H. (2001). Everyday mathematical knowledge: Asking children what is developmentally appropriate. In S. L. Golbeck (Ed.), *Psychological perspectives on early childhood education* (pp. 181–219). Mahwah, NJ: Lawrence Erlbaum Associates.

Greenes, C. (1999). The Boston University—Chelsea project. In J. V. Copely (Ed.), *Mathematics in the Early Years* (pp. 151–155). Virginia: National Council of Teachers of Mathematics; Washington, DC: National Association for the Education of Young Children.

Greer, B. (1997). Modeling reality in mathematics classrooms: The case of word problems. *Learning and Instruction, 7*(4), 293–307.

Hatano, G., & Inagaki, K. (1997). Qualitative changes in intuitive biology. *European Journal of Psychology of Education, 12*(2), 111–130.

Henningsen, M., & Stein, M. K. (1997). Mathematical tasks and student cognition: Classroom-based factors that support and inhibit high-level mathematical thinking and reasoning. *Journal for Research in Mathematics Education, 28*(5), 524–549.

Hiebert, J., & Carpenter, T. P. (1992). Learning and teaching with understanding. In D. A. Grouws (Ed.), *Handbook of research on mathematics teaching and learning* (pp. 65–97). New York: Macmillan.

Hiebert, J., Carpenter, T. P., Fennema, E., Fuson, K. C., Wearne, D., Murray, H., Olivier, A., & Human, P. (1997). *Making sense: Teaching and learning mathematics with understanding*. Portsmouth, NH: Heinemann.

Klein, A., & Starkey, P. (2003). Fostering Preschool Children's Mathematical Knowledge: Findings from the Berkeley Math Readiness Project. In D. H. Clements, J. Sarama, & A. M. DiBiase (Eds.), *Engaging young children in mathematics: Findings of the 2000 National Conference on Standards for Preschool and Kindergarten Mathematics Education*. Mahwah, NJ: Lawrence Erlbaum Associates.

Lesh, R. A., Doerr, H. A., Carmona, G., & Hjalmarson, M. (in press). Beyond constructivism. *Mathematical Thinking and Learning, 5*(2 & 3).

Ma, L. (1999). *Knowing and teaching elementary mathematics: Teachers' understanding of fundamental mathematics in China and the United States*. Mahwah, NJ: Lawrence Erlbaum Associates.

National Association for the Education of Young Children. (2002, April). *Early childhood mathematics: Promoting good beginnings*. A joint position statement of the National Association for the Education of Young Children and the National Council of Teachers of Mathematics (www.naeyc.org/resources/position_statements/psmath.htm)

National Council of Teachers of Mathematics. (2000). *Principles and standards for school mathematics*. Reston, VA: Author.

Nesher, P. (1980). The stereotyped nature of school word problems. *For the Learning of Mathematics, 1*(1), 41–48.

Perry, B., & Dockett, S. (2002). Young children's access to powerful mathematical ideas. In L. D. English (Ed.), *Handbook of international research in mathematics education* (pp. 81–111). Mahwah, NJ: Lawrence Erlbaum Associates.

Sowder, L. (1988). Children's solutions of story problems. *Journal of Mathematical Behavior, 7,* 227–238.

Stein, M. K., Schwan, M., Smith, M., & Silver, E. A. (1999). The development of professional developers: Learning to assist teachers in new settings in new ways. *Harvard Educational Review, 69*(3), 237–260.

Trafton, P., Reys, B. J., & Wasman, D. G. (2001). Standards-based mathematics curriculum materials: A phrase in search of a definition. *Phi Delta Kappan, 8*(3), 259–264.

Weissglass, J. (1998). Maintaining our integrity amidst controversy and attacks. *Teaching Children Mathematics, 4*(8), 438–440.

White, C. S., & Caropreso, E. J. (1989). Training in analogical reasoning processes: Effects on low socioeconomic status preschool children. *Journal of Educational Research, 83*(2), 112–118.

Author Index

Schwartz, J., 130, 131
Seo, K. H., 1, 15, 77, 202, 203, 208
Sharry, P., 50
Sherman, H., 130
Siebert, D., 7
Sigman, M., 177
Silver, E. A., 5, 11, 13, 184, 209
Singer-Freeman, K., 176, 184
Smith, M., 209
Smither, D., 11
Sophian, K., 14
Sowder, L., 204
Staessens, K., 106
Starkey, P., 76, 203, 204
Stavy, R., 5, 11
Steffe, L. P., 75
Stein, M. K., 203, 209
Sternberg, R. J., 3, 4, 10, 13, 25, 28, 35, 48, 50, 78
Stewart, I., 35
Stiff, L. V., 12, 13, 49
Stiles, J., 15
Stipek, D. J., 129
Swingen, C. C., 49

T

Tang, E. P., 77
Thagard, P., 2, 5, 10, 27, 47, 48, 169, 170, 180, 194
Thomason, R., 49
Thomasson, R. H., 129, 130
Thompson, A., 130, 131
Thompson, C. S, 105
Thompson, P. W., 8
Thornton, C., 75
Tirosh, D., 5, 11
Toupin, C., 11, 28
Tron, M., 70, 196
Turner, J. C., 79

U

Underhill, R., 130, 131

V

Valsiner, J., 76
Van der Veer, R., 76
Vartuli, S., 129, 130
Verschaffel, L., 191
von Glasersfeld, E., 75
Vosnaidou, S., 8, 10, 11, 16, 23, 47, 189
Voss, A. A., 7
Vygotsky, L., 24, 76

W

Wade, B., 50
Warfield, J., 3
Wasman, D. G., 203
Watters, J. M., 207
Wearne, D., 10, 203
Webb, N., 13, 49
Weiss, R. S., 132
Weissglass, J., 203
Wertsch, J. V., 179
White, C. S., 2, 5, 11, 12, 15, 16, 24–26, 28, 29, 36, 48, 50, 56, 59, 64, 70, 78, 79, 83, 123, 172, 187, 188, 190, 193, 205
Whitenack, J., 17, 75, 76
Wilcox-Herzog, A., 128–130
Wilkins, J. L. M., 77
William, D., 130
Willson, V. L., 11, 12, 24–26, 30, 48, 78, 79, 123, 172
Wilson, A. F., 11, 12, 32, 48, 78, 123, 172
Wilson. F., 48, 172
Wong, E. D., 8
Wood, T., 131, 132
Wright, N. L., 28, 205
Wright, R. J., 10
Wynn, K., 14, 24, 49, 173

Y

Yackel, E., 131, 132
Yamauchi, A., 196, 198
Yanowitz, K. L., 11
Yin, R., 104
Yttri, M. J., 3

Subject Index

224

Reasoning *(cont.)*
  informal, 99, 104
  spatial, 49
  similarity-based, 170
Relational thinking, 28, 78, 95, 192
  higher-order relations, 4, 79, 85
  lower-order relations, 4–5, 79
Relations
  abilities, 52
  causal, 3
  corresponding, 16
  higher order, 4, 11, 28–29, 79, 85, 182
  lower order, 4, 28–29, 79
Relationships
  mathematical and analogical, 16, 50, 52, 56, 58, 60, 70, 91, 123, 134, 189, 191, 202, 210
Representation, 35–36, 180
Risk taking, 134, 136, 140–141

S

Scaffolding, 145
School culture, 106–107
Second order domain generality, 191
Semiotic mediation, 76
Similarity
  low, 28–29
  high, 28–29
  surface, 170
  structural, 6, 170
  see also Relational thinking
Social interaction, 76
Spontaneity, 85
Street mathematics, 195
Structural alignment, *see* Mapping
Structure
  generalisable, 7
  relational, 7, 11, 170, 192

T

Target, 5–7, 206
Teacher practices, 158, 163, 166, 168
Teachers
  beliefs, 127–130, 156, 161, 165
  discourse, 207
  influence of, 128, 202
  orientation, 67
  pedagogical knowledge, 49, 127–130, 132, 139, 148, 208
  professional development, 211
  roles of, 16, 49, 70, 75, 138–139, 147–148, 155, 202, 207
  types
    experiential, 159–163, 188
    intuitive, 163–167, 188
    theoretical, 153–159, 188
Tests
  Georgia Kindergarten Assessment Program (GKAP), 36
  Mathematical Reasoning Test for Young Students (MRTYS2), 36–39, 42, 51–52, 69, 80, 114, 187–188
    components of, 187, 180
  Mathematical Reasoning Test for Young Students (MRTYS3), 39–40
  Test of Analogical Reasoning in Children (TARC), 30–32, 42, 48, 51–52, 69, 80, 114, 181, 187–188
Theories
  componential, 4, 28, 78
  Piaget's, 1, 10, 77, 170, 179–180, 183
Thinking processes, 13, 36
Training, 11
Transfer, 7
Translation, 35–36, 180